"The risk of not trying converts to regret. Regret is stronger and consumes more of your internal resources for a longer time than what you would have spent trying. Sometimes regret lasts forever."

-Erik A. Kaiser

Dedicated to my toughest
bosses and best employess,
Wanchen, Issaya, and Malis.

FOR OFFICE USE ONLY

The 100 Point Guide to Navigating
Everyday Differences Between Employers
and Employees

ERIK A. KAISER

A **GLAMCOR** Publication

FOR OFFICE USE ONLY

FOR OFFICE USE ONLY. Copyright © 2009, 2023 by Erik A. Kaiser.
All rights reserved.

SECOND EDITION PRINTING
The first edition was released in 2009. This is the updated version that brings current references to social media and Internet-related commentary. Also, my voice of my late 30's has been updated without changing the context of information.

This book has two types of content:
1) a storyline tale
2) employer/employee opposing viewpoints

Regarding the storyline tale: the story, all names, characters, and incidents portrayed in this book are fictitious. No identification with actual persons (living or deceased), places, buildings, and products is intended or should be inferred.

Printed in the PRC. No part of this book may be used or reproduced in any manner whatsoever without written permission except in the case of brief quotations embodied in critical articles or reviews.

Books are available for bulk purchases at special discounts. Custom branded editions are available to specification.

For information contact www.**erikkaiserventures**.com

ISBN 979-8-218-17896-3

GLAMCOR GLOBAL LLC
New York, NY
www.erikkaiserventures.com

Printed in PRC

Author's remark

This book has been designed to deliver information in the manner that mimics how we often receive information today. With the proliferation of the Internet, we are now accustomed to using our own incredible processing power to digest concentrated information in short bursts. We can choose to remain engaged on a topic to investigate further, or we can decide to immediately navigate somewhere else in a random fashion. The print book accomplishes the ability for the reader to surf the pages at random, or read it from cover to cover.

Inside the print book, the upper information on each page is a distillation of a topic that addresses the core of that matter. On the bottom of each page is a running conversation between six common individual profiles regarding the general topic of the page spread. The casual exchange between the six individuals makes for entertaining reading while describing real life applications of the topic. The conversation begins on the following page and continues without interruption to the last page.

Wherever a reader opens the book, the format will remain the same. On the left hand side of the page is the point of view of an employer regarding the topic. On the right hand side of the page is the employee point of view regarding the same topic. The balance of information should prove to be very valuable to gaining insight about the behavior or employers and employees.

-Erik A. Kaiser

Introduction

It is important to put any type of relationship into context in order to bring order to your thoughts about it. If you were to consider that any relationship is between two or more "entities", you will find that less emotion will cloud your understanding of the purpose of the relationship and how it can be managed. To productively unpack this idea for our intentions, "entities" can be people, groups of people, organizations, et al. You, personally, are also an entity.

The spectrum of relationship types is very broad. There is likely a common list of the most popular "base relationship" features which exist in humanity, and we can assume some of the list would include being dependent, symbiotic, ideological, and political. The "employer entity" / "employee entity" relationship is just one expected experience in life. Grossly speaking, the other most common entity relationships are interpersonal (marriage or family), work, religious, and friendship. Each of the aforementioned entities involved in a relationship have some natural inequalities. Differences of knowledge, personality, or experience, create friction leading to conflict.

The perspective of an "employer entity" / "employee entity" relationship is not difficult for each independent entity to understand. Each entity typically knows what it wants and needs to fulfill an independent and collective purpose. The balancing act of getting it right is where the opportunities and difficulties exist. The independent ideals, goals, expectations, pride, knowledge, ideologies, work ethics, skill sets, emotions, experiences, dreams, attitudes, perceptions, chemistry, and feelings of each entity create imbalance. Compexity amplifies the imbalances.

Since all relationships can have the propensity to be a giant chess game, building a business and building a career also get played out in unison. From the perspective of an employee, it is difficult to deal with the corporate ups and downs. Employees are reliant on the company for income and job security while they rarely perceive being paid enough. Leadership may be too tough or soft. Companies can experience greatness and desperation sometimes in the same day. Employees just never know what to predict. One day, an employee is a titan on Wall Street at Lehman Brothers, and the next day, she is scratching her head, wondering what job security means. If a firm that has been in business since 1850 can close its doors very rapidly because of a changed market condition, where is it safe to work and build a career? What does it mean to be a great company?

In contrast, employers need to think in the abstract to fulfill the vision of the "big idea" or whatever the goal may be. The kinetic energy expended is applied to navigating the often unpredictable waters of sales, marketing, R&D, HR, operations, customer service, customer acquisition, capital investments, joint ventures, intellectual property, financing, investor relations, et al. Business, in general, has a lot of moving parts, and as unknowns increase, so does the part count. There is potential risk, and there is potential reward. Monkey wrenches get thrown, and companies need to figure out how to pivot to survive. Now add in the importance of seating the right people in the right positions, and the landscape becomes more tenuous. It is no wonder that employees sometimes never understand why the employer makes certain decisions, and that is because full transparency is difficult to achieve. It becomes hard to understand why anyone would start a business in the first place.

The evolution of business has divided employers and employees into separate armies. There are exceptions, but this is pretty clear. Employees often claim that employers don't understand or care about them. Employers often claim that employees don't see past their own needs to the larger picture. At the core of the differences is both parties' apparent inability or disinterest to be honest with one another about each party's true intentions. What if we were all really truthful about what we think, desire, or need? One might think that this approach would help clear up confusion and get us back to the simplicity of "I work, you pay" and "I pay, you work." Well, such disclosure might backfire on everyone, because the revelation of those hidden agendas would likely work against each party and incite even more confusion and frustration. Chess is always in play.

Business management and employee rights will continuously evolve. There is always pressure from each side to gain better understanding of one another. Different versions of the "I work, you pay" and "I pay, you work" platform are tested (like the "we work, we pay" and "we pay, we work"), but none has successfully eliminated the core differences that drive the everyday perceived struggles between employers and employees.

For two summers prior to graduating college in 1992, I worked on Wall Street in an attempt to fulfill a dream of developing a career alongside the finance titans about whom I read in newspapers and magazines. There was such an allure for me, and I wanted to work for a New York City powerhouse investment firm making brilliant stock and bond transactions that would make me rich, and revered. It only took one summer between high school and college working as a clerk at a boutique bond brokerage to help me begin rewriting my career goals. It was after the second summer of working in the same environment that the absolute and final nail was driven into the coffin of my Wall Street dreams. My decision was also final about never wanting to be an employee again. However, what I learned from my coworkers and about myself in contrast to the outlook of our employer proved to be invaluable information on which I would capitalize soon thereafter.

In retrospect I expected to be in control of my day-to-day career according to my terms. I worked very hard at being the best at my given role, and I was surrounded by others who were all older, but not necessarily smarter. The experience of the amount of work I was doing, what I was being paid to do it, and the exposure to coworkers with whom my energy and interests were not shared ultimately challenged my desires. What was it about working on Wall Street that was so attractive? It was no longer the type of work, and it was clearly no longer the people. It was really my perception of how big money was made, and that is where I wanted to be. Except when I got there I no longer wanted Wall Street to be how I earned my future expected fortune. I wanted to do it on my own in my own way, whatever that would eventually be. So I decided that I would try whatever I thought would be profitable which led me to real estate years later.

From humble beginnings of buying distressed condominiums I bought land for development usually plowing near 100% of the equity and profits into the next deal. Through that process I started taking on construction until I had a steady crew of workers. Those relationships with the construction crew gave me insights into the homeownership desire of less financially saavy individuals. I built a mortgage bank to service those borrowers. Those borrowers led me to building out a real estate brokerage business. And the real estate brokerage business led me to building a title agency.

When the crash of 2008 occured, it wiped me out completely, and I had to start again. Except this time I switched careers and went into manufacturing by taking my ideas, moving to China in 2010 and developing a new company to design, market, and sell finished product ideas to any market in the world. This gave me intellectual leverage to find problems in markets and develop solutions quickly to see how needy the market really was. Starting a company in China and hiring local was another data point for how different the developed western world of employer/employee relationships is compared to Asia and Southeast Asia in general.

My experience building companies from the ground up has given me the most education about the employer/employee balance, not school. Since graduating college in 1992 I have employed over 1,000 different individuals across multiple different companies at different times in different countries both developed and emerging. I was never exactly prepared to manage people. I did not have a mentor or a guide to advise me on how to properly do much of anything when it came to business. My father was a doctor, and you know the rest of the story. Through years and years of trial and error, mistakes, successes and maturity I was fortunate enough to evolve into what others consider a great manager of people, and an effective leader an CEO. Once I reached a point of feeling confident about my management abilities, it became apparent to me that the maze of madness that delivered me here was very complicated and confusing with the requirement of making a lot of quick decisions. I learned that to be effective as an employer, I had to think like an employee while educating the employees to see the world through my eyes. My short stint working for two summers was my crash course in being on the other side.

What is clear is that there has been, and will continue to be, some division between employers and employees, as long as both parties continue to rely on one another. However, if each side understood why the other party does what it does, think about the confusion that would be eradicated. Mutual understanding would go a long way in improving employer/employee relationships.

I know a lot of people in general, and it is easy for me to describe the different profiles of employers and employees in a spectrum. When developing how to put together an entertaining format to bring to life examples of the 100 topics hereafter, I decided to synthesize people, places, events, and ideas into a tale. The tale is an experience in my creative writing using all of real life experience, and with hope, the profiles of the individuals are familiar to you. The people and story are purposely ficticious, but as in The Fountainhead, the characters are built from the foundations of personalities that are everywhere we look. Opposing points of view and the ability to express oneself without suffering retaliation are how better ideas germinate and grow.

The Tale

Here begins our journey. After all, what could be more fun than to hear brutal honesty from people on both sides of the divide? How interesting it would be to assemble people who represent both sides and let them be as revealing as possible. Add some great food, wine, and cocktails in a private place where everyone can talk freely, and the results should be amazing.

But we have to be fair. We can't just have employers talking about their ideas. No, this would require a real slice of people from good to bad. Great, average, and horrible employers and employees must all be represented in order to have a truly balanced and open conversation. There is little value in merely listening to one type of person talk about an experience; indeed, there are always two or more versions of the same story!

After scouring my database of hundreds of personal relationships, I made a shortlist of candidates. It took time to really think about who has a horrible track record as a boss but still operates a decent business. You can't really tell someone that he or she is a tough, selfish, and unfair boss and expect him/her to acknowledge such qualities and respond openly. The same goes for a bad employee profile, as well as the typical employee or employer profile. "Come join us, Average Employee, and let's talk about your work perceptions as an average person" just doesn't have a productive ring to it. However, telling them all that they would be privy to a decadent night of verbal freedom did the trick. All parties involved were promised that they could say everything and anything in confidence without their identities revealed to the rest of the world about what they really think. This openness served as a stress reliever and a catharsis of sorts. Each final candidate was eager to talk openly, without judgment, about successes, failures, ideas, stories, perceptions, and thoughts about being on one side of the employer/employee table.

The team quickly confirmed a date to meet, and I arranged to transport everyone to a private retreat in a private second home the Catskill Mountains for an overnight culinary experience, tucked comfortably away from any distractions. Like a good host should, I used every culinary talent and bartending skill I had to keep them interested in spilling their most honest thoughts on 100 different topics of employer/employee relationships. What started as a civil gathering quickly devolved to a theme of "in vino veritas," where an internationally-regarded Fortune 500 CEO and an unscrupulous blue-collar worker simultaneously traded high-fives and insults.

The lodge in the Catskills is a farmhouse built in the late 1800's that was saved from decades of neglect. It was purchased generations ago and left to a family trust, and occaisionally it is availalbe to rent to friends. The family restored the house and updated the interior style to reflect a casual contemporary feel that mixes old, hand-carved beams with modern furniture and slick surfaces. It is the perfect balance of a rough, authentic, rustic barn board structure with modern sophistication, one which makes everyone who enters the door feel right at home.

Consequently, it was hardly a surprise when Lenny, the first to arrive through the door, immediately dropped his overnight black knapsack onto the beautifully-restored pine floors and fell backwards onto the plush sofa that, he claimed, was "callin' his name." He had picked up his rental car from Newark Airport and probably sped the entire way to the lodge. His old knapsack was bulging, stretching the Dallas Cowboys embroidery to its limits. After telling him to remove his boots from the couch, I questioned him on what was nearly tearing apart his knapsack. He proceeded to tell me in his hard, southern voice that his knife had been confiscated at the airport terminal in Dallas, and he tried to bribe the official who took it from him. His knife had sentimental value because, he said, "his neighbor gave it to him to hide before the cops showed up." He opened the bag, excitedly saying, "Oh, yeah! I totally forgot. Check this out." He held up a beach towel that displayed a topless girl on a beach blowing a kiss to the words "Puerto Rico" emblazoned at the top. "I knew there was something else in there. Got this from a guy at the airport, too. Said he couldn't bring it home. Never seen nothin' like it! Got to hide it from my girl."

Needless to say, Lenny is not an avid traveler, but he was clearly the right person to represent the unscrupulous faction of the general employee base. He arrived in a version of what he has always worn whenever I have seen him - a worn pair of jeans, a pair of well-used boots or sneakers, an untucked t-shirt, and a cap. The cap he was wearing today was black with the letters "TMP" stamped on the front. His t-shirt was crisp and white, bearing the name of a lumber yard and logo depicting a bulldog chomping a wood plank in half. He was sporting a neatly-trimmed moustache that was thin and lean because, as he explained, "My goatee was givin' my girlfriend a rash." Regardless of his seemingly tough guy appearance with his inset eyes, he conveys a sense of adoration to those whom he trusts. Indeed, he is very loyal and protective of people he likes. On the other side, however, is a guy who has little sympathy for people whom he believes have victimized him or treated him unfairly, even if he was the cause. I know this because I approached him for help years ago while he worked for a competitor in exchange for a future favor; after keeping my word, he felt aligned to me. Simply put, he is one step away from being a henchman who says "yeah, boss, yeah, boss" between snickers. The troubles he had with the law when he was a teen have kept him interested in abiding by the law as he approaches 30 next year. His future is written with more of the same behavior.

We sat outside, catching up in a pair of comfortable Adirondack chairs while the summer Friday morning approached noon. The temperature was idyllic, and the sky was a crystal blue that appeared muddier in the distance from an approaching car on the long, dry dirt road leading to the lodge. The car's horn was honking in a playful manner, and Lenny and I went to the approaching vehicle to greet a mud-coated white SUV with lightly tinted windows.

The first person to emerge from the car was Lauren, who immediately started telling us about how they took a wrong turn, got stuck on the side of the road near a "brook or something," and was laughing about how filthy the car was. It was obvious from the pattern of mud around the tires that the driver had spun the vehicle's tires in an effort to escape a marshy area.

As the story was told, the passenger, Chandra, was laughing from the front seat and repeating, "Oh, my God, oh, my God." The driver, Glen, one of the most respected CEO's in the nation, was just grinning with that look in his eye that communicated to Lenny and me that as soon as the girls were done "acting like girls," he was going to tell us exactly how he had it under control.

Glen was the most difficult person with whom to arrange a date to visit the lodge. Nearly everyone had been presented with dates for this overnight excursion based entirely on Glen's availability. As the CEO of a very successful corporation headquartered in New Jersey with thousands of employees operating nationally and internationally, his days off away from his family are very limited.

Glen is responsible for the growth and sale of two important companies during his career; in the process, he has amassed wealth and experience that only handfuls of people ever acquire. Beginning as a stockroom clerk, he paid his way through school by earning scholarships, working at night, and eventually earning a business management and law degree. He surfaced from retirement only years ago after turning 68 in response to the request of a major corporation to help it reinvent itself. The board of directors developed a list of 3 names, of which his was their first choice. The salary, benefits, and opportunities required to lure him out of retirement must have been substantial. He is known for his unbelievable talent of managing employees and has developed an employee fan club that blindly follows him from company to company as positions arise. His mastery of personality, politics, motivation, innovation, and leadership has earned him the highest recognition from inside and outside the companies for which he has worked. Having him as part of our overnight conversation was an honor to everyone. He picked up Chandra at the train station and Lauren from the airport in an effort to be a team player, even though the detours added an hour to his ride. He would normally travel this distance by helicopter.

The two-hour ride to the lodge was hopefully fun for all of them. Chandra likes to talk when the topic is something that interests her. She is not a great small-talker. Her interests are essentially confined to weekend fun with friends, decent sitcom television shows, social media, and eating. She and I share a food connection. I have never known her to have a boyfriend lasting longer than a few weeks. She has a solid yet arguably idle mind. Her personality can be somewhat rigid, leaving little room for the point of view of another, which has perhaps restricted her romantic opportunities. Nevertheless, she is a good worker when given a task. She contributes the requisite amount of time at a decent pace during standard work hours. Staying overtime or working weekends is not part of her employment vocabulary because such acts hold no value to her. Work is a means to earn money, and when the proverbial whistle blows, Chandra punches out on the dot. She will arrive promptly the next day to do her job, at her own pace and in a diligent manner, but getting anything more out of her is an exercise in futility.

My relationship with Chandra began when she worked for my company years ago after leaving her previous job because it was boring. She worked for a variety of companies until her mid-thirties, when she decided that she wanted to establish a more long-term relationship with a company. We put her to work, and she did a good job for two straight years. After closing the company, I recommended her to friends who were looking for a stable worker who would "do the job" as it was described. Chandra and I always stayed in touch, and I found her insight and thought process to be typical of so many employees in the workforce. I knew I could count on her to be open about her points of view related to working. She has since expanded her social media interests into becoming a food influencer.

Lauren, on the other hand, is a single woman in her early 40's who has been an entrepreneur for about 10 years. She worked in the catering business and eventually started her own company with money she borrowed from her father. I met Lauren through her father, a retiree with whom I have been friends since 1991. He made a lot of money early in life and retired in his late 40's, raising his only daughter while traveling the world together with his wife. I met Lauren in the mid 1990's after he recommended I speak with her about catering a fundraiser. She was employed with a good catering company that served as the training ground for her to open up her own catering business years later. Her father confessed to me that he gave her the money with little expectation that she would be successful at starting and operating a catering company on her own, given that she lacked real management or practical business experience; he had believed that she would get frustrated and go back to a traditional job. But, he contended, the money did not mean anything to him, and he preferred to give her a forgivable loan over conveying the impression that he didn't believe in her.

Well, Lauren proved her father wrong. When Lauren decides to do something, she does it. Within two years, her fledgling catering business in New York City grew to employ 30 people on a regular basis and up to 30 more on a part-time basis when extra hands are needed for larger jobs. I have had the good fortune of watching her business develop because I became one of her first customers and, at her father's urging, somewhat of a business consultant. She had to develop her own managerial style and skills on the job, a process in which she engages even today. The affluent lifestyle she experienced while growing up detached her from the regular lives of most everyone else. Combined with her affable personality, her management style is essentially an experiment of trial and error as her business continues to grow organically. Becoming an entrepreneur was an entirely new education in life for Lauren, and her experiences mimic those of an entire cross-section of employers in the world who are learning about what to do as their business matures. Her business has made it near impossible for her to meet someone, and she faces a life likely of no children and marriage.

At around 2 p.m., Grace and Vinny arrived. This was quite the sight to see. Grace is everything her name describes. She is pretty, sexy, gentle in speech, well-mannered, and non-confrontational. Vinny is pretty much her antithesis; he is a testosterone-driven, big, burly, unrefined, cigar-chomping man's man with a personality of a ghost-driven concrete truck. When the two of them pulled up in another white SUV – this one clean – it looked like they were in a conversation that needed to be finished before they got out. Knowing that Vinny has an audacious personality, I figured that he had the chance to irritate Grace with a controversial conversation on the ride up, and she was giving him a piece of her mind. When I went outside to meet them, I discovered that they had stopped at the local farmers' market on the way up and bought bushels of fresh vegetables and an enormous, stunning arrangement of flowers. Somehow, Grace and Vinny managed to coalesce during the ride up and were inspired to contribute to the mounting supply of food already at the lodge.

When I had asked Grace to be part of the dinner, she immediately confirmed and mentioned that she was looking forward to meeting everyone. She loved the idea and, with her characteristic efficiency, wanted to help in the organization and execution of the entire project, from coordinating flights to New York to dietary restrictions for the dinner.

One October Sunday, about five years earlier, I had my first introduction to Grace without ever actually meeting her. On an especially turbulent flight back to New York from Miami, many of the passengers had become upset. When the plane landed, the captain required everyone to remain seated to allow a very slow elderly woman off of the plane first because she had suffered severe nausea from the turbulence. The old woman made it through the plane assisted by her granddaughter. She was put into a wheelchair and wheeled away.

The next day, I had a meeting with the CEO of an investment firm in NYC to discuss the funding of a new project. When I arrived, the CEO's assistant greeted me and escorted me to the conference room, and I commented on her tan. She explained to me that she had just returned from Florida the day earlier to help teach basic math to struggling first generation children as part of a charity organization. As we traded Florida stories, she mentioned taking care of an old woman seated next to her who had become ill during an unusually turbulent flight. I remembered, of course, and confessed that I had thought she was her granddaughter. But Grace had not even known the old lady; she had simply felt awful that the woman had been alone and scared. She helped keep her calm and requested to allow her to get off the plane first. I was amazed at how considerate and thoughtful she had been in taking care of a complete stranger.

As her boss and I continued to work on a few deals, Grace and I were able to really get to know each other. Her diligence, work ethic, honesty, and thoroughness helped facilitate the deals, and as a result, we became social friends as well. I wish I had a sea of employees like her, and I know her boss wishes he had another one of her as well. He and I have spoken about Grace many times, and he has revealed that without her, he wouldn't know what to do at this point in his career. He claims that they share a brain, and he can use all of his processing power at work with the assistance of Grace. She has dutifully earned the name Amazing Grace by her friends and colleagues.

When Vinny stepped out of the car, I was very excited to see him. He had just become a father two months ago, and he could not have been prouder to talk about his baby girl. His girlfriend, the mother of the baby, had already sent several e-mails with pictures of the baby and asked me when I was going to visit Boston to meet Francy, short for Francesca.

Vinny seems to love his girlfriend, but he will not get married to her because he believes that he will lose the benefits he enjoys by retaining the status of being technically single. Practically speaking, he is married. He has lived with his girlfriend for over five years, he has a child with her, and they act and do everything that a normal married couple does. His family is concerned because he has not followed the trend of his brothers and sister, who have all taken the traditional path of marriage. Yet the commitment holds Vinny back, even though he has been known to introduce his girlfriend as his wife just because he claims that it is easier.

When Vinny turned 40 a few years ago, he celebrated with only a few people, of which I was one. A milestone birthday usually brings out wishes from lots of friends and family, but such was not the case for Vinny, who doesn't seem to keep friends easily and has had a lot of conflict with his family for the past decade as a result of his financial success. He grew up with an abusive Irish father and an Italian mother in a poor section of Boston. He was named Vincent after his mother's father, who was the patriarch of the family. It was Vincent Senior who contributed to raising the young Vinny when Vinny's father was incapacitated from drinking too much, working overnight shifts, or being too exhausted. After his grandfather's death when Vinny was around 24 years old, Vinny became, as it has been told to me, tougher and more intolerant. As one of five children, he vowed to make his own money so he would never again have to live in the kind of squalor he experienced as a youth. He barely finished high school and never considered college, forecasting it to be a roadblock to quickly becoming financially independent. Without any formal business training, he worked himself into some lucrative businesses that earned him a small fortune. He worked every day after school from the age of 14 right up until the day he graduated high school. He went on to drive tow trucks on the night shift for a local garage. After saving enough money, he purchased his own tow truck, and then another and another, until he had the largest fleet in the area. By the age of 27, he had earned his first million dollars and a reputation for being an extremely hard worker. He worked alongside his drivers on night shifts and signed lucrative contracts with municipalities for their towing needs.

He then decided to make some small real estate investments for his towing business. He purchased a warehouse for his vehicles and an enormous piece of unwanted industrial land on which to store the towed cars. As the real estate boom grew, so did the number and value of his property acquisitions. He sold some of them at the height of a cyclicl real estate boom to a real estate developer, realizing millions of dollars in profit. He reinvested some of the money in other properties and businesses that he understood.

Vinny doesn't understand high-level management or have a lot of people skills; rather, he gravitates to businesses that share similar employee profiles: those who earn a low wage, are non-technical, are not educated, and can drive a truck. He bought a minority share of a vending machine business that he eventually purchased in full because he thought the operators of the business were "too nice" to the employees and could have been making more money with a different approach. His investment of $250,000 in the vending business is worth close to $8,000,000 now because of his retooling of the operations.

But Vinny's financial reputation is at odds with his managerial reputation. He became known in his late 20's as the "Tyrant of Towing" because he would hire and fire employees with all the care and deliberation of selecting an item on a breakfast menu. He has hired and fired nearly all of his family members. He sees employees in his business as dispensable because, for every person who will do the job, "there are five lined up behind them to do it as well." His gauge on employee performance starts with the level of the employee's hard work as compared to Vinny's. He doesn't want to hear about other management ideas; he feels that his financial success is the result of his style, which is one that others would do well to adopt.

Vinny has become a very successful businessman but remains a bit of a loner. He has a small yet diverse group of friends who revere him for his amazing success story and his fun social personality. His wealth allows him to be a spectacle at times and, like Lenny, is loyal for life to his friends. How he and I became friends is purely by chance. We met at a famous steakhouse on a Saturday night in Boston because our significant others struck up a conversation in the bathroom about lighted RIKI LOVES RIKI beauty mirrors. They are both passionate people and carried the conversation from the bathroom to the bar; before I knew it, the four of us were having dinner together.

I was initially hesitant to dine with strangers based on a shared love of a a mirror; furthermore, based on the restaurant staff's treatment of Vinny, I knew he either scared them, or he was a regular. I remember thinking that he was a mobster, and I determined that under no circumstances would I stand alongside him on the sidewalk in front of the restaurant in case there was a drive-by like the one that took down Paul Castellano after a steak dinner at Spark's in NYC.

The night turned out to be a lot of fun, and Vinny and I shared light stories about business as we watched our ladies chat away the night. They seemed to have far more in common than we did; nevertheless, the love affair with food that we all seemed to share was evident as we ate family-style and ordered loads of delicious items from the menu in a rush of excitement. It became readily apparent that one could say anything to Vinny, no matter how gross, off-color, politically incorrect, stupid, or vulgar, and he wouldn't flinch. Yet I noticed a sobering change in him when I ruminated on some random tidbit of wisdom during our casual conversation. The comment made him introspective and somewhat uncomfortable. From that moment on, I assumed the role of his freelance psychologist. He fired off questions at me, asking my opinion on topics that intrigued him. There must have been something in me that made him feel comfortable discussing the intimate details of his life; whatever it was, it extended the evening's events from the restaurant to two other venues that night. At the end of the evening, Vinny made it clear that he wanted to get together again. From that night on, we have built a very open and direct friendship. I can tell him point-blank that he truly is the unfair tyrant and dirtbag for which he is known, and he yells back in defense, right before we both hang up the phone laughing. He is open to learn, but only from those whom he trusts.

Seeing Vinny the Tyrant and Amazing Grace arrive in one piece after two hours in the car was a highlight for me. Knowing the worst employer and the best employee would be forced to engage in conversation was equally as humorous and dangerous. Yet they seemed to get along fine and looked even happy to have spent the time together. This was an obvious relief.

It did not take long for everyone to settle in and be introduced to one another. Shoes were removed, cocktails were served, and everyone began to relax, surrounded by the calmness of the light breeze that wafted a light pine fragrance into the air from the bordering hemlocks. There were lots of awkward silences that crept into the conversations as the group absorbed the perfect weather and the coziness of the fluffy couches and rocking chairs outside. Colorful flower gardens that bordered the lodge were glowing in the sun, and I could see that each minute that passed further melted the stresses that had accompanied each guest to the mountains. This was precisely the reason I chose the lodge for the retreat. Having been there many times in the past and experienced the same deceleration, I knew my friends would be eased into the state of comfort needed to contribute openly to the conversations at dinner. Distractions were minimized as cell phones flirted with one inconsistent bar of service, and the sole landline at the lodge held little appeal due to its public location and short cord. It is too far off the grid for Internet, so our interruptions were reduced to distant animal calls and creeks in the floors.

As the afternoon faded, I retreated to the kitchen to make last-minute preparations for the decadent dinner that would be served promptly at 7 p.m. With the exception of Arctic char and oysters, all of the food was purchased from local markets and farms on windy roads with weather-battered farm signs. Stopping at every good opportunity along the way, I amassed the impressive summer harvests and fresh meats for which the region is known. Over the next couple of hours, I roasted, baked, sliced, and diced to perfection several interesting dishes that aimed to please the palate of every guest. Chandra made her way into the kitchen and was stupefied at the array of foods that were being prepared. She loves food and puts on a few new pounds each year as a result. She has an enormous appreciation for the culinary arts but does not know how to prepare anything beyond the basics. So when she saw the tower of oysters on ice and the marinating pork chops cut that morning from a slaughterhouse down the road from the lodge, her eyes lit up with excitement. "Let me get my phone. I have to take a picture of this," she said.

After she left, she made an announcement to the others about what she had just seen, and the five others immediately paraded into the kitchen. They immediately swarmed around the food on the counter. Vinny and Lenny jockeyed for position in front of the oysters. Grace started cleaning up the items in the sink, and Glen, not used to being in the kitchen, took a seat at the counter to watch. Lauren, the caterer, wanted to learn about each of the dishes in hopes of inspiration for her business. Chandra pushed through the kitchen doors with her phone ready, shouting, "Easy cheese!" and taking the first picture of everyone moving about the kitchen. She then exclaimed, "Wait, wait, we have to do it again so I'm in the picture! Let me get my SUNRISE." She returned with her social media light, mounted her phone into her GLAMCOR SUNRISE on the counter, paired the phone with her light, grabbed her remote control, and jumped back into the frame next to the sea salt, pepper, and fresh, herb-crusted Arctic char. She posed as a game show assistant displaying the possible prizes, with her palms up in a sweeping motion over the fish taking pictures the entire time with the remote control. Glen thought this was particularly funny and encouraged everyone to pose with a kitchen utensil for another photograph. Lenny and Lauren grabbed long chefs knives and held them high like crossed swords, while Vinny found a huge spatula and posed like a tennis player returning a serve, ready to hit Chandra in the rear. Chandra got on her knees on the counter, holding a rolling pin above her head in a reproduced pose from the last musical note of a Fame performance. Then there was Grace, scrambling around the kitchen looking for the perfect kitchen prop for the photo. "Wait, wait, I am still looking!" she said.

"Y'all come on, I can't hold up my arm like this forever," Lenny exclaimed.

"Let me help you, Grace. Here, what is in this cabinet?" asked Glen in his helpful, fatherly tone. He opened up a long cabinet that was equipped with every baking supply imaginable. He pulled out three white identical chefs hats, quickly putting one on Grace, another on Vinny, and the last on himself. He found two oversized batter spatulas and threw one to Grace, who caught it upside-down.

Everyone struck hysterical poses, and as Chandra said, "OK, ready, 3…2…" Lenny took a large measuring cup of flour and, at "1," tossed the contents high into the air. It was a hysterical collection of images that will forever be burned into our memories.

If there were any tensions or hidden inhibitions among the group before the picture, they were definitely gone now. Everyone broke into deep laughter and threw their arms around each other's shoulders as they wiped flour from each other's eyes. Chandra continued to take pictures because the aftermath was as entertaining as the prize photo. "Look at my hair! I look like an old woman! Is this what I am going to look like when I get old?! This is great content!" shrieked Chandra. Glen cleverly recruited Lauren and Vinny to even the score with Lenny, who didn't have a speck of flour on him. Within seconds, Lauren was in front of Lenny, laughing and telling him how funny he was. She raised her hands up to solicit two "high fives" from him. Just has Lenny put his hands up to reciprocate, Glen pulled back on the rear center belt loop of Lenny's jeans, while Vinny dumped a heaping clump of flour down his pants. They smacked him on the pockets and watched a plume of flour rise from his jeans. The laughter continued when Lenny confessed to bringing only one pair of pants.

We never made it to the dining room to eat that night. The kitchen became a playground, and everyone felt more comfortable as they cleaned up and took seats at the counter. Chandra really wanted to watch the food cook and capture more content for her social media outlets, and there were enough seats at the counter for everyone. Glen took over as bartender, mixing drinks using a Finger Lakes wine. He was really creative and kept everyone interested in his delicious concoctions.

Grace and Chandra organized the food and set places for everyone around the counter. The layout was perfectly designed, promoting both eating and communication as we sat high up in tall chairs.

Lenny excused himself after the kitchen was cleaned up because he wanted to beat his jeans to get out the flour. He had to go outside at the back of the lodge to do it and didn't want anyone to "come lookin,' because I ain't wearing no underwear." When he returned, he had with him a slightly-worn CPR dummy he had found in a closet. "Hey, look at what I found. I'm bringing this dummy to dinner. C'mon, stupid, say something," he joked.

"Let's find him a good shirt," Glen suggested.

"Yeah, put some clothes on Stupid. I don't want to stare at that dummy's nipples all night," Vinny added.

"I saw a closet with some old clothes in it upstairs right by my room," Chandra said.

"I'll go with you! Come on!" Lauren said.

When Lauren and Chandra returned, they were laughing at what they found. They told everyone not to look as they dressed "Stupid," as everyone referred it to now. When we all turned around, Stupid was propped up in the eighth chair wearing a red and blue flannel shirt and a tweed cap adorned with a peacock feather. Lenny completed the look by adding his orange reflective sunglasses. Stupid looked ridiculous and was a comical addition to the dinner. Glen filled a martini glass with water and set it in front of Stupid as he pretended to have a conversation with him about the state of the stock market. "I bet you know all about the market crashes," Glen stated to Stupid.

The group began eating between sips of Glen's cocktails. Lauren referred to Glen's drinks as "Big Shot Cocktails," which prompted Chandra and Lenny to ask her from where she got the name. "Because Glen is a big shot in the real world. He is one of the top CEO's in his industry, and there is even a book on him!" Lauren replied.

"No way! What is it? Bartending for Dummies?" teased Lenny as he pointed to Stupid's martini glass and let out his distinctive, crow-like laugh.

"Did you really write a book, Glen?" said Lauren.

"No, no. A book was written about my previous company and my iron-fisted reigning over the masses," Glen said jokingly.

"I don't do a lot of reading, Glen, so what's it about? I mean, is it any good? Because I can make my girlfriend read it and tell me about it," Vinny said, only half joking.

"It's basically about the changes I made to our corporate culture and our operations when I took the CEO position at a new company. You know, I was eager to perform after being promoted at the company. I knew I could do the work, but there were parts of the company I just didn't understand because I didn't have any experience with certain operations. And when I don't understand something, I recruit everyone I know to help me understand it. The book is sort of about that," he said as he put his arm around Lenny, "and mixing cocktails!" The grouped laughed at Glen's humble presence and his ability to make Lenny laugh.

Continued

VINNY: What was the first thing that you did? What'dja do first, Glen? Fire everyone? That's what I woulda done!

GLEN: [responding smoothly] No, that came later, actually. There were a lot of people who had to go but you don't know that the day you walk through the door. The first thing I do is get my office in order. You know, you have to make sure you have everything in line to do your job. You need the basics to make decisions and analyze what's going on. So whenever I have a new position or go into a new company, I spend the first day getting my systems up and running. Telephones have to be working, I need to know how to transfer calls, call other departments, you know. Then I need spiral binders that I write everything in. They are my bibles. And my computer needs to be working with all of the programs I need and email up and running on my computer and my phone. Oh, so that is where it starts. Day two is when I go after everyone who contributed to any problem on day one. Like the tech department.

LAUREN: So why the book on you? That doesn't seem like anything special.

VINNY: Yeah, that ain't special.

GLEN: The book is not on that. The book is about how I took over the CEO position and figured out the moving parts, the problems and turned it around.

CHANDRA: If you don't know how the company works, how did you figure it out?

Employer

Consider Hiring A Consultant To Analyze Your Company

The sheer mention of the suggestion of hiring a business consultant often elicits an eye rolls from the C-suite. However what should be recognized is that consultancy of your/the business is often not formalized; it's often a casual conversation among peers in order to test if the sensibilities of your executive team and you are sane. This is peer-to-peer consultancy which is usually embellished or missing critical information in order to protect one's own image.

How comfortable are you opening up your books and putting your business decisions on display? Unless you are feeling a burn, it's unlikely. Do you want to acquire another company? Do you want to sell your company? Is your operation optimized for a buyer? Have you looked at your company through the lens of a buyer? Do you know what you should be doing with recent market changes? How much do you really think you know versus what you think you know?

You should consider hiring a professional consultant to objectively review your operation to illuminate that which you have not yet seen. Early efforts should include introductory conversations with consultants to develop a cost-benefit analysis.

GLEN: Well, the same thing I do when I don't know much about moving parts of any company or if I want to do something that we don't do everyday. I hire consultants who know it. You know, it is my job to have the best information provided to me.

CHANDRA: Aren't you supposed to know everything about how the business works? You *are* the boss.

GLEN: Oh, come on, that's not realistic. Let me give you an example. When I took the CEO position, I was in charge of preparing the company for sale. The guy who had the position before me started the ball rolling by talking to different investment bankers and other interested parties. So when I got on board, I had no idea what was going on, and neither did the board of directors. Everyone was concerned about what was happening and how we were preparing.

CHANDRA: Why were they trying selling the company?

GLEN: Because the board of directors believed that the value created was at a peak and the market climate was good for a company like ours. The previous CEO wasn't equipped to handle a sale. He had never done it before, and it seemed there

Employee

Has Your Company Hired A Consultant?

If your company has hired a consultant who is working to better understand the company for which you work, you may have mixed feelings about it. You may be wondering exactly why your boss hired a consultant and why that consultant is asking you all sorts of questions that seem irrelevant to his/her supposed purpose.

Many times, consultants are hired to prepare a company for sale, to provide insights into how certain company departments can operate better, to perform important tasks that are not in the skill set or allotted time for current employees, and to make suggestions on what the company needs to do to get to the next level. Consultants are generally professionals who are hired for specific tasks with which your employer needs professional help.

You may feel that you are not being given straight information on why the consultants are there. If you feel like you are being given the run around, it may be because there may be confidentiality issues or that your job is in jeopardy. Consultants are generally under confidentiality agreements, so you will most likely not get any relevant information from them. But you can hammer them with questions to see which ones they do not answer.

was one mistake after another. When I took over, I immediately hired a top consulting firm that prepared our company for sale.

LAUREN: What do they know that you don't know?

GLEN: A lot. We don't sell our company everyday because we are focused on growing it. It's like selling a house. You live there for years and then you want to sell, so you hire a real estate agent to tell you the value. Then they make recommendations on how you can increase the value to the buyers in the market. The consultants did a comprehensive review of every department and all profitability per department.

LAUREN: What was the outcome?

GLEN: We realized we were losing money in some divisions because we took on too many growth projects. Some departments were a mess and totally mismanaged. We ended up not selling and fixed the departments that were hemorrhaging. We had to get the divisions back to their core business and in a better, more streamlined way. It took the consultants two months to make recommendations and a year to fix.

LAUREN: Well, that is what happens when

Erik A. Kaiser

Employer

Are You Understaffed?

It can be difficult to determine whether or not you are understaffed especially if you have already optimized for efficiency. Your employees might complain that there is too much to do, and you see that the work is not getting done as quickly as you need it. You may think that the employees are lazy or are not doing as much as they should, and that their lack of effort is the problem, not the manpower. But if they are working hard and still cannot keep up with the work without spending inordinate amounts of time to finish it, you are most likely understaffed.

Be sure to act quickly in either case. If your employees are not getting the work done when they have the ability to do so, you are not understaffed. You just have the wrong staff.

If your employees are legitimately understaffed, consider solving through temporary hires while recruiting additional permanent staff if the work is more specialized. Otherwise, you will face declining productivity as your overworked staff begins to fatigue and burn out.

---

you make too much work for yourself. It's no different in the catering business. In the beginning, I took on too many jobs for the amount of people that I had. We had three deliveries on one night, and my people were working night and day. I didn't sleep for weeks. I would sleep in the shop for a few hours, and so would some of the other people as well.

LENNY: So how much more did they get paid to do all that work?

CHANDRA: You wouldn't get me sleeping at the office! [laughing]

LAUREN: Well, it was in the beginning and we were really growing, and it was all sort of new to me. It was an exciting time for the business, probably more exciting for me than my employees, so I expected them to want to work more.

CHANDRA: My boss tried that with me when I started working at my current job. At 5 o'clock, I was packing up and out the door, and everyone was looking at me like, "Who let you go?" Yeah, there was a lot of work to do, but it's not my fault if you don't want to hire enough people to do it. After 5 o'clock, it's my time. **You want to fire me,**

Employee

Are You Buried in Work?

Staying late? Working weekends? Stressed about not getting the job done? Having dreams about what needs to get done at work? Can't find time to spend the money that you are making? You could either be really busy, or you could be experiencing the effects of working in an understaffed environment.

Distinguishing between the two is relatively simple. Busy is when you feel you can get caught up with some extra effort. Working in an understaffed environment is when you know that there isn't any way you are going to get all of the work done, and the prospect of even trying to is daunting.

The result of being part of an understaffed team is never positive for the quality of work. You run a high risk of producing lower-quality work and burning out more quickly.

If you find yourself in this situation, recommend to your boss that he or she consider hiring some temporary help. Many growing companies go through periods of being understaffed; this is normal. What is not normal is allowing this situation to become the status quo.

---

go ahead. Fire me because you don't want to hire enough people to do the work. That's just cheap.
GLEN: Or maybe the others can't work as quickly as you. Your boss may just have the wrong people.
GRACE: When I first started out working after college, I worked at a temp agency because it was hard to get a job. I went to a couple of places but found that the companies I worked for treated me like gold because they needed people so bad. The other workers complained about having too much work and they were stressed out, but I never complained. I was happy to have a job, and if it meant staying later, that was fine with me. The last place I worked kept me, and I ended up working there for two years before getting another job.
LENNY: So I guess y'all ain't never played roller hockey in the parking lot with that amount of work to do? I like working for those type of guys, you know, the ones that let me do other stuff on company time.
VINNY: Oh yeah, right. Try that one by me, and you'll be under the truck instead of driving it.

Erik A. Kaiser

Employer

Are You Overstaffed?

Too many people on the payroll can be deceiving. When business is going well, money tends to wash away more problems, and there is a higher tolerance for non-critical expenditures. No one seems to question the number of people working at the company because it appears that everyone is working and all is good.

But when cash flow declines and you are forced to get reacquainted with your company's books to determine how to keep the bottom line positive, you have to ensure that all of your staff is necessary. Payroll costs are expensive, and companies that are top-heavy with payroll are more keen to controlling employee costs.

One of the least disruptive tests you can give your company to determine if it is overstaffed is to use employee vacations as a start. Let certain people take substantial vacations (two weeks), and while they are away, determine how valuable they really are to the organization. If you find that other employees pick up the work without much extra effort, you most likely do not need that person. If while the employee is on vacation, you actually begin to forget about him or her and realize that it does not make a difference to your business if he or she ever returns, you are clearly overstaffed. Cut the payroll cost and give the employee an opportunity to find employment in an environment where he or she will be needed and appreciated.

LENNY: *Whatever, dude. Work is boring if it is just work. Who wants to do that?*

VINNY: If I ever see a guy standin' around or doing something other than working, he's gone. Boom! Right there, I fire him on the spot. That means that you got too many people or not enough work if someone's got time for screwing around.

LENNY: Check this out, then. So, a few years ago, I was working for this rug company in the warehouse moving rugs and stupid crap like that with a bunch of guys. They were a big company with a bunch of people in the office, and when there was nothin' to do, we set up in the warehouse a room made out of rugs in the back. We took these big area rugs on the racks and made them sorta square to each other and made a room. And we put one of them big iPads in there from the office. When the boss was away, everyone would go in there and watch movies and play games. This guy Joe in sales brought a old mini fridge, and we put beer in it. It was awesome in there. We used to watch everything in there. It's cool, too, because the rugs absorbed the sound, so you could really have a cool surround sound. We had

Employee

Not Enough Work To do?

Extra coffee breaks don't put a dent in accomplishing your work? Able to meander around? More personal time on the Internet? All of your work still getting done with more distractions? Your company is either slow, or you a part of an overstaffed team.

Watch out. Employers have a radar on employee productivity, and they know the costs of payroll. Most employers will do anything to cut down on payroll costs. If you know you are in an overstaffed environment, you have to be prepared for the idea that your job will might be eliminated.

To try and safeguard against being terminated, approach your boss and describe how you can take on the work of other employees and work harder so the company can save on employment costs. If your boss sees that you are aware of the problem, he or she will be happy and will most likely consider saving you first, since you were first to approach.

Don't let another employee identify that the team is overstaffed and make the suggestion to reduce the number of people before you do. People will eventually be terminated, so jockey into position to keep your job with this adult approach.

---

all these chairs with the rollers on 'em from the office in there. That was awesome.

VINNY: I woulda cracked your skull.
You gotta be kidding me? How did you get busted you bonehead?

LENNY: We never got busted, no way! Bro, everybody was in on this. No one was ratting this out. This was half the reason those dudes came to work.

GLEN: So why did you leave?

LENNY: I got fired.

GLEN: For what?

LENNY: The guy who owned it just got rid of a bunch of people because he said the business wasn't doing good. That, and because I used to take the install trucks home on the weekends to do my own thing, and he said something about it being a problem. Whatever. He thought it was like the best place on earth to work. Who the hell wants to work for a carpet company forever? Who does that?

LAUREN: Well, when you build a business, it is very personal to you. I was, like, *totally* into everything with my business and thought everyone else was going to be as

---

Erik A. Kaiser

Employer

Think Your Company Is So Great No One Wants To Leave?

Are you high on your own company? Are you under the impression that your company's practices and success makes it so attractive that losing an employee by death would be the only acceptable reason for a departure? This is a certain recipe for your extremely rude awakening.

Employers who adopt this delusional attitude will find themselves thrown for a loop when an employee submits his or her two weeks' notice for reasons related to the company. When employers are riding high with confidence, a departing employee can be a major blow to the ego, and it will make the employer question exactly what it means for the organization.

Your company may be great already or have great promise. There is a thrill to building a company, and engaging the commitment of the employees is crucial. But don't be alarmed if your ideas of success are not aligned with those of each of your employees. You could be building an exciting product that will change the world or providing a service that is in demand. But what you think is great and tolerable about the business may not have the same payoff for those working for you. They just might not be as excited about everything as you are. Always remember that, and you will be more aware of changing attitudes that

excited as me. It never dawned on me that the people who worked for me didn't think the same thing.

LENNY: Yeah, that's how this guy was. He was always talking about how great the company was compared to other companies because... I don't know why.

LAUREN: That could be a good or a bad thing. When I started, we kept building and growing, and there was one point that we were rocking. And I remember thinking that I had a good thing going and other people from other catering companies wanted to work for me. That felt really good, and it was like, "I never have to worry about finding people to work again like when I started." And then one day, this girl who was one of my best workers, who had been with me since the beginning, told me she was going to a bigger catering company.

"Whenever I climb, I am followed by a dog called 'Ego'."
Friedrich Nietzsche

24   For Office Use Only

Employee

Is Your Employer Delusional About Your Commitment To The Company?

Without question, there are times when your employer will be super-confident and amazed by the company. The company may get a lot of press or experience huge growth, both of which spell success to your employer. Those events may infuse your employer with a sense of bravado that, while energizing, can lead to a disconnection to reality.

You may witness this during a revealing moment in which the employer perceives that the company is of greater value to you than it actually is. This means that your employer is operating in the clouds, unless your situation is so unique and fabulous that you know it is true.

Other ways you may experience this type of thinking is if your employer becomes more demanding while holding the scepter of job loss over your head as motivation. If your employer is so confident that you would not want to lose your opportunity at the company, it is only a matter of time before your boss gets a reality check.

GLEN: Let me guess, you thought about what could go wrong next?

LAUREN: Worse, I felt like really stupid. [pointing to Stupid at the table] Like him. And I walked around with sunglasses on for weeks so if someone asked me about what happened to her, they couldn't see my expression. I was afraid the others would leave, and then it would get around that people are leaving the company, and I would have to shut down because no one would give us business.

CHANDRA: Why did she leave?

LAUREN: You know, **I begged her to stay**. She said that my business was not consistent enough and she wanted something more steady. We would have a rush of jobs, and then sometimes we would have only a few, and she would have to chase the money. We were always just making payroll, and that made her nervous. She was looking for more "stability" and went to one of the biggest catering companies in the city. Oh, and she never got any time off, but what did she expect?

VINNY: Yeah, you try and take a vacation, and the work doesn't get done right. You

Erik A. Kaiser

Employer

Hostage to Your Employees?

Do you feel like you are owned by your employees? Do you feel trapped? Do you feel like they control your destiny and that your world would crumble without them? If so, then either you do not have proper control over your company, or you may not fully understand your industry.

It takes a long time to build a company and to find the right people, but you did not go this distance only to be taken hostage. If you are feeling this way, you need to quietly go out into the market and do some undercover research. Think of it this way; if all of your employees failed to return to work one day and you had to replace them, what would you do? Do you already know replacements, or would you have to look for them?

Venture into the market and look for new people as if you have to replace them all. Make time to meet and greet others in the industry and begin to build relationships. Get others excited about what you are doing, and leave the conversation open to the possibility of joining your company. Build a database of the people you meet, and build relationships with them.

Having replacement employees will give you confidence and relax your mind. You will regain some control over your destiny and you will have sourced other people who can work for the company.

---

know how long it was before I could take a day off and not have those monkeys screw somethin' up? It was forever. *Years.*

CHANDRA: Well, what do you think it is like for us not taking time off because if we do, you'll get rid of us? That's the real problem. It's just a job. You don't own me, so if I want to take a few days off and do something, why are you always wanting to replace me?

VINNY: Because you either work or you don't. **I don't get this vacation time crap. You work, you get paid. You don't work, you don't get paid.** I don't get paid if I don't bring in work. Who's payin' me? You? I don't think so.

CHANDRA: My sister broke her foot. After surgery, she had to wait until I finished work to pick her up at the hospital because if I left work early to get her, I would have gotten a pay cut again. That's what these creeps did to me when I had to stay home with the flu for a couple of days. They said I was being unreliable and I could have come to work.

GLEN: I don't agree with the part about you having to get a pay cut, but employers have to go to work sometimes when they are sick because if they don't, their business

Employee

Hostage To Your Company?

Are you in a position where you are afraid to leave your company? You may be satisfied with your company but not thrilled with your job, and if you were even caught thinking about leaving, there would be serious consequences to opportunity. Perhaps you feel trapped at the company because of a loyalty issue. Or maybe you are getting paid above-market, and replacing your current income is close to impossible for what you do.

You first need to determine if you are happy with your job. If you are not, then you are not working to your potential. It is up to you to make a plan to find employment that will make you happy doing what you love to do.

If you are being paid more than you can earn somewhere else and you are unhappy, you will be terminated eventually. It is almost inevitable. It is easy to find someone who will replace you for less money and be happy about it.

You also need to determine if you are feeling like a hostage because of your perception of what people will think about you leaving your job. You may be identified with your job and believe that losing that identity will negatively impact you in some manner. Don't be so convinced of this. People generally revere others who take control and initiative in their lives.

---

won't work.

LAUREN: That's how it was for me! Seriously! If I took a day off, there was no one there to run the operation who knew what I knew. Every day that I had to be out of the shop was a day we were essentially closed.

VINNY: The same here. I could never leave for a day, let alone an hour. It took a long time to find someone I could trust who would run it the way I wanted it run.

LAUREN: Yes, me too. It was years of trying to figure out what to do and who to trust. It wasn't easy. And I always had to show up because it was like babysitting. They needed someone telling them what to do everyday and to make sure there was someone there to answer questions.

LENNY: Sounds like you were a really crappy boss.

LAUREN: No, not a crappy one. I wasn't sure if I could lead the people the right way. What did I know? I never had employees before. I knew the catering business and I knew how to get the business, but I never went to school to learn how to manage a whole bunch of people.

Erik A. Kaiser

Are You Fit To Lead?

Business owners, entrepreneurs, and bosses may all appear be smart people, but that doesn't mean they are necessarily equipped or prepared to lead the overall operations of a company. Entrepreneurs are especially prone to the idea that they have to know how to do everything or else be perceived as vulnerable.

You need to be honest with yourself and to your employees about your capabilities and your ability to be the leader of the company. Are you able to lead and control people properly, or do you let your employees walk all over you out of fear of losing them? Do you feel that you are effective in motivating your employees and that they look to you for guidance? Do you take criticism well, or do you think that you know everything better than everyone else? Do your employees respect you? Are you more of a friend than you are a boss?

Founding a company is not a prerequisite or an ingredient to acheiving good leadership. Founding is more static project while ongoing governing is dynamic. Take your ego out of the equation and ask if you're actually a leader or you're someone who needs a leader to interface. If the latter, you can hire someone to whom you can relinquish the company leadership so you can focus on what you actually do best.

GRACE: I am sure you are not a crappy boss, Lauren. You were just learning.

LAUREN: And I still am. I realized that I was really good at some of the business and not other parts. I can design menus and bring in business, and I know the whole preparation-delivery thing. But I realized that **my workers did not listen to me or take me seriously** all the time. That was a huge problem. I used to cry at night sometimes, wondering what I did wrong.

GLEN: What was it, then?

LAUREN: Well, I just wasn't good at connecting with the workers. But I hired this girl, Sylvia, who did, and she was the one who- I don't want to say stuck up for me- but she was the one who made the workers do what I wanted them to do.

GLEN: So you are not a people person?

LAUREN: Yes, yes, I am. Just not with every people... person. Sylvia just gets along with them better, and they listen to her more than they do me. I know you are thinking like, this is backwards, but it works.

VINNY: Yeah, as long as she listens to you.

CHANDRA: I know what you are talking

Employee

Is Your Boss A Good Leader?

There are many grades of leadership and as many personalities to match. But there are some underlying principles that you can examine to determine whether or not your boss is a good leader.

A good boss will accept responsibility for the employees and for the work. He or she will acknowledge and address any problems and challenges the company faces.

A boss who leads well knows how to motivate you and is able to expose your strengths and weaknesses as a positive exercise, not a humiliating one. He or she helps you create new opportunities for yourself by learning from your mistakes.

A boss who leads well acts professionally to you and to the other employees and makes you feel as though you are working together. He or she also leads by example, engages you, and wants to help you grow.

A great leader is a mentor people want to emulate and from whom everyone wants to learn. If your boss is not a great leader, you risk not fully developing your professional skills.

---

about, Lauren. But you don't seem like the weak type. You seem to have that look.

LAUREN: Over the years, it has gotten much better. It was mostly for the first couple of years. But once you get to know the workers and they get to know you, it seemed to get better.

CHANDRA: Plus, you sound like you had to figure out what to do.

LAUREN: Yes, the stress of it was so bad that I wanted to close the business just to stop the insanity.

VINNY: You never give up. You hear me? You *never* give up. You know what? I thought about the same thing a lot of times. Just have to keep pushing on. If it was easy, then everybody would be doin' it.

LAUREN: I just couldn't handle it

"Leadership is the art of getting someone else to do something you want done because he wants to do it."
Dwight D. Eisenhower

Erik A. Kaiser

Employer

Do You Stress Out Your Employees?

Are you the type of boss who thinks that yelling and causing drama is how you earn respect? Do you feed your employees stressful information in an effort to motivate them? Are you considered threatening? If you recognize that you create stress for your employees, your employees will become less productive and disinterested in working for you.

Bosses who stress out employees find themselves with the highest turnover rate and the least amount of productivity. If you find yourself in altercations with your employees, or if you create an environment in which people consider their work a job rather that a path of a career, you are getting a low return on the input of your company.

With a higher employee turnover rate, more of your time will be committed to finding and training replacement employees. Take into consideration the amount of time and money you must spend to find replacements. It is a distraction from your company operations.

There is a significant cost to stressing out your employees; you are losing money because of the environment you are creating. Improve your behavior, and you will be more profitable.

---

sometimes. I used to freak out and do amateur stuff and get all dramatic, but I realized later that was just dumb. I didn't know how to handle stress like I do now.

CHANDRA: Everyone gets stressed out. My coworkers and I get stressed, and so does the boss. My boss is great, but he is under a lot of pressure, and I know when he gets really pissed at us, sometimes it is his way of blowing off steam.

VINNY: Hang around my place, and you'll see blowing off steam! [everyone laughs]

CHANDRA: I see a lot of my coworkers cause dramas to get attention. They go to the boss and tell them something that stresses out the boss, like it is something important when there is really nothing. I never understood why people think that stressing out the boss is going to be good for you.

LENNY: Well, if the boss stressed you out, it is only fair that y'all stress him out. I had a girl boss that would get all crazy if you told her that someone stole something, so **we used to steal stuff for fun and blame it on someone we thought was a dick.** She used to freak out! It was awesome. She

Employee

Do You Stress Out Your Coworkers And Boss?

Work environments can be very stressful places at times. In good and bad times there is always something challenging that will heighten sensitivities at the workplace. Be careful that your actions do not contribute to the stress of your environment. You will be identified as a cause of stress, and not a provider of solutions. Your actions and what you say have enormous impacts on how you are judged.

Here are some common examples of how you may contribute to the stress of your coworkers and boss without knowing it:

- If you prefer to deliver news you consider to be bad to your coworkers or boss by saying, "I have bad news."
- Being late to work, meetings, presentations and scheduled events. If people rely on you to be somewhere at a certain time, be there on-time. Your lateness is costly.
- Being inconsistent with the quality and completeness of your work.
- Doing part of your job and leaving the balance for others to finish.
- Being disruptive, overly opinionated, or intolerant.
- If you exaggerate situations, or create doubts in people because you believe that it increases your value.

---

would start screaming and get all red in the face and yell at the dude we named. It was hysterical. She laced into this one dude and he was like, "Screw this, I'm out!" And he quit. He couldn't take this girl boss yelling at him no more.

GLEN: There is obviously a more effective way to chew someone out. That was her fault for yelling. I never saw the reason to do it that way. Let's say someone really screws up something. They are going to be stressed about it when they find out. Adding to that stress isn't going to be any better. So what I have always done is

The three types of stress:
- Psychological
- Physical
- Emotional

Common side effects:
- Compulsive Behaviors
- Headaches
- Anxiety

Erik A. Kaiser

Employer

Yell At Someone Without Yelling

An employee is screwing up for one reason or another, but you think the situation can be improved. The reaction most employers have is to call the person into the office and ream him or her out. You are frustrated because the person is costing you time or money or is in need of an attitude adjustment. Typically, employers think yelling is the way to get the message across and, indeed, it is true at times. But the real power to improve the situation is in how you communicate with the employee. Remember, no one likes to get yelled at, especially at work.

Here is a great method to turn a negative into a positive. Change your approach to the situation by calling the person into your office, and start the conversation by telling him or her that you are glad he/she is on the team and growing. Then mention how you have detected an area for improvement. Make the employee understand that you have been in the same situation and are giving advice that applied to you. This relaxes the employee and makes him/her more open to hearing suggestions for improvement. You will positively empower the employee and leave the discussion on a positive note. But remember, if you are attempting to rehabilitate an employee who is not right for the job, and that is the reason for the problems, focus on replacing the employee. Don't waste the employee's or your energy unnecessarily.

---

something more... I guess you would say it is more psychological.

LAUREN: Like what! Tell us!

GLEN: I look at it this way. I know what happens in my head when I screw up something. It is terrible. **Getting reamed out has never motivated me**. So what I do is instead, to get my point across to the employee to not do it again, is to tell them that they have done a good job first.

VINNY: What?! Are you nuts?

GLEN: Hear me out. I will sit them down and tell them that they have done great at work, and that disarms them. They get relaxed knowing they won't get fired. And then I tell them about how I screwed up something in the past and offer them some real constructive advice on how they can prevent the mistake they just made.

CHANDRA: When you say it that way, it makes it seem like you actually care.

GLEN: I do. I do care. I want them to improve, and you have to leave room for errors. That is how most people learn. Look, everybody screws something up at some point. I don't care what your position is. It is a fact. So deal with it, and think about

---

For Office Use Only

Employee

What To Do When Getting Yelled At

No one likes getting yelled at, but it does happen. And because bosses are people too, we cannot always expect them to behave appropriately all of the time.

If your boss or employer decides to unload on you for something you have done, there is probably a good reason why he/she is so upset. It's important to remember that the workplace can be an emotional place in which there is a lot of vested interest. If you get ripped a new one by your boss, take this advice:

- Do not yell back. Remain quiet and listen, because the yelling cannot go on forever.
- Do not respond in kind. Let him or her ride out the anger as quickly as possible.
- If others are present, calmly ask to speak in private.
- Remaining calm will defuse the situation faster. Calmness promotes calmness, but craziness instigates craziness.

Once your boss's anger subsides and you are able to speak to one another, start to discuss the situation. Mention that you appreciate your boss's frustration, but you would be much more motivated and encouraged to respond if he/she approached you in a calmer manner next time. You can then determine, based on your relationship with the company or your boss, about your potential options.

---

being on the other side of the desk in that conversation. What would you want to hear that would keep you motivated?

VINNY: *Gooooooooodbye.* That's what I would have said. Adios, stupid.

GLEN: That is your style, but you can get replacements easily. In my industry, you want to keep people and help them get over mistakes. Once they own those mistakes, they can help others prevent them from making the same.

VINNY: I am so tired of idiots screwing up. You give people a simple job, and they screw it up. They don't care about anything long-term. They want their paycheck. Sometimes these idiots don't come back to work. They just disappear. Poof, like the magic dragon.

CHANDRA: It's "Puff" the Magic Dragon.

VINNY: Stupid the Magic Dickweed, I don't care what you call 'em. [everyone laughs as Vinny slaps the back of Stupid's head]

CHANDRA: You probably burn them out, and they don't want to come back.

VINNY: They burn me out.

CHANDRA: Maybe they do, but you are too

Erik A. Kaiser

Employer

Are You Burning Out?

Being a key person responsible for a company is quite a challenge. That weight alone can be ominous. What once made you enthusiastic now may give you chest pains, and as the stress builds, you may question if the effort is really worth all the trouble. Your employees have started to really irritate you, and you don't want to be around them. Maybe, after vacations are over, you still do not want to return to work, and you fantasize about living a simpler life doing something that has more meaning to you. Your patience is shorter, and you are tired - exhausted tired - and you don't want to give any more than you have to. You are getting sick more often, and you may have turned to substances like alcohol or drugs to numb your reality.

If you are exhibiting any of these signs, you are most likely experiencing work-related depression, commonly referred to as "burnout." There are three hard and fast ways to cure it:

1. Leave your job and do something completely different.
2. Rehabilitate yourself. Get rest, exercise, change your lifestyle, and begin to reinvent yourself.
3. See a psychologist to help you identify the specific factors that are causing the burnout.

Letting burnout become your lifestyle will only drag your company and your employees down with you. It will slowly eat away at you, and your negative energy will spread fast.

---

tough on them, it sounds like to me. Maybe they are like, "Forget this. I'm out of here" after you yell at them. You sound like you are burning out.

VINNY: I went through that. I remember... Seriously, stop laughing, Lenny. I remember when I was ready to pack it in. I was goin' to get all my money outta the bank, close the business, and move to Florida. I had it. I spent almost a year not caring about what was going on until I realized that I was bored every day. That's when I got into another business, and I got my energy back. I got interested in stuff again.

GLEN: Well, you worked a lot and were under a great deal of stress. I have been there, too. **I went into retirement early** because I had it the same way. I was sick of the last business. There was nothing interesting left for me to do. This stays between us here. I thought about going to Florida too.

LENNY: What's the deal with Florida?

GLEN: [laughing] You know, I have no idea. It's close and it's warm. I like Palm Beach.

VINNY: And it's cheaper than up here. And I can sit on the beach and count bikinis.

For Office Use Only

Is Your Boss Burning Out?

Work may be great, and your company may be doing fine, but you have begun to notice that your boss is less and less interested in what is happening. You may notice that he or she is tired all of the time and is missing that energy that you once witnessed. Maybe you notice that he or she is coming in later and later and leaving earlier and earlier. He/she may be overly critical and irritated by your presence. If you are noticing these changes, your boss could be taking drugs or experiencing the effects of what is called "burnout."

It is not uncommon for bosses to burn out. They live personal lives that are full of all of the same problems as everyone else. They have enormous responsibility, for they are the people to whom everyone turns for leadership and guidance. They carry a lot of weight on their shoulders. They usually work more than everyone else, and they are subjected to stresses that are not experienced by others in the workplace.

If you have a boss who is burning out or has burned out, you need to be conscious of what it means for you. If you are close enough to your boss to help him or her out, by all means, show some thoughtfulness and offer to lend a hand. But if you see the situation deteriorating and your job severely at risk, don't wait until the company falls apart. Don't be the last one standing.

LENNY: [to Glen] So, why'd you go back to work if you got out of it all?

GLEN: Because I knew that it wasn't the business that did it to me as much as I did it to myself. You know, you have to reinvent yourself sometimes, and after retiring, I realized that I wanted to be working again. But, I had to change what I was doing. The business used to control me, and I had to make sure it didn't do that again.

GRACE: I watched one of my bosses burn herself out and take others with her. She was such a nice person and took her job so seriously. But she kept getting more responsibility than she was capable of handling, and she drove so many people from the company.

CHANDRA: Sounds like a woman Vinny!

GRACE: She was just a little bit different [playfully pointing to Vinny]. She pushed people to the point of them just bolting from the company. She would work them to the bone and made it seem as though it was what they should have been doing. She wasn't bad; she was just unhappy with herself and her life I think.

GLEN: So she took it out on her

Erik A. Kaiser

Employer

Are You Burning Out Your Employees?

High productivity in the workplace is so important that there are numerous indexes by which to measure it. Reaching a high level is always a challenge, and it is important enough that many large companies have dedicated Productivity Managers.

If you are pushing your people to be more productive, many times that means extended business hours, overtime, fewer breaks, no vacations, and more stress. Even though you may believe your productivity is high, your employees will burn out faster, leaving you with severely decreased productivity.

You can detect burnout if your employees are:

- More volatile
- Snappy
- Temperamental
- Late to work
- Less energetic
- Having much less fun
- Gaining or losing weight
- Working less

If you observe these signs, especially under intense conditions, your employees are facing burnout. Identify appropriate methods to improve it by adding staff and allowing employees to get proper rest. Don't forget, they bring their work lives home with them, which perpetuates the burnout cycle.

---

employees. She had some control.

GRACE: I watched people who worked for her literally go from happy people to being miserable. They just lost interest and didn't think it was worth it anymore.

GLEN: She fried those people, then, and she did it fast. Burning out took years of development, in my case. Years. Stuff just starts building inside your head until finally, **you have to make a drastic change or face monsters.**

GRACE: This woman really rode the employees. She wasn't a bad person inside, but she was when it all started to change. And everyone started to feel the same way.

LAUREN: Even you?

GRACE: Not me as much as the others. I don't know why it didn't affect me as much. I did what I was told, but deep down, I knew that it was going to change for the better. It had to.

GLEN: I have seen that a number of times in my career. It usually starts to set in after someone is promoted and they can't do the work. They start riding everyone, thinking that by doing that, they will gain respect

Employee

Is Your Boss Burning You Out?

There are always objectives to reach at work, but if you find yourself becoming miserable from the amount of work and stress associated with doing it, you could be burning out. It is not unusual to become fatigued from being overworked.

You can cease your burnout by immediately getting rest. It means that you have to take time off of work, without any work-related interruptions. If this is not possible, then you have to determine whether your life is worth giving to your company or keeping for yourself.

The work lifestyle you are living is essentially unhealthy. To counteract the effects, you have to begin to be as healthy as possible. Eat well, exercise, listen to music, see a psychologist, and learn to set boundaries around you at work. Could you be jeopardizing your job? Possibly. But a smart boss will know exactly what is going on and will support you in your efforts to improve your health.

If you leave burnout to manifest, you will be breaking down your body and your mind, and you will have a negative impact on your relationships at work and at home. Illness is a common side effect of burnout, and that should be a clear sign that a change needs to be instituted.

---

and the work will magically get better. It never does. You have to be careful not to burn out your good employees. Some of them will burn out naturally. They just can't handle the amount of stress.

GRACE: Yeah, she was all over everyone. It got to be a little unbearable, to the point that you couldn't really get your job done.

GLEN: Like how?

GRACE: Like making everyone fill out reports. She had this one report we called the "amnesty" report that instructed everyone to claim how many times they arrive to the office after 9 a.m. People were freaked out to know if she knew or not, and they wouldn't know what to write.

LENNY: Did they have cameras watching over the people?

GRACE: I don't think so. Why?

LENNY: Because unless someone is watching you, it doesn't matter what you put down. Check this out. When I worked at that rug place, they had cameras all over the place, but no one ever looked at them. So we tied plastic bags around them, and no one ever picked up on it. I bet you they

Erik A. Kaiser

Employer

Keep An Eye On Your People

Trusting your employees to do what they are supposed to be doing should not be left untested. Developing a pattern of trust with them is great because it relaxes you and enables you to do your job. But never let trust go unchecked. Always keep an eye on your people. Stories about the most trusted employee at the company being caught stealing are not new.

- Be unpredictable with your policy to test your trust. They will be aware that a test can occur randomly.
- Monitor emails, Slack. You can pick up a lot about potential wrongdoings from what employees are writing.
- Monitor website traffic. Find out to where your employees are navigating and for what purposes.
- Know when people are coming and going through your workplace. Keyless entry readers log employee traffic.
- Keep tracking devices in employee vehicles to pinpoint where they really are while they are using the company car.
- Install video cameras at key locations.
- Review phone call logs and individual numbers.
- Perform random accounting audits of your books.
- Make sure that your employee manual gives you the right to perform all of the monitoring tasks that you desire.

---

are still on them right now.

CHANDRA: That's not as bad as having your computer constantly monitored. Where I work now is good, but they told me when I got hired that they monitor internet usage and emails. And they *do*.

LENNY: How are they going to watch what you do on the computer? They can't have someone stand there all day watching y'all.

GLEN: It is done with software. We have it as well, and it is really important for us to have. Here's the reason. When you want a job promotion because you claim to work hard, **we are going to run a report on the websites you visit** on the company computer, the telephone numbers you call, and your entry and exit times at the office.

CHANDRA: Wow! That's crazy!

GLEN: It isn't. We don't tell the employees that is what we do and what we know, but we do disclose it to them in the HR manual. We just never mention it, ever. This way, we get to see who is real.

CHANDRA: Who watches all of this stuff? You have so many people.

GLEN: Everything is digital now, so all of

For Office Use Only

Employee

You Are Being Watched

Companies don't want to be sued for your wrongdoings. To prevent against your infidelity, they monitor what you do. Even if you are the most honest person in the world, your company is probably watching you for any breaches of security.

Even though you may not see them, there are most likely numerous systems tracking your every move. Software on your computer knows to which websites you navigate from your work computer, how long you spend on those websites, and potentially, the personal usernames and passwords you use.

Video cameras around your workplace are there to record events and keep you from behaving dishonestly. Your emails and phone records are reviewed to ensure their proper use.

Security and copier codes are also recorded and can tell the company where you were at a specific time. If you drive a company car, your whereabouts can also be tracked.

If you are an honest person and you are doing what you are supposed to be doing, you will find that increased security measures will benefit you. If a false claim is ever made against you, company security tools can verify what you were doing and where you were during the time in question.

---

the phones and internet and entry systems use the same routing hardware. Look, we have offices all over the country. We can find out in five minutes with one call to the IT department about what is really going on in our Arizona location. Not everyone tells the truth all the time, and these systems keep honest people honest.

CHANDRA: But you don't look unless you want to?

GLEN: Basically. But we do run reports on when people arrive to work by job title. We know if our managers are arriving late, and we can measure if that affects the revenue of that location.

LENNY: I never worked in a office, and it sounds like if I did, I would get booted the first day!

VINNY: Yeah, I can imagine the porn sites you visit on your computer. LustylovehosfromTexas dot com. Right?

LENNY: Ohhhhhhhh yeah!!!! [feeling up Stupid like a sex doll]

GRACE: Lenny! That's a guy doll!

LENNY: Well, so far from home, I'll take what I can get! [everyone laughs while Glen refills cocktail glasses]

Erik A. Kaiser

Employer

Monitor Employee Internet Usage

The Internet has become the number-one distraction in the workplace. In context, employees have access to everything that the outside world offered before computers, and now the outside world is also an office. Computers are instant television sets, porn magazines, photo albums, joke centers, newspapers, retail stores, social parties, and music centers. With all of these opportunities in the hands of your employees on demand, do you really trust them to resist the temptation of using them inappropriately? The answer is rarely "yes," or you are likely naive or delusional.

Companies need to protect themselves from improper usage of employee Internet access. Clear liabilities exist from decreased productivity, wasted time, and the potential of sexual harassment lawsuits from inappropriate Internet activity.

Plus, with email hosts like Gmail and file transfer sites, your employees can be using these personal accounts to transfer out proprietary company information without being traceable. It is a regular occurance.

If trust is an issue, install tracking software on all of the employee computers. The software is inexpensive and very advanced. You can then monitor what your employees are viewing and what they are doing at a level you believe is necessary to protect your company and keep your productivity high.

GLEN: We laugh, but **porn sites are the most visited** that we have. We have a program that sweeps the most commonly-visited site by the employees, and it blocks it if it isn't related to the business. We had to block YouTube, Instagram, Facebook, Twitter, and tons of porn sites. They are like roaches. People were spending serious time on those sites during work, and what happens is that once one person looks at those sites, they recruit someone else from the office to look at their computer, which wastes their time, too. It is a real problem. People can get distracted very easily with cheap entertainment.

CHANDRA: We used to have instant messenger, but our company deleted it from the computers. I am glad they did because you would get these random messages from people at work when you were trying to get something done. Other people loved it, but it was annoying for me.

GRACE: Every company is different because at one company, we used Slack all the time, especially with the boss. It was great when I could IM him that someone was on hold when he was already on the phone and stuff like that. But most

Employee

Your Internet Usage Is Being Watched

Your employer has the ability to know everything about every key you press and every web page you see if you're using a company-issued computer. There is a deluge of simple software that captures all of this information without you ever knowing.

You may think that clearing your browser history, emptying the cache, deleting the cookies, and restarting your computer will wipe your trail clean. It won't. The programs that monitor your activity are collecting the information and storing it in another place. If you are connected to a server, the information is probably being stored away from your actual computer.

Companies want to know if you are using their work computer productively. They also want to limit their liability for personal activity that you do at work over the Internet. They want to know if you have an online gambling problem that prevents you from doing the work or if you are sharing online porn with your coworkers, creating an environment that is ripe for a sexual harassment suit.

If you want to bypass these systems use your own laptop or computer for work and plug into the their network. This way, you can do whatever you want on your own computer without having a much of a trace at the company level.

---

companies have to watch what their people are doing on the computer for liability reasons. I get that. But my last **employer went too far** with some of the people. They were paranoid about their company image and they wanted to be seen as this important company where the employees were really committed to the company. It was like they were trying to get some award, so they were really sensitive to anything bad that they heard about the company from any source. If you mentioned you thought the company was just "OK," they would sit you down and really want to understand what they could do to make it better.

GLEN: Sounds like the were doing the right thing for their company.

GRACE: Yes, but they were paranoid. They went too far with some of the people, and it turned out to be a huge problem for them. They almost got sued. There were two guys at work who were both having girl problems, and they became friends. No big deal. They would go to lunch together and stuff like that. They worked in different departments, but everyone talked, so it was normal. So it turns out that the guy I

Erik A. Kaiser

Employer

Search For Negative Blogs By Your Employees

You should regularly take a minute to search the Internet for what is being said about your company. If you never have, you may be in for some interesting surprises when you do go searching.

It does not matter what type or size of business you run, from where it operates, or the number of employees you have. Someone, somewhere will most likely have written something about your company or you. And more often than not, it will be an existing or former employee.

Usually, if an employee is motivated to write anything about a company, it is usually the result of an experience he or she considers unfair or abusive - regardless of whether there's any validity to their version of events. When those words hit the Internet, the authenticity of the facts are generally misinterpreted and embellished.

This type of behavior can be harmful to your company's image. It can make it more difficult to sell your product or services and hire and retain employees, and it causes undue stress on the organization. You will have to combat comments that may be true or untrue, which will cost you time, energy, and money.

Keep up to date about when your company is mentioned on the Internet by using Google Alerts. Make your employees sign confidentiality agreements that help protect the image of your company in the public eye.

---

worked for thought that they were posting about the company, saying all of this bad stuff. I don't know why they thought it was those two guys, but however they did it, **the boss went into their personal Gmail accounts** and read all of their emails! Can you believe that! Isn't that illegal!

CHANDRA: Oh, my God, no they didn't!

GRACE: Yes! Everyone checks personal email accounts at work, and the boss got their passwords off of their computers and looked at personal email and then stupidly went to them and accused them of putting the company down on Glassdoor, even though there wasn't any evidence from what they said.

LENNY: Well, did they do it?

GRACE: I don't know for sure, but I don't think so. They weren't those type of guys. They wouldn't do something like that, and from what they told me, they were accused of other things, too, that had nothing to do with them.

VINNY: Who cares what they say? Like it really matters what a bunch'a babies write online.

GLEN: Oh, it matters to most companies.

For Office Use Only

Negative Blogging About Your Company

Keep negative comments about your company to yourself when it comes to the Internet. Blogs, company review sites, and social media, have become dumping grounds for employees to air a company's dirty laundry without independent verification or a balanced response from the company. Be careful.

Often, you may feel that you have been treated unfairly or have experienced an incident that impacted you negatively. With the ease of posting anything today, distributing that information to the public in real time could not be more efficient. Before you make any such moves, you need to take into consideration the company documents that you signed during the course of your employment. If you do not have to uphold any confidential or privileged information, take into consideration how the company may retaliate once they are in receipt of your comments. There are circumstances that create slander liabilities for you if you are out to purposely do harm to the company by fabricating or materially misrepresenting information.

If you are going to disseminate information, maintain a level of anonymity that will make it harder for your company to identify you as the author. Once you are identified, trying to erase your comments from the Internet might just be impossible. Maybe you need to just write it out, leave it, and return later... like with an angry text message to someone. You might just need to vent.

You would be surprised to see the lengths people will go to keep their name clean and the information about them online good. We had to threaten to sue a guy who had a blog that has a lot of bad information about the company that was just simply untrue. It made a difference to us because our Recruiting Department would report back to us that people in interviews would complain that our company would never give vacation time or personal time because they read it on some employment blog that job seekers use. We knew that if people were bringing it up, some people were not interviewing with us because of it. That's when it is a problem.

LENNY: Well, is it true?

GLEN: Not even close. We have a great vacation policy and have never had a problem with it.

VINNY: Yeah, I got a great vacation policy, too. Here it is. You take a vacation, and stay there. [Vinny lets out a huge laugh, and the others start to laugh]

CHANDRA: You don't mean that.

VINNY: Oh, yeah I do. Look, if you are a good guy and you have to **take a day off**

Employer

Afraid To Go On Vacation?

If you are afraid to take a vacation, then you do not have a company; you have a job. If you cannot disconnect yourself from your company for a week or two without causing yourself panic about what is going to happen, you have hired the wrong people. If you know that the business cannot run without you on a daily basis, you are essentially a glorified babysitter and traffic cop.

You may also be incorrect in your assumption that you cannot take off time. You may not be giving your employees a chance to demonstrate their capabilities. Many times, employers are micromanagers who believe that they are so critical to day-to-day operations that they actually interfere with employee success. Take your hands off the wheel to see who can drive.

If this sounds familiar, test it. Take a long weekend, and see how your employees perform while you are away. Give objectives to reach while making sure that you can independently verify how the work was performed.

If you have a manager of your operation and you feel like you still cannot leave, you do not have a true manager. Make sure you have a proper chain of command. Replacing a manager may be only move you really need to take.

---

because your mother died, OK, take it off. You can get your job back tomorrow, but I ain't payin' you. Got it?

CHANDRA: How do your people survive working everyday? How could you not allow for a day off?

VINNY: Look, in my business, you got to work. I did it without vacations because I had to. So if I had to do it, so do they. There's some equality for ya.

GLEN: So if a guy calls in sick, is he automatically fired?

VINNY: Yep.

GLEN: So what if he shows up the next day back at work?

VINNY: If I need him and I'm in a good mood, I will give him the job back. He can keep working. Same price.

GLEN: What happens when you are on vacation and someone calls in sick? Who makes the decision then?

VINNY: Well, now we got so many people. I don't know them all, so I have a few guys who run the day-to-day business for me.

LENNY: Oh boy, I bet those guys never take a day off because they will be fired by

---

For Office Use Only

Employee

Afraid To Take Time Off From Work?

There are clearly times you can take off work and times you can't. If you are nearing a critical stage in a time-sensitive sales season or in an important project of which you are part, it is irresponsible to take off unnecessarily until the objective has been reached.

But if you are just generally scared to take time off because you think that it will send the impression to your employer that you don't care about your job or that you have something else more important in your life, you need to take a deep breath.

To be happy and productive at work, everyone, including employers, needs time off to recharge the brain and have some fun. Don't be afraid to take your vacation to do something other than work. Good employers look for you to be balanced. They know that all work and no play makes you a dull employee who is not contributing at a high level. You will find that disconnecting from work will only make you more productive and happy at work while working.

There is one caveat: be responsible about how you take off your time. Don't leave your employer hanging. There is a right and wrong time to take off; make sure you choose your vacations properly. Otherwise, you will be perceived as irresponsible.

you if they do.

VINNY: Somethin' like that. Hey, they have to work five out of seven days a week, and they rotate weekends. That's enough free time for anybody.

GLEN: Why don't you let your managers take any real time off? Why wouldn't you want them to get recharged?

VINNY: Because they roll on you and leave you hangin'. I tried this whole "vacation" thing before. They all took off at the same time, and I had to cover all of their jobs and do the work myself. One of the busiest times is around major holidays. We tow frickin' everybody, and these clowns all decide that is when they are taking a vacation. Yeah, no longer, thank you.

GLEN: Oh, I get it. You didn't tell them when they couldn't take a vacation, so you just canned the entire idea.

VINNY: Yep.

GLEN: Why didn't you structure it better?

VINNY: Why should I? They screwed me once. This way, it ain't gonna happen again.

GLEN: You have to **manage how and when people can take vacations**. It is just

Employer

Controlling Employee Vacations

Why is it that employees decide they are going to take a vacation at one of the most critical times in the business cycle or at times that are clearly expected to be crunch times? Even better is when a group of employees decide to all take their vacations at the same time, leaving the company to flounder for a week or two.

The best prevention against having the company suffer is to create a system of selecting vacation days. You can devise a policy that does not allow managers, executives, or other employees to have identical vacation days, and you can also include overall company vacation blackout dates. This will prevent "missing management" at critical times.

There are also systems that can be implemented to have the employees bid on vacation dates. The higher-ups have first pick for days, and then so on down the totem pole. You can control the dates available to the employees based on how your company operates. If your company's busiest time in the business cycle is in December, and that is when a significant amount of money is made for the year, your vacation calendar should blackout all of December as ineligible. Also, eliminating the opportunity for employees to accrue vacation days, or clearly delineating how these days can be used, will ensure that you don't lose an employee for an extended period of time.

---

that simple. The business needs people to operate continually.

VINNY: The way I look at it is simple. If they are goin' on vacation and the business still runs, I didn't need 'em anyway.

LAUREN: I know what you mean, but there are busy times and slow times, and it is good to let people take vacation during the slow times. I need a break from them, too.

VINNY: Yeah, and they go look for another job when they are on vacation.

LAUREN: People are going to look for another job. You can't prevent that.

VINNY: It makes it harder.

LAUREN: Who makes all the hiring and firing decisions for your companies?

VINNY: Me and a couple of people, but mostly me. I make the call.

GLEN: How many people do you employ?

VINNY: About 400, including the illegals.

GLEN: How do you do it without a full time HR department?

LAUREN: You can't possibly do it all without an HR department. Who administers all of the benefits?

---

46 **For Office Use Only**

Employee

Taking Your Vacations

Vacation time is a normal benefit that companies offer to employees as an incentive and that they use to make sure you have enough time off to stay interested in working. Vacations are a time to recharge, focus on what you like to do, travel, and contribute to your personal and family life.

The three most obvious days that you can take off are vacation days, personal days, and sick days. Some companies allow these days to accrue, which is to your benefit. This means that if you accrue 30 of those days over the years, you may be able to take a month straight off of work.

Some companies will try and limit when (and sometimes where) you can take your vacation. They do not want you disappearing when you are needed most or during the busiest time of the year. There are other conditions that can be implemented, like not being able to take a vacation should certain events occur, like a company audit or the launch of a new product.

If your company does not have a vacation schedule policy, then you are free to take vacation as you please. But if your intention is to grow with the company and be perceived as reliable, coordinate with your boss the best times to take vacation in advance so you appear concerned about the interests of the company.

VINNY: That's where you got it all wrong. You don't need an HR department.
GLEN: With 400 people, I would think it is hard to manage.
VINNY: You let your people have control over you. Not me.
GLEN: How so?
VINNY: Because they have all these holidays and vacations and benefits and guidelines and crap. I don't have any of that.
LAUREN: You don't have benefits?
VINNY: Nope.
LAUREN: Don't you have a hard time keeping your executives?
VINNY: Executives? You mean the guys who want all the fancy stuff? **Yeah, this**

"It used to take me all vacation to grow a new hide in place of the one they flogged off me during school term."
Mark Twain

Erik A. Kaiser

Employer

Is HR In Control Of Your Company?

If your company is large enough to have an HR department, you may find that it is dictating to you appropriate courses of action for the company that are based on their beliefs rather than your experiences. HR departments tend to know everything about everyone, in addition to the hiring and firing pattern of the company. Self-serving HR departments sometimes get intoxicated with the power of knowledge and believe they know what is better for the company than the employer.

If you are faced with this cancerous situation, you need to take very direct action. Some situations may be easily handled, but some may be very severe and may involve disruption of company operations.

First, perform a manual review of the confidentiality documents that have been signed by the staff in your HR department. Have your legal counsel review them to make sure that they specifically address any and all information dissemination about the company. If your employees have not signed one, they must sign one before you make any waves.

When you have confirmed receipt of signed confidentiality agreements, either hire an outside consultant to review your HR department under some innocuous pretense, or do it yourself. Otherwise, you need to make slow and strategic replacements so as not to disrupt the organization.

---

is what I tell them when they ask for all the stuff. I say, "**Here's an extra $1,000** a month; **go get it yourself.**"

LAUREN: And that works?

VINNY: Every single time. I save myself the headache of all that crap of health insurance and figuring out who has to contribute and all that. Been down that road. No more.

GLEN: You are the HR department, then?

LAUREN: He has to be!

VINNY: Yep. The vending machine company I bought had an HR department. You should have seen these people. When I got more involved, they would tell me - TELL ME - what I should be doing. They were telling me that we needed better health insurance because the employees were complaining about the doctors they could see and how

"Power does not corrupt. Fear corrupts... perhaps the fear of a loss of power."
John Steinbeck

For Office Use Only

Employee

Is HR The Most Powerful Department?

You need to be alert to your relationship with your HR department. If you have mild interactions that seem appropriate, your company is probably in balance. But if you find that your relationship with your HR department is the defining relationship that you have with your company, there may be a few hidden reasons why.

First, your company may be poorly run, and the HR department needs to be involved with so many employees in order to help maintain morale. Be concerned that your company is not managed properly at the top level with bigger issues lurking.

Second, the management at your company may be weak and directly relies upon HR to actually manage the employees. This is a very common problem at larger companies, where weak managers want to avoid conflict and instead try to transfer their unpleasant responsibilities to HR.

Third, some or all of the people in the HR department have their own agenda for increasing their own compensation, security, and power at the company. They will befriend and engage the employees so the employees build allegiance to them personally rather than to the company.

Do your own research so you are aware of what it all means for your job and you.

---

far they had to travel to see them. Babies.
CHANDRA: That's important stuff.
VINNY: No it's not.
CHANDRA: Yes, it is. HR is like the eyes and ears of the company, and they know what the employees want and need.
VINNY: Exactly. They know what the employees need, not the company.
GLEN: So how did you handle them from that point?
VINNY: Fired 'em all and told everyone my "new policy" in a meeting.

CHANDRA: Did everyone quit?
VINNY: Nope. Only a few people, and that told me that the rest needed the jobs. And then I kept firing people and replacing them with ones who complained less.
GLEN: You know, this reminds me of a story of when I was younger and was promoted by the board of directors to my company as CEO. Now that I was in charge, I found out about all of the other people who thought they were in charge, too.
GRACE: Like who?
GLEN: Like the HR department. They were

Erik A. Kaiser

Employer

HR or Recruiter Holding Staff Hostage Against You?

Good HR directors and recruiters will build relationships with the employees on behalf of the company. They start the second they are selling the company to new employees and engaging the employees about the superiority of your company. But be careful; those relationships can be very empowering to the HR director or recruiter, and sometimes, it will be used to hold you hostage during a negotiation.

When you employ someone to attract people to your company, that person has an important job on which you rely to grow your business. Sometimes, the director or recruiter will believe that he or she is worth more than you can, or are willing, to pay, and if they don't get what they want, they threaten to leave and take the employees to the competition, who will gladly pay their price. Don't fall for that trap if you have a good, healthy company. What these director and recruiters fail to see is that the company as a team keeps the people in place. Employees don't just jump ship for another company because the HR director or recruiter leaves. The director or recruiter is not the employer, and his/her following is never as deep as they believe it to be.

But be careful; if your company is not well-run and you are not a great boss, you will certainly have a problem when a better competitor makes the sale to your HR director or recruiter easy. The following sale to your employees will be that much easier.

---

amazing. I worked with them, and they were very private about what they were talking to the employees about. It was like there was this wall between upper management and the HR department.

VINNY: You see, you're provin' my point.

GLEN: Oh, it gets much better. So HR was responsible for recruiting new employees, but most importantly, new salespeople for the company. And they really did a great job on selling the company and keeping them happy. So then one day, my head recruiter makes an appointment with me and shows me the numbers of the people he recruited, and they were awesome. And then he says to me that he deserves a raise because he brought in all of these people who are making money, so he should get paid a percentage **or he was going to take them to the competition,** and they would gladly pay him for it.

VINNY: That's why I keep a gun at the office. For guys like that.

GLEN: I couldn't believe what I was hearing. I ended up having to explain that it was not him that kept them at the company. It was everyone. I had to drive this home and flip the script on him.

Employee

Do You Believe In HR Or Recruiting More Than Your Boss?

If you have an open dialogue with your HR department or the recruiter at the company who hired you, you will likely have a good relationship with them. Often, you will hear from either of those departments about what they believe to be the health of the company. You may be receiving great reports on the company, and you are eager to do your job. They may develop new programs to keep you happy, and they represent themselves as your advocate.

But remember, they are employees as well, and they have their own objectives to perform at their own jobs. If they become unhappy, you could end up in their mess without knowing it. They may begin to consider you as part of their personal work domain, not the company domain. When you first arrived, they sold you on how great your company was. But if they become disgruntled, they might sell you on why the company is terrible. The result usually finds them terminated, or they leave for a competitor. Then they contact you to try and sell you on moving to where they landed because of the improved benefits.

Use your own head and analyze your own job. If they left because of the same issues you are experiencing with the company, then they have some credibility. But if your experience at work is different, be careful about what you believe from someone who is no longer at the company. It is a common practice for companies to poach recruiters and HR directors from competitors to be purposely disruptive.

VINNY: That's outta control.

GLEN: No, that was just stupid. Out of control was the IT department at the time. Those guys were the real crooks.

CHANDRA: I have yet to meet a normal IT guy.

GLEN: There was a huge problem with the IT department. The CEO who had the position before me started this campaign to bring the company into the future with all of these new proprietary programs, and he hired a team of programmers to write all of this stuff. When I got on board, I had no idea what was going on. Everyone was complaining about the IT department.

LAUREN: Preaching to the choir.

GLEN: I got so mad at these guys. The money that they spent was ridiculous,

"An illusion which makes me happy is worth a verity which drags me to the ground."
Christopher Martin-Wieland

Erik A. Kaiser

Employer

Has Your IT Department Gotten Out Of Control?

Once you become confused about IT costs or you hear conflicting suggestions about how to handle technology issues, you are facing problems. If you are not an IT expert, you need to rely on someone else.

IT personnel tend to be a very territorial group of people who will never implement something to save the company money if it means that they lose a job. They often know usernames and passwords and can "get into your system" at will. With access to sometimes all of the critical information at the company they feel powerful and know that if you screw with them, they can get back at you without you even knowing it. This simple fact keeps you hostage to them because you lack IT knowledge.

If you find resistance to your technology ideas, an unwillingness by your administrator to give you user names and passwords to your own systems, or challenges to your money-saving ideas by outsourcing, you need to get your IT monster under control.

Hire a few outside consultants to give you a complete analysis of your IT department and recommend suggestions on how you can get it under control. There will be overall savings to the company, and you will likely find that new technology will be available to replace, not supplement, multiple costlly systems.

---

and I could never get a straight answer out of them on anything. So I hired a tech consultant. They came into the office, did a full evaluation of their work - everything - the hardware, the software, what they were doing. You know what we found out? **The IT guys were control freaks who created a monster** on their own and cost the company a fortune when they could have done it all for cheap. We ended up outsourcing a lot of the services we thought we did better in-house and gained control of what we did best. Our core business isn't IT.

VINNY: I woulda killed those guys. How much was it costing you?

GLEN: We went from $4 million a year to $400,000 in a matter of six months, once our consultant gave us the information. And the consultant cost the company $40,000, or something like that. We had a sea of guys working in the office. The payroll was just ridiculous, and they kept justifying adding more people. The consultant said he never saw such an incredible volume of work that needed to get done with half of the people needed to do it. And the cost to the company was just staggering. There

---

For Office Use Only

Is The Company IT Department Difficult?

Information technology personnel are an interesting group. They typically speak a foreign computer language, are quirky, and are extremely opinionated about what they think is good, bad, right, wrong, smart, and stupid when it comes to technology and the illogical end-users.

Your company may be progressive in every way, but when dealing with the IT department on any issue, you wonder if they work for the same company or remember you're there to work.

Sometimes IT departments exacerbate an already frustrating situation by being rude or dismissive. You can't understand why they are even employed at the company.

Don't fret; you are not alone. You can be sure that everyone in the chain of command at your company feels the same way. The problem is that IT is a specialized area that even your bosses know is temperamental and strange.

If you are offended by the way you are treated, file a complaint. The more people who complain about a bad experience with IT, the sooner the pressure will build on the IT department to either improve or be replaced.

---

were rooms of guys who were working like a boiler room because they never had the proper management. There wasn't anyone there who could lead properly. It was a disaster.

LAUREN: Who was in charge of it?

GLEN: That was part of the problem. There were multiple people in charge, to the point that they all thought it was the other person's responsibility, even though they would all address it.

LAUREN: That is when **you need a clear job description** and the duties that go along with it.

GLEN: You are correct. That was another issue. I ended up rewriting my job description, and I did the same for the other executives so they were all clear on what they actually were being judged. The previous CEO took charge of different departments at whim and sent the message that he was now responsible for them. He never made it clear to his managers what he wanted to have happen.

LAUREN: That must have led to confusion.

GLEN: Yes, of course. When I took over,

Employer

Do You Supply Clear Job Descriptions?

Job titles are often important to employees, however the actual job descriptions behind the titles have become increasingly ambiguous. Even though a title is supposed to imply certain responsibility, it is often only a vague general description. Sometimes it means nothing.

Some companies believe everyone should have a job description. Other companies refuse to utilize them because those job descriptions change fast, especially as companies evolve.

Clear job descriptions benefit the company and the employee in a few significant ways:

1. They keep the employees focused on what they should and should not be doing.
2. They boost employee morale by giving agency to the employee to know when to assume a responsibility.
3. They give you an excellent understanding of whether the employee is capable of carrying out his/her required responsibilities.

Employees can typically do more for the company than the job description they were given. You don't want to stifle the growth of the company by boxing in an employee's responsibilities so much that you miss the opportunity to be pleasantly surprised.

---

people were asking me what they were supposed to be doing now that the other guy was gone. It started to get obvious real fast that the other guy couldn't get it together.

CHANDRA: I always want to know exactly what I am supposed to be doing. That's how you get judged.

GRACE: I agree. It makes life easier.

GLEN: You just need to be clear with people. If the job changes, that is OK but they need to know where they start. Employees walking around wondering what they need to be responsible for is not good

"I distrust anyone with a slash in their job description. I've met too many actor/waiters and too many rock musician/electricians."
Brad Holland

Employee

Do You Have A Clear Job Description?

Allowing your employer the pleasure of letting you work without a clear job description has the tendency to work against you. It should be a requirement of yours to know the exact duties that encompass the expectations on which you will be judged for future promotions and pay raises. Without it, you are taking the chance that your employer is unaware of the extra work you may be contributing and value you create.

There are circumstances when an ambiguous job description is beneficial. It can create a platform to demonstrate a full spectrum of your capabilities. Internships offer you to embrace the ambiguity. And in fast-paced companies or evolving industries, you will find new tasks that will test your skills but foster "job creep".

In contrast, a strict job description will make it easier for your employer to measure your output and performance. And it makes it easier for you to identify the specific value you create. The "jack of all trades" position is honored at home but is absent from company rosters for a reason; it's not a valued position.

---

when you need to manage. Whenever you change job descriptions or make new rules, you have to make people aware of them.

GRACE: Yes, and you have to enforce them, or they don't mean anything.

GLEN: Exactly. Otherwise, it is a total waste of energy.

GRACE: Some bosses do a good job at it, and others don't. The ones who know what they are doing usually have the most impact.

LAUREN: It is also a function of the employees. If you decide to change something up, like the time of lunch breaks, it doesn't mean everyone will follow. Sometimes, the employees decide that they want to continue to do what they did because they don't like change.

GLEN: Right, **but if you let them get away with it over and over, then you aren't a good manager.**

LENNY: That's what we call a "big softee ice cream guy" where I come from. In Texas, it's hotter'n hell, and the ice cream melts all over the place. **So we call bosses that when we call the shots** more than them.

Erik A. Kaiser

Employer

Do You Set New Guidelines And Not Enforce Them?

As your company embraces change to strengthen, protect, or enable itself to evolve, new employee guidelines to follow will evolve. But enforcing new guidelines can be a complete job of its own that requires additional work from your staff and from you.

Consider any example of employee theft which can range from hard cash to toilet paper, office supplies, inventory, resoures, et al. Identification of the theft causes management to react with a new set of "effective immediately" advertisements. If you're relying on trust in following the new rules as a solution, there is no enforcement, and therfore no compliance.

Forced change in any process should demonstrate to those affected a higher utility and a benefit when implemented. You need a system in place to monitor the effectiveness of the new guideline. You may get employees to follow it, but without constant enforcement they will most likely return to the default.

If you develop a history of creating new rules that are not enforced, your employees will know, and they will not take new rules seriously, regardless of how emphatic you are about them.

VINNY: I know the type. Have to get rid of guys like that.

CHANDRA: Vinny, you want to get rid of everybody.

VINNY: That's because I *can't* get rid of 'em!

LENNY: Check this out. There was this one guy we worked for that tried to change up using cell phones at work, and this other guy at work told him that he would get his ass beat if he got in trouble for using his cell phone because he has a sick daughter and needed to be on call for her.

LAUREN: So, what happened?

"Start with good people, lay out the rules, communicate with your employees, motivate them, and reward them. If you do all those things effectively, you can't miss."
Lee Iacocca

For Office Use Only

Employee

Are New Guidelines Not Enforced?

Evolving companies change, and with changes come new rules that will be established for what appears to be the improvement of the company. Often, however, you will witness that there are lots of new rules that seems to make sense, but no one follows them.

If your employer does not implement a system to monitor the guidelines and reprimand employees for not following them, then you can bet that those new rules are not serious.

Unenforced or overlooked guidelines are often regarding someting personal during work hours. Add cigarette and coffee breaks into the mix, and there is a lot of room for acceptable noncompliance.

Before you ingore new rule, you need to be aware that your noncompliance may come back to haunt you one day. Even though everyone else may be negligent by not following the new guidelines, it does not mean your employer will not try to use your noncompliance against you. If you want a raise or promotion, for example, your boss could cite this as an example of your irresponsibility and deny your request.

LENNY: Nothing. We all just used our phones like regular, and nothing ever happened.
GLEN: Mr. Softee sounded pretty weak.
LENNY: Yep. Those are the easy guys to deal with. **You just have to intimidate them**, that's all.
GRACE: Lenny! That's terrible.
LENNY: No, that's business and working for the man.
GRACE: That is an awful work environment!
LENNY: I don't care. Workin' sucks, but you gotta do it.
GRACE: I just couldn't imagine working in a place like that. Seriously. It sounds so mean.
LENNY: It ain't mean, it just sucks. I can't understand how you like work.
GRACE: Because I like it! I work for a great company, and I like going to work and seeing everyone and doing what I do. It is not great every day, but I have been around the block and worked for a bunch of people, and this company knows how to keep me interested.

Erik A. Kaiser

Employer

How Is The Energy Of Your Company?

Your employees' personality types are irrelevant when determining whether or not your company has good energy. Ask yourself if your company is a place where you can feel the energy of people being engaged in what they are doing? Do they look forward to their work?

Companies that have good energy share similar employee traits. Those employees:

- Care about the work
- Want to do a good job at work
- Are interested in the company objective
- Have good self-esteem
- Are confident
- Are happy at work
- Are proud of what they know or do
- Care about their individual and team performance

If you think your company could have better energy, you have the power to improve it by making contributions to the above list. The most powerful recharge occurs by hiring fresh blood. New, eager employees tend to jump-start their environment and activate the other employees around them. After time, you will be able to clearly see who needs to stay and who needs to go.

LENNY: Yeah, well, if it's work, it ain't fun. And if it ain't fun, I don't wanna do it.

GRACE: Maybe you still haven't found what you want to do.

LENNY: I want to ride my dirt bike.

GRACE: Then maybe you should find a way to do that for a job.

LENNY: Yeah, but I broke my leg once, and the doctor told me it was bad and to stay off of those things.

GRACE: Why is it that you don't like to work so much? Work can be really great and fulfilling. I know I feel good at the end of the week if I did a good job. I look forward to the next week and doing more of the same.

LENNY: Yeah, but I don't work in a place like you. I had so many jobs already, it's crazy. And the bosses are all the same. No matter what goes on, we're always to blame for everything. I'm sick of gettin' yelled at.

CHANDRA: Why do you get yelled at all the time?

LENNY: Well, for one, bosses are always yellin'. It's stupid.

VINNY: So what? They have a right to yell.

For Office Use Only

Employee

Does Your Company Have Good Energy?

Does the company at which you work drag you down, but you don't know why? You may like the work, but you may not like the people because they are not like you or they are lazy. If so, the energy of your company is probably low, and it is likely affecting you in many ways.

The difference between a low-energy company and a high-energy company is easy to spot. A high-energy company does not mean that you walk through the door at work and people are swinging from the chandelier. It means that the people at the company are engaged and interested in what they do. They want to succeed at their work, and they want to grow. The environment is inspiring and open to new ideas that embrace what everyone has to offer.

Conversely, a low-energy company is one where you will find that the people are not necessarily engaged in, inspired by, or connected to their work. If you do not look forward to going to work because the people are a drag, then you are part of that same low-energy machine. The faster you get out of a low-energy work environment, the better. Otherwise, you run the risk of adopting the same unattractive, low-energy traits.

"I found that the men and women who got to the top were those who did the jobs they had in hand, with everything they had of energy and enthusiasm and hard work."
Harry S. Truman

LENNY: Yeah, but how is your screw up my fault? That's what bothers me more than anything. These **bosses are slicker than an eel in a oil bucket**. They turn everything around and make us the reason they screwed up. You know what I'm talking about?

CHANDRA: I've been there before. They don't hit their sales targets and they freak out on you, but it wasn't you.
LENNY: Yeah, it's BS.
VINNY: Well, it's usually the workers screwin' up, so they deserve it.
GLEN: Oh, that's not true all the time. I

Erik A. Kaiser

Do You Blame Your Employees For Business Problems?

There are ups and downs in every business. The ups are always great, but the downs cause stress. Sometimes, in your mind, the trail of responsibility for the downs leads directly to your employees. Be careful not to blame employees when the decisions you've made are really at fault or there has been a fundamental change in the market in which your company operates.

Owners are ultimately held responsible for just about everything that goes right and wrong with a company. Carefully analyze your role in business problems so you do not ostracize your employees because of your own failure. It is easy to point a finger to your employees as a contributor to business problems.

Changing market conditions can bring on stress to any organization. When those market conditions contribute to your company stress, don't blame your employees for not anticipating the change. They are hired to perform job functions, not act as individual oracles.

"Blame where you must, be candid where you can, and be each critic the good-natured man."
Robert Burns

have seen my managers screw something up and then blame their staff to hide it. Sometimes it works, but the truth eventually comes out. It make take years, or sometimes you hear it from a former employee, but that is a tough way to manage people if you are always blaming them for your problems.

LAUREN: But sometimes they *are* to blame. You can do your best as a boss, and your people can still screw up something. Then you can blame them.

GLEN: Ultimately, you are to blame because you are the one who is taking responsibility as the face of the company. Blaming employees for too long is a battle that you can never win. You have to fix the problem and move on, or you have to deal

Do You Get Blamed For Business Problems?

According to your boss, are your fellow employees and you the sole cause of certain problems? You may be. But that does not mean that you are wrong all of the time.

Bosses are under different types of stress than employees when it comes to work. As the leaders and guides of the company, the higher-ups are responsible for performance. That means when employee underperformance causes the company ills, someone higher-up is to blame.

Employees get the blame a lot, but many times, the cause of the problem is the management behind the employees. Business problems may be the cause of unprepared employees who are under-trained and under-qualified. Unless you lied about your skills when you took the job, or unless the job requirements have accelerated past your skill set, your boss needs to put the proper people in the right positions to help solve business problems.

---

with it. If you choose to deal with it, then you accept your own fate.

LAUREN: Well, sometimes you have to deal with it, and it sucks the life out of you because you have to manage every little detail.

CHANDRA: Like what?

LAUREN: In the catering business, you are feeding people. The food has to be cooked so no one gets sick. It needs to be clean. It needs to be prepared according to my plan. It has to be presented well. There is all this stuff that goes into it.

GLEN: It sounds like every other business.

LAUREN: Yes, but when someone is screwing up, you have to watch every little thing that they are doing to prevent them from screwing up again. It is ridiculous.

GLEN: So you have to micromanage the entire process. Why don't you just get rid of the person and find a replacement?

VINNY: [throwing a fist into the air, excited] YEAH! **NOW YOU ARE TALKING LIKE THE BOSS I WANNA KNOW!**

GLEN: [laughing] Yes, I am going the Vinny route with this one. That type of person can

---

Erik A. Kaiser

Employer

Do You Have To Micromanage Employees?

Micromanagement is probably the least efficient and most wasteful form of management. It really means that either you are a control freak, or you don't have qualified people working for you.

If you find yourself unable to trust the work of your employees, doing their work for them because you think you can do it better, taking their calls, or making them account for every minute in the day, you are probably not an effective boss.

Being able to relinquish tasks to employees is the reason for having employees. They are hired to do the work with standard supervision. If your micromanagement of them occurs because they are not qualified, then you need to hire better.

There is an enormous difference between a micromanager and a perfectionist. A perfectionist will not release the final product unless it reaches a high standard. A micromanager is a person who cannot relinquish control of the process.

bring you down.
LAUREN: I know, but it takes time to find a suitable replacement. **You can't just fire the guy and then not be able to get the job done**. If it means that I have to stand over the guy to make sure he is skewering the meat in the right spot or layering the vegetables in the dish the right way, then I have to stand over him and direct.
VINNY: How the hell do you find the time for that? Forget it. Fire the person and do it yourself is what I say. You are standin' there anyway, so you might as well do it.

LAUREN: How am I supposed to do that when it is busy? As soon as it slows down, then I can find the time to look for another person, but that takes time, like I said. I wish it was that easy.
CHANDRA: Don't you have a manager to take care of that stuff?
LAUREN: Yes, now I do. But before, I didn't. That's the hard part of running a business. There is so much more to do than I originally thought. You have to be on top of everything all of the time.
VINNY: That's every business.

For Office Use Only

Are You Micromanaged?

Of all of the management styles one of the most disconcerting styles with which some employees must deal is the suffocating micromanagement technique.

When you feel that your manager is there at every step you take, finishing your work, wondering why you were a minute late back from lunch, and getting in your hair about everything you do at the company, you are being micromanaged. Be careful that your micromanager does not prohibit you from advancing at your current job or in your career.

Because micromanagers tend to create an environment in which all of the work produced is really a result of their own efforts, you should be aware that they are taking credit for work that you should have been able to finish and for which you should have received credit.

But also beware that if you are being micromanaged, you actually may not be qualified for the responsibilities of the job. Sometimes, superiors have to micromanage you when you are not performing as expected. They will want to control the output of your work so it reaches a certain standard that you are not meeting. Be sure to understand the difference.

GLEN: Oh, definitely. Every business.

LAUREN: I tried letting my workers do their own thing. They told me they could handle it on their own and they knew what to do. So I listened to them, and I didn't get involved in any of their work. I let them work like they said they would.

VINNY: Right, and then the hands-off approach didn't work.

LAUREN: You got it. Once I started picking up on their mistakes, I got blamed that I wasn't involved enough and they weren't told what to do. I mean, come on, are you kidding me?

GLEN: You just learned that you have to manage your people to the level they need to be managed. **You can't afford to micromanage, but you can't afford to be hands-off, either**.

LAUREN: There is no such thing as hands-off, as far as I am concerned. If I take the money, I am responsible. And, if I am not managing my people the way I need to, then I am not doing my job.

GLEN: Well, even if your managers are managing, you still have to manage them,

Employer

Do You Manage Your Employees Enough?

There are employers who desire a working model of absentee ownership. It offers delusions of sitting on the beach without a care in the world while a machine just pumps out cash for you without any effort. Although this has been possible for heirs of major corporations, for the rest of the us, reality is quite different.

As long as you have employees, you will have to manage them. And you should. Although there are different intensity levels of management, for you to maintain an orderly system of operations, you will absolutely need to keep your people in line with your ideas and your style.

Employees, including managers, need guidance and need to know if they are doing a good job. That information needs to come from the top down. Learning how to fine-tune the amount of management needed to keep your employees on track and keep you at ease is a trial-and-error process. To start the process, let your employees work without your input for a week at a time until they get used to less management. When they start making mistakes, it will be obvious, and you will then determine the amount of management for which you need to be responsible. You will also determine if your managers have the skills to get you one step closer to the elusive absentee-owner dream.

so you need to build that skill no matter what.

CHANDRA: I don't want to be left to figure it out on my own. I want my boss to tell me exactly what I am supposed to be doing so there isn't any confusion. I want to get my work done and leave. I don't want to sit around all day wondering if what I am doing is the right thing. That's a waste of my time.

VINNY: How can pickin' up a paycheck be a waste of time? I don't get how your boss is wasting your time. How is that possible?

CHANDRA: Well, let me tell you about my old boss who did a lot of pitching of clients for new work. I was part of the team that did the presentation and knew more about the client and what they wanted more than the boss. Whenever we had a presentation

> "Once you have missed the first buttonhole, you'll never manage to button up."
> Johann Wolfgang von Goethe

For Office Use Only

Employee

Do You Expect To Be Managed More?

Everyone is happy not to deal with a micromanager at work. But having an absent manager who does not provide direction can also be daunting.

Your management is the source of information about almost everything you need to know to do your job well. If you are not properly managed, your employment security and on-the-job learning will be compromised.

Companies design standards and expect work to be completed at or above the standard. If you find yourself confused about your work, or you have been reprimanded for making mistakes because you have not had the proper training, you need to be managed more.

Your employer should be giving you direction on performance expectations. Doing the work over and over until you get it right by trial and error is inefficient and does not make you look good. When you are properly managed, you will be able to perform better at your job.

If you find yourself under-managed, approach your superiors and request a meeting regarding your performance so you know whether or not you are doing what is expected of you. If they want more, demand

---

with the client, he asked me and a couple of others from the team to be part. I thought it was cool that he wanted us there in the beginning because he needed us for backup. *Wrong*.

GRACE: So why did he have you there?

CHANDRA: Well, I thought at first to fill up the room and show the client that the company was more than my boss. But then he would do the presentation, and we would just sit there waiting for him to ask us a question or something, but he never acknowledged us.

GRACE: Didn't that seem weird to the you were presenting to?

CHANDRA: Totally. My coworkers and I saw it. The client would ask us a question, wanting to hear what we thought, and my boss would just immediately talk right over us and take the stage again. And the client was as confused as us why we were there.

GLEN: That could mean that your boss was an egomaniac or didn't trust you to represent the idea.

CHANDRA: We knew the stuff better than he did.

Erik A. Kaiser

Employer

Do You Let Your Staff Speak In Meetings?

Inviting your staff to join you for meetings and presentations is customary. But only inviting them to have them fill up seats and nod affirmatively at everything you say makes you look more like an egomaniac than an equal collaborator. If your staff is there and you don't want them to speak, why have them there in the first place?

Leaving your colleagues in the meeting dust will make the people on the other side of the table question the show of force on your part. It will appear that your colleagues do not have any original or important input, even if they were the ones who did the work. The cosmetics of having your staff with you will quickly lose effect once it is obvious that you are the only one allowed to speak. Your messages and presentation will be not be effective.

Each time that you act in this manner, you will decrease the morale of your colleagues and make them feel less valuable as part of the organization. Employees need to feel like part of the whole to keep them interested and productive. Keeping them caged up will enforce qualities you most likely already want to eradicate from your company.

GLEN: But he gets all the credit. I know; I've seen it before.

CHANDRA: So, that's a waste of time. Yeah, I am getting paid to sit there, **but it is boring and makes us look dumb.**

GRACE: Didn't you ever say something to your boss about what the deal with the meetings is?

CHANDRA: No. I figured that it didn't matter. It's not my company. **As long as I keep getting paid is all I care about.** If you want me to sit like a prop in a meeting and tell you how great you did after, fine. Just don't skip a payroll on me.

LENNY: That's bosses for y'all.

GLEN: That's not bosses for you, Lenny. That is the case with some people. It depends on how the boss interacts with the team. This guy was a team player, Chandra?

CHANDRA: What do you mean when you say "team player"?

GLEN: Was he a guy that you worked with instead of you working for?

CHANDRA: That's a good question. I think it was both, but it depended on the situation.

For Office Use Only

Employee

Are Meetings All About The Boss?

When your boss asks you to join meetings with clients or others, does he or she dominate the entire conversation? Do you find yourself spoken over, your sentences finished for you, and your ability to contribute overridden at every juncture?

If you are experiencing a boss who keeps you at these meetings for no apparent reason at all, you should calmly describe to him or her your experience either in writing or privately face-to-face.

Sometimes, employers think they need to do all of the talking because they believe themselves to be more effective. This can be the case in many situations, but it does not mean that you have to sit there and suffer through it, especially if the other side of the table directly asks you a question and your boss answers it for you. You have something to offer, and you should be heard.

If it was to his advantage, he worked with you, but anything else, it was working for him. I don't want to say he was two-faced, but I wouldn't say that he didn't care. I think he did, but only if it meant something for him.

VINNY: Hear, hear.

CHANDRA: So I learned that about him.

GLEN: Did it make a difference to you?

CHANDRA: Not really.

GRACE: You definitely didn't get the most from that boss.

GLEN: Definitely. And that is why there are so many books on leadership. It is important to have a team spirit when working together. It makes for a much better turnout when the people are as committed to the goals as the boss is.

GRACE: One of the companies I temped for when I got out of college was a small company that basically was mostly a sales force going out and getting business. The sales girls all competed with each other, but they also worked together, and the boss was out there everyday bringing in business just like the others.

Erik A. Kaiser

Employer

Do Your Employees See You As Part Of The Team?

It is important to make the impression to your employees that you are a team player, even if you are competing with them for the same kind of business. Although you may consider yourself a team player with your staff, you need to demonstrate it to them continually.

A good boss will create teams, and those teams have leaders who manage other people to accommodate the size of the organization. Being part of the team means that you are in continual communication with the other members of the team and that you can be relied upon for leadership.

Each of the teams you design should have a clear purpose. Team players focus on the purpose and the execution, while team leaders help the employees guide the team to accomplish the goal.

If you are not responsive to your employees or your team, you may be the leader, but you are not being followed.

GLEN: So the boss was competing with the sales force for the same business?

GRACE: Exactly, but everyone liked the boss, and she helped with her sales force getting business and went on pitches with them whenever they wanted.

VINNY: Why would she waste her time teachin' the others how to get business she could get herself? That don't make any sense. They could just go out and make their own business. That's how I got started.

GRACE: I think it was because she couldn't cover as much territory as her sales force.

GLEN: And not everyone has the same entrepreneurial instincts as you do, Vinny. It is good to find a boss who will invest the time to help you develop your job.

"If everyone is moving forward together, then success takes care of itself."
Henry Ford

Employee

Is Your Boss Part Of The Team?

Bosses are expected to be the team leaders. They are expected to give their employees guidance to reach the goals necessary to keep the company in business. But your experience may be different. Your boss is the leader of the team, but he or she is not really there when it matters.

Consider what you need from your boss. You need guidance on work, motivation, clarifying and reaching objectives, communication, availability, feedback, education, and reliability.

Sadly, not all bosses are team players. Identifying that your boss is either on or off the team will help you be clear about how you should handle your job. You will probably make more mistakes because you have to take the risks of doing the job incorrectly without the proper team leader.

If your boss isn't the owner of the company, then look for the opportunity to do a better job than your boss by learning everything that you can to take over the job. Once you are confident you can lead better, even if you do not know as much, approach his or her superior with a formal application and presentation detailing each point that would make you a better choice and the reason why they should listen to you.

GRACE: It was neat because what she did, others would do. She taught one person something new, and they taught the others. Everyone worked as a team.

GLEN: So she had a lot of influence over her people?

GRACE: Definitely. They all wanted to be like her. She was good at what she did, and she was respected in the industry. She set the bar high, and once you are around that, you start to set the bar higher as well. They started acting like her. Some of them even started dressing like her. She was a really great influence, and it showed.

LENNY: I hope she was a good dresser!

GRACE: She was an impeccable dresser, and you could see some of the more sloppy people in the office start to be more concerned with what they were wearing.

GLEN: Bosses have powerful positions, and people want to be like them.

VINNY: Hey, even I would agree with that. I see it with some of my people. They think my success is cool, and they try to be like me. It's funny.

GRACE: I think it is flattering, Vinny. Doesn't that make you proud that other

---

Erik A. Kaiser

Employer

Your Employees Are An Image Of You

You set the basic standards of how employees conduct themselves at your company. You may not know it, but you influence their work ethic, their behavior, and their self-image. Your acts send a signal to your employees to tell them that it is acceptable to dress, behave, and speak in a certain manner.

For instance, think about something simple, like the time at which you arrive to work every day. If you are not strict about the time of your daily arrival into the workplace, it sends a signal to your employees that arriving punctually is not important to you. And, if you don't care about punctuality that much, you are basically telling your employees not to worry about it that much, either.

Your influence extends to your employees in just about everything that you do. Your employees will follow your lead whether or not you intend for them to do so. Be sure that if they are following your lead, your lead is one that you want followed.

---

people want to be like you?

VINNY: No. Who cares?

GLEN: Well, it works both ways. Your company is an image of your employees. There are a lot of companies that have profiles of people that are all a certain way. Like, **some are full of only smart people, and others are full of convicts.** You know the deal.

VINNY: Yeah, I got the all the convicts. *And* the idiots.

GLEN: Why did I know you were going to say that?! [laughs]

GRACE: Vinny, tell me, how do you dress for work every day? Is it like what you are wearing right now, or is it something different?

VINNY: I dress the same every day, except if I am going out to dinner with my girlfriend or to a party or somethin' like that. You know, a pair of jeans, sneakers, and a button-down shirt. That's a big upgrade from what I used to wear.

GRACE: What was it?

VINNY: [pointing at Lenny] *That!*

LENNY: Hey, what's wrong with this outfit?

For Office Use Only

Employee

Your Boss And Company Are Images Of You

You are judged by the association you have with your boss. How many times have you been aware of a really bad boss or a really bad company and wondered why someone would work for either? It is easy to believe that there is something wrong with those people. It is only natural to think that like-minded people find each other, and that if the boss or company is a jerk, then the people working there must of the same caliber.

Companies can be compared to street gangs or church choirs in the way that each only admit members based on a set of behaviors and beliefs. Simple consumer logic is that a great company is full of great people, and a bad company is full of bad people. You are a representation of the company and the company is a representation of you.

The job you do will be judged by others who will consider you as part of the company's directive. Ask yourself, is you company image your own self-image? If it is not, remember that guilt by association can stay with you forever. You may sweep floors, but if you sweep them at a company that is involved in fradulent activity, you will be considered supporting that effort.

"The herd seek out the great, not for their sake but for their influence; and the great welcome them out of vanity or need."
Napoleon Bonaparte

This is a new t-shirt.
VINNY: I'm just joking, kid. I like the bulldog. I used to wear whatever, but once the business started growing, **my mother told me I needed to start wearing better clothes** to meetings, and I couldn't go dirty. So I got into the habit of wearing a button-down everyday. Now it's like nothing.

LENNY: Hey, Glen, what do you wear every day? A tie? You dress up?
GLEN: Every day without a question. I want to. In my position, you never know who you are going to meet and if you will end up in a photo or on TV. You have to be prepared. Plus, "dressing up," as you call it, shows respect for others because it shows

Erik A. Kaiser

Employer

Dress For Your Job As A Boss

Most jobs have a different requirement for one's own personal appearance. Dress appropriately for yours. Remember that you are the top image of your company, and how you dress sets the standard for all of the other employees. Your employees will follow after your image without you having to do anything.

If you want to dress up your company appearance, start by dressing up yourself. Look the part of your company's leader. You will be treated more professionally and earn more respect.

If you wear a uniform as a boss and require your employees to wear one as well, they will be more comfortable wearing their uniform knowing that you are leading the group in one. If you have your shirt untucked, you are setting the standard for all of your employees to wear shirts untucked.

If you arrive to the office on Fridays without a tie because you take off the afternoon to make a long weekend, you are essentially broadcasting to your employees that "no-tie Fridays" is acceptable. If you don't want to broadcast this message, wear your tie to work. Most employees who are not allowed to wear regular everyday clothes to work will take the first chance they get to wear street gear. Don't be the reason why they get comfortable doing something you don't want them to do.

---

respect for yourself.

LENNY: I don't even own a jacket. Whenever I gotta go to someplace and I have to wear a jacket, I always borrow one.

GLEN: Well, that seems like a luxury to me these days. I don't mind, but the second I am home, I am in my comfortable clothing and out of a suit.

LAUREN: But that is normal for a person of your position.

CHANDRA: It's not like you are running an Internet startup or something with a bunch of kids. You are an important person.

GLEN: There are a lot of important people who do not choose to wear a suit every day. That doesn't mean they are any less serious about what they are doing or about what they can do.

VINNY: Hey, Lenny, you ever go in front of a judge?

LENNY: Yeah, why?

VINNY: What did you wear? Did you get all cleaned up and look like you were about to get married?

LENNY: Yeah, why?

VINNY: Just checkin'.

For Office Use Only

Employee

Dress For Your Job As An Employee

Dress for you own success and for how you want to be received, and dress for the part of your job in your company. Look as professional as you can and choose to wear well-fitting clothing that is not offensive or distracting. If you wear clothing that is two sizes too big, you look sloppy and will be perceived as sloppy. Wear clothes that are too tight, and you look like a sausage. Be "well put-together". You will earn respect, and you will appear to be in better control of your life and job. Self care reflects as respect for another.

Your boss will generally set the tone by what he or she wears. Take cues from how he or she dresses to determine what is acceptable.

Styles change, and so do trends. Be sure to ask a superior about changing your style if you want to wear something that is a potential conflict to what you have already been wearing or is common in the office.

Don't assume Friday is casual unless the policy is clear to you. Many times, an employee takes it upon himself or herself to establish Friday as a dress-down day, even though no one complains and some others in the office follow that rule. If the conditions of casual Fridays are not spelled out for you, especially if you are a new employee to an organization, ask your superior for the guidelines and clearance to dress down.

GLEN: [looking at Lenny] He means that when you are standing in front of a judge, you want to look as respectful as possible. Is that what you meant, Vinny?

VINNY: You could say it that way. Or you could say that you are tryin' to get the judge to respect you and believe your story and that you are sorry. You go there lookin' like a hoodlum, and you'll get treated like one.

CHANDRA: It's the same thing going on a job interview. You don't dress down. You dress up to look more professional.

GLEN: It is also important in my eyes for me to always look the part that I play because I represent the company and the employees.

CHANDRA: One of my old bosses never got dressed for the clients when we went

"You cannot climb the ladder of success dressed in the costume of failure."
Zig Ziglar

Erik A. Kaiser

Employer

Do You Present Well As A Boss?

Just because a boss may be the owner or operator of a company, that does not qualify him or her to automatically be a presentable representative of the company. Some founder/employers are geniuses with a brainchild product, but they are disastrous in front of bankers, investors, or other professional types. Others may always be hungover, sleepy, overly energetic, nervous, or have a neck full of hickeys. And still others dress, speak, act, or smell terrible enough that employees do not want to introduce them to clients or customers.

Since business is an art and a science, you should want to know if your employees think of you as presentable in some or all circumstances. You should be clear on the topic in order delineate when your presence is helpful and when it is not.

You have to put your ego aside and have a very transparent conversation with your employees about your presentability. A great leader is a great follower, and if you can shelve the megalomania, your employees will be critical in a constructive manner. You may not hear what you want all of the time, but you will hear the truth about their experiences and perceptions.

---

into meetings. Everyone else did, but he thought it didn't make a difference. I don't know, but we were always worried that his appearance would make it harder for the company to get the business.

LAUREN: That's OK, but what about your boss showing up with hickeys on her neck!

GRACE: No!

LAUREN: Yes! Before I left to start my own business, **my boss attended a meeting with hickeys on her neck.** She tried to put makeup on them, but you could tell. She told people they were bug bites from the beach, but we weren't stupid.

GRACE: That's so gross! Why didn't she wear a turtleneck?

LAUREN: It was summer, so that was out of the question. And she had clients into the office and thought nothing of it.

LENNY: One of my old bosses tried to change the dress code for everybody. I was workin' in the warehouse part, and they wanted us to dress in this one pair of work pants and a company shirt that we had to buy. No way was that happening.

GRACE: Why didn't you want to do it?

74　　　For Office Use Only

Employee

Do You Present Well As An Employee?

You may be awesome at your job. You may know the computer program better than anyone else at the company. You can be the best generator of new ideas. But, you never get invited to meetings outside of your department to present yourself to others. Maybe it is because you are not presentable to anyone other than your colleagues.

If you have questioned this and never get a straight answer, it is time that you find someone at your company who cares enough to give you some honest feedback. You would hope that your boss would tell you. If not, and you think it is because you may not be presentable in the way that your boss wants you to be, then you need to be an adult and not resent the truth when you hear it.

A good boss will be receptive to telling you the reasons why he or she does not find you presentable. If you show a sincere interest in improving yourself, more often than not, you will be supported by your boss and your company.

What you hear may be the result of old habits that are hard to break, but the advice will be important. Listen to it and appreciate that someone is investing the time to help you learn about yourself.

LENNY: Because it cost money, and they didn't want to give us the shirts. We were gonna have to go out and buy all new pants that they wanted. What for? So they could control us more? I don't think so.

GLEN: So let me guess. You told the guy **you were going to beat him up** if he made you buy new clothes?

LENNY: Close. All the guys in the warehouse got together and told the dude that there was no way we could afford it, and the company was goin' to have to give us the clothes if they wanted us to wear them everyday.

VINNY: That's called a union. I hate them.

LENNY: Call it whatever you want, bro.

GLEN: So the company paid for the clothes?

LENNY: No way! They were too cheap. They were trying to get us to, but the shirts- you know they were making a profit on 'em. I didn't want to wear that crap. So we told 'em "no," and they wanted to fire us for it. Go ahead, I said.

GLEN: They sounded cheap.

LENNY: They were. That was the only company I ever got excited about joining

---

Erik A. Kaiser

Employer

Do Your Employees Form Gangs To Gain Influence?

Employees can be very cliquey. Over time, they may band together in different factions and use their strength in numbers to wield influence over the employer. Essentially, an employer can end up with micro-unions, which can be unpredictable.

Always be on the lookout for the signs of a nascent group of employees banding together. You will see them taking lunches together, leaving at the same time, and generally adhering to a similar pattern of behavior. They may be quiet, but there is always an authority who will lead the charge and act as the spokesperson for the group. Many times, a higher-spirited employee who does not get his or her way and begins to register complaints will begin to question other employees on the same topics. If he or she believes that there is an opportunity to effect change by forming a group, expect it to happen.

You can detect through targeted or random monitoring of communications and through personal interviews with any parties in question an uprising in the make. Your best bet to halt the formation of a group is by removing the leader; you can always find a replacement. You can expect that the leader will continue to exhibit the same behavior, if you keep the him or her employed.

---

because they said I could be a manager one day. Yeah, right. There was no way to be a manager. I got assigned in the warehouse to this guy, and he said to me the first day that I worked for him, not the company. I was like, "Um, OK, whatever you say, Pops."

CHANDRA: That's just wrong. You don't work for that guy.

LENNY: Yeah, well, the whole idea of me going there was that I could get out of the warehouse and move up at some point **because I want more money.** This dude, you could never get past him.

GLEN: That's not true. If you do a good job, your efforts should be seen.

LENNY: Oh, yeah? I don't think so. Don't you think some of the people who work for you steal the work of other people and claim they did it?

GLEN: I know what you are talking about.

LENNY: In the first year I was there, I did all this stuff trying to make more money. You know, get noticed. I didn't want to work in no warehouse no more, you know?

GLEN: So, what did you do?

LENNY: There was one part of the

Employee

Do You Gang Up With Coworkers On Your Boss?

Usually, you have a few choices when there is dissatisfaction among coworkers about certain conditions that exist at the company: enter a complaint about the condition and ask for improvement, deal with it, or leave the job. Dealing and leaving are not usually the preferred choices. But there is another choice, and that is to band together as a group to make the employer understand that the condition is serious enough for people to assemble and demand change. This can be very effective, but it is not without risk.

When you band together, you are not seen individually, but as a group. If you believe that your jobs are critical to the operation of the company, you are effectively creating a micro-union specifically to address certain conditions you collectively want improved. Unless your company is a unionized company, most employers will not know how to address the group. They will usually respond out of fear of losing the employees and money. Most of the time, you will get a version of what you want.

But, banding together can work against you. Employers have the ability to fire one or all of the people involved because they may want to prove that no one will threaten the company in a gang type of formation. In weaker economies, employers would rather fire the gang, as replacements are more easily found. In better times, your success ratio improves.

"Sometimes I've been to a party where no one spoke to me for a whole evening. The men, frightened by their wives or sweeties...the ladies would gang up in a corner and discuss my dangerous character."

Marilyn Monroe

---

warehouse that was a total mess. Boxes everywhere. People didn't even know what was in there. Crap everywhere. So I started opening up the boxes and saw all this good stuff they were trying to sell. So I started stacking all of it real neat and puttin' labels on everything. I was trying to make it look like it was supposed to.

VINNY: Did you ask anybody, or did you just go off and do this on your own?

LENNY: I didn't ask nobody because I

Erik A. Kaiser

Employer

Do Your Senior Execs Hold Back Junior Employees?

If you are finding evidence that some of your non-executive employees are exhibiting great ideas and work results, but you are finding out about them by accident or through channels other than their direct managers, you need to do some investigation.

Many times, managers and executives will attempt to pass off their subordinates' creative ideas and work as their own. You will not have any idea about the origin or the authenticity of the work because you may not have any reason to ask. If you do, you will be told by the manager or executive that it is his or her original creation. This is a very common practice in an leader-subordinate structured company.

This occurs generally because the senior person is usually trying to secure current and future employment. This comes at the expense of your company, because if you were to perform a value analysis on the managers or executives against the people for whom they are responsible, you would probably be in for a major surprise.

The best way to be sure is to actually spend time with the people on the team to hear their ideas and witness for yourself if you have a manager or executive in a position that is not of value to the company. Do not let your managers take credit for all of the work done under them. You could be missing many diamonds in the rough.

---

wanted them to be surprised. You know, get the right attention.

GLEN: But...

LENNY: Yeah, so I did it all. It looked beautiful. I did it in about three weeks on lunch breaks, you know, a little after the whistle blew, and I go to my boss and tell him to check it out. I show him everything I did, and he was like, "Good, that needed to be done." Then that next Monday, I see him going over there with his boss, and he was telling him all how he just did the stacking of the boxes and found a whole bunch of stuff they can sell.

CHANDRA: You got punked, boy.

GRACE: Oh, that's terrible, Lenny!

LENNY: This cracker went and sold what I did to his boss, and the guy walked right past me. My boss didn't tell him I did it.

VINNY: That's 'cause you were the new guy. He probably thought you wouldn't last long, and why should he promote you when he can take the credit and make his position more secure?

LENNY: Yeah, I learned that the hard way. I ain't doing that again.

VINNY: I know that feeling. When I got my

Employee

Are You Held Back By Your Superiors?

There is nothing worse than being great at your job, producing great results, and then having your superior take direct credit for your work without recognizing you. There are times that you may find this behavior acceptable, like when you are a new employee or are training for a new job. But, if after a period of time, you see that this trend is now an expectation, you are essentially allowing your career to remain in neutral when you have the chance to put it into drive.

Superiors are also employed by the same company and have financial motives in mind as well. If they are able to increase their own job security and pay scale by directly leveraging your work, you should expect it. But that does not mean you have to stand for it.

If you find yourself in this situation, you have to be careful of the politics of the company and the strategy you will need to implement to get the recognition you deserve. If you feel that you are as qualified or better qualified for your superior's position, consider making a bold move to deliver an unsolicited application to fill the position. On your resume, you will detail out all of the directly applicable information you have developed that was branded by your superior to fit his or her image. This will get the attention of upper management and most likely result in a conversation that will allow you to professionally deliver the information in an appropriate setting.

---

first towing job, the other tow operators didn't want anythin' to do with me. They treated me like some pain-in-the-ass kid and tried to keep me from going on tow runs because they wanted them all to themselves.
LENNY: So what did you do?
VINNY: Screw them. I went right above their heads. You don't think some middle-manager dick is getting in my way? I went right above him to the big boss, and that got me recognized.
LENNY: I woulda gotten fired.
VINNY: Are you working there now?
LENNY: No.
VINNY: So what would it have mattered in the long run? You know, you gotta take

> "Has fear ever held a man back from anything he really wanted?"
> George Bernard Shaw

Erik A. Kaiser

Employer

Senior Staff Isolating New Employees?

There are times when your managers or executives will not agree with the hiring of a particular new employee and will protest by isolating him or her. The threat of being replaced, or training a potential successor, is something that comes and goes with your employees. Everyone is territorial, especially when it comes to making money and keeping a job. If you do not challenge the isolation techniques, you will endorse the practice and indicate this poor behavior is acceptable.

Managers or executives will isolate a new hire because they either want to voice their general difference of opinion about hiring the person, or they fear that their own job will be in jeopardy. They will be on a mission to prove to you that the new hire is not suitable for the job by citing a list of reasons, some of which will seem emotionally charged. Remember, people don't like change. If your managers or executives sense that a new hire is not going to be as productive to the organization as you do, you may find yourself having to sell the idea to them, and to support the new employee.

Senior staff will also be hypersensitive to the addition of a team member when they know that their job is in jeopardy. Even if your intention is to bring on someone new to replace the manager under the guise of just adding another person to the team, you need to personally convince the manager that the new person is not a threat. Otherwise, you risk disruption.

---

those chances. I wasn't lettin' anyone get in my way. Screw it. I could have gotten another job. You know, we're lucky because we can do that. There are guys I worked with who can't call any shot.

LENNY: Yeah, you're right. **My girlfriend is** like that. She is **Mexican** and she is illegal, but she is gettin' her papers. She has to do everything her boss tells her to do because it's hard for her to find a job.

VINNY: Exactly. **I have a lot of illegal guys** working in the garage fixing tow trucks and doing other work. You know, mechanics, laborers moving stuff around, fixing trucks and vending machines. These guys are my best guys. They don't talk back, they show up, stay quiet. All you gotta do is pay 'em.

GRACE: Don't you run the risk of getting caught?

VINNY: Yeah, whatever. Most of the illegals speak Spanish. They are from Mexico and the Dominican Republic. I have guys from Poland, too. They are all the best workers I have, hands down. No one is takin' them away from me, you hear?

GRACE: But it is illegal to hire them, isn't it?

For Office Use Only

Employee

Are You Isolated By Senior Staff?

If you were recently hired and find that your superior does not have regard for you and seems to constantly remind you that you are not doing the job correctly, he or she may be purposely setting you up to fail.

New hires are sometimes welcomed by managers with open arms and other times greeted with sneers and mumbled anger. Take note when the feeling is not so warm and fuzzy, because your superior is probably fearful that you will take his/her job or advance at a higher rate than he or she will.

You may be given tasks that you are absolutely certain could only be completed by your manager because your manager holds the knowledge. You may not have the opportunity to learn important information that he/she doesn't want you to learn.

Ultimately, your performance will be judged by your superior, and that information will be delivered to his or her superior, and so on. Be sure to protect yourself by registering complaints with your HR department or your manager's superior if you feel that you are being kept as an outsider. If you are not given the opportunity to properly integrate into the organization, you may unfairly find yourself out of a job.

"Anger is a natural response when something you value is taken away from you. You may feel alone, isolated, or not understood."

Anne Grant

VINNY: Here's what I know: I got a job to do. If you want to do it, I don't care what color you are, where you come from, whatcha did, whatja doing. **This is how much I pay, this is the job, go do it.**

CHANDRA: Well, I think illegal immigrants shouldn't take our jobs.

VINNY: What jobs? The jobs that regular "citizens" don't want to do? Do you realize that illegals run this country? They are everywhere.

LENNY: What's it like working with Polish guys? They eat sausage, what's it called...

VINNY: Kielbasa. Stuff is great.

LENNY: Yeah, I had that at a pig roast once.

Erik A. Kaiser

Employer

Hiring Illegal Immigrants

There will always be a debate about whether hiring illegal workers is right or wrong. There is a split between those who think it is morally and constitutionally wrong and those who find illegal workers indispensable and necessary. The right answer is the one with which you, the employer, is most comfortable.

Illegal workers are not authorized to work legally, which creates clear liability for the employer. The employer can be fined and face real jail time as a result. Each state approaches the employment of illegal workers differently and with different interest at different times. In bad economic times, there are more enforcement crackdowns than in good times. Your local political climate also plays a significant role in the interest of policing authorities identifying employers of illegal workers.

The unfortunate truth is that illegal workers fill many of the gaps that cannot easily or effectively be filled by legal status workers. Even though the act of hiring undocumented workers is illegal, companies across all sectors have found benefits that outweigh the risks. And, on many occasions, companies will sponsor the illegal worker for working papers with the federal government. Employers see the worker for his or her work ethic and skill, not for his or her legal status.

That's good stuff.

VINNY: They are some of the hardest working guys I ever saw. They don't stop unless you tell them to stop.

CHANDRA: Well, I just don't think it is right.

LENNY: My girlfriend is illegal, but she is the same as everyone else. She works two jobs and knows English better than me or my friends. She wants to be a nurse, and she can't get into school until she gets her papers. She is payin' her boss to sponsor her, and she's been doing it for years.

CHANDRA: Yeah, but she isn't supposed to be here.

LENNY: She isn't supposed to or not supposed to, Chandra? She's not supposed to be here, but she is, so deal with it.

CHANDRA: Don't you think that she is taking a potential job away from you?

LENNY: No.

CHANDRA: Well, I wouldn't put up with my boss hiring illegal immigrants to do my job.

GLEN: What if they were illegal yesterday but got their work papers today? Would you still feel the same way?

Employee

Working With Illegal Immigrants

Some companies will hire illegal workers on a part-time or full-time basis. Illegal workers may fill a void at the company that is not easily filled and may be less expensive than a documented worker. Your reaction will depend on your personal view of the hiring of undocumented workers and your relationship with your company.

In many cases, undocumented workers mix with legal workers without any friction and enjoy the camaraderie of a working team. But in other cases, undocumented workers can be threatening to the existing jobs of legal workers who may just cost the company more money. Unfortunately, there is not a hard and fast rule regarding what you should do about illegal coworkers.

If you find yourself at ease coexisting with an illegal worker, your employer may sponsor him or her in support of obtaining legal work status. But if you feel threatened, you should approach your employer and be candid about your thoughts. As a worst-case scenario, you can anonymously report your employer to the proper authorities for an investigation.

CHANDRA: Yes, because they're illegal.

LAUREN: I hear what everyone is saying, but the fact is that illegals are hired everywhere. I have hired them to help around the shop. I mean, there is a luxury to having them around. **You don't have to make a commitment to them,** and they are always around and willing to earn the money for working.

VINNY: Yeah, and there's no payroll taxes and vacations and all that crap. They just get the job done. And they don't care about raises and promotions. They are sending all the money back home to their families, so they will do more than the average guy.

LENNY: My girl has to do all the stuff nobody wants to do, but she does it. She knows it'll pay off for her once she has her papers. But when she gets them, she has to leave this job and get something where she can grow and get experience to become a nurse. She wants to get into nursing school and work at the same time, so she needs a place to go. That's her biggest problem coming up in the next year when she gets her papers.

CHANDRA: Well, she better not apply at Vinny's company unless she wants to do

Erik A. Kaiser

Employer

Handling Discrimination Among Employees

There are unfortunately some very strong sentiments employees can have against one another because of race, religion, ethnic origin, color, gender preference, disability, and weight, to name only a few. It is not uncommon for discrimination to leave the home and arrive at your place of work. Identifying and navigating it can be a tricky road, indeed.

The most popular discrimination at work is between employees of different ethnicity. Many first-generation employees from foreign countries can develop a deep sense of disrespect for other cultures and maintain that emotion at work. Other domestic discrimination appears between those who distinguish based on gender, weight, religion, clothing, attractiveness, age, and intelligence. It may not be obvious to you if you do not have discriminatory beliefs.

Discrimination creates a hostile work environment, and your employees will have recourse against you if you do not act to eliminate the problem. If you know that certain classes will not mix, don't try and become a crusader by trying to defeat centuries-old cultural disagreements at the expense of your company. You are running a company, not a rehabilitation clinic. Have a policy in your employment manual that makes any discrimination a terminable event.

"I have no race prejudice. I think I have no color prejudices nor caste prejudices nor creed prejudices. Indeed, I know it. I can stand any society. All that I care to know is that a man is a human being -- that is enough for me; he can't be any worse."

Mark Twain

the same thing forever or get fired.
VINNY: I take that as a compliment, Chandra. [with a British accent] Thank you.
LENNY: No way, she ain't moving up here!

I want her to make something of herself.
VINNY: Can she drive a truck? [everyone laughs]
GRACE: Well, I think that is great for her,

For Office Use Only

Discrimination Against Other Employees

It is not uncommon to be discriminated against at work by other employees. It can be delivered in the form of racial slurs or attacks on your character because you belong to a different religion or a different culture. You could be discriminated against because of your spoken language, your ethnicity, or your gender preference. Discrimination can prevent you from being able to perform your job properly and cause you hardship.

If you find yourself in a position of discomfort because of discrimination, you need to put your employer on alert. Your employer will want to know about the individuals who are acting in a discriminatory manner because a good employer will know that you may not be the only person who feels this way. Other employees will most likely witness the discrimination and will feel uncomfortable about it, but ultimately, they are not the ones who are actually affected. You will be responsible to report your experience to your employer so proper action can be taken.

If your employer is unresponsive and the abuse you are taking is significant, seek advice from an attorney about any options you may have against your employer. There are laws that protect employees from working in a hostile environment.

---

and I wish her the best. It has to be tough trying to get papers and working a dead-end job in a place where you don't want to work. I hope she persists.

GLEN: Some people need to have a stable job that they can keep and not have the pressure of growing. We have factory workers who really just need to keep assembling the goods. A lot of these folks just want a good job that will stay around awhile.

GRACE: I never looked at it that way. I always thought that you have to keep growing in your job or you lose value.

VINNY: No way. I would rather have everyone just doin' the same thing. All the guys who want a bigger position are a pain. Those are the ones who end up leavin' you fast. You can figure out who is sticking around longer.

GRACE: But you aren't giving them opportunity for growth.

VINNY: Who says I gotta do anything? I pay these guys. I make the decisions on who does what in my company. I don't owe anything except a paycheck at the end of the week for the work done. That's it.

Erik A. Kaiser

Employer

Creating A No-Growth Environment

Certain companies require a no-growth environment to be able to provide a good or a service in the market. Many factory jobs rely on the consistency of groups of people performing the same task diligently, day in and day out. We don't want these people to grow out of the position because it will have a incure retraining costs.

A no-growth environment may be excellent for some types of people. Seniors, for instance, are often looking for something steady that demands a consistent and stable work output without the distraction of climbing the corporate ladder. Other types of people just want the reliability of knowing they only need to know one job and do it well. They may just be working to live and not living to work. No-growth situations do not offer much in the way of promise to the employees involved.

To create a no-growth environment with the most output, create teams to compete against one another internally. Let them engage their senses of competition and work ethic to increase performance while feeling a sense of pride. If they know they do not face a more profitable future but enjoy the job, make it as interesting as you can to keep the morale high. And whatever you do, do not make the mistake of tempting them with any growth opportunities.

GRACE: I see.

LAUREN: That's *your* style. That isn't everyone's style. I want my people to grow, but not to grow out of my company and leave me hanging, looking for new people. Grace, look at it from the employer's perspective. All we really want is people we can rely on to do a good job consistently.

VINNY: Look, you give people more, they want more. You gotta train people to be the way that you want. I learned that at an early age. When I started working for my old boss as a tow truck driver, I wanted to be like him. He had a fancy office and kept things real neat. So that was what I wanted, and that's what I set my target on. If this guy had a yacht, I woulda wanted one of them, too.

CHANDRA: So you made your place nice or not?

VINNY: No way. I don't want my guys gettin' the same idea, so the first crappy office I had is the only office we got. You giv'em the Taj Mahal, and they are going to start wanting more stuff. No way. You don't need to spoil people.

GLEN: In my business, the workplace is

For Office Use Only

Employee

Working In A No-Growth Environment

Positions that can offer stability and other benefits without personal growth potential are sometimes the right jobs to have. Not everyone wants to climb the corporate ladder or has the same work interests as more aggressive people. You may need something predictable and steady that earns you what you need so you can go off and spend your personal time doing what you really want to be doing. You might want to work for a pension or benefits.

You will not have the opportunity to advance at your job, but a good company will keep you regularly entertained and interested in what you are doing.

If you find yourself working in a no-growth environment and decide you want growth, you need to find a way to move on as quickly as possible. You can determine whether or not you are in a no-growth company if you are discovering ways to advance but are kept in the same position because that is where you are needed and expected. Get out as soon as possible, and find something interesting that has growth potential. Once you are in a proper growth environment, you will start to realize your potential.

"A steady salary is an invitation to mediocrity."
Unknown

a factor that makes us more competitive in the market when we are recruiting employees. We believe that a good workplace promotes good work, and people feel good about coming to work.

GRACE: I have never worked in a bad office or anything like that. But **I judge a company based on how it looks.** You have to. It's an impression that people get. I think it tells a lot about the people who work there and about the management.

GLEN: Yes, indeed. We are always thinking about how we can create a better work environment. I know what Vinny is saying about expectation, but we want our people to want to work to get to a corner office. That is important to us.

LAUREN: When I started the company, I got a space that I thought was really good, but after working there for months, it was getting to be pretty obvious that it was a problem. I got space in a building in the

Erik A. Kaiser

Employer

Do You Have An Appropriate Work Environment?

Do you provide a work environment that makes it easy or difficult for your employees to perform their basic job functions and maintain a decent level of morale? Creating an optimal work environment is important to keep productivity levels high.

The clash is most easily recognizable in start-up environments. An energetic entrepreneur will work from a basement and then transition to a small, cheap office to keep overhead low. Then come the employees who have to work in a place that was never given any thought because space was not the main focus. But, now the company has grown, and the entrepreneur expects the employees to overlook the office squalor and adapt the same way he or she has. Unfortunately, the employees don't see it the same way because they may not be as invested in the company. It is still just a job to them.

It is important to try to match the environment to the work. Don't operate in an environment (unless there are no other choices) that makes it harder for the employees to do their jobs. Environment matters. There are numerous studies that show the correlation between of natural light, ventilation, heating, and air conditioning to morale and productivity. Employees consider these factors as benefits when the competition's pay is the same.

40's on the West Side that was really cheap and had what I needed to get started. I was surprised about how cheap it was. That was until my employees got mugged a few weeks after we opened for business. I was so scared after I signed the lease, so we used to all have to leave together sometimes.

GRACE: Oh, that's terrible! You must have been terrified.

LAUREN: I was scared. I wanted to move out right away, and I had my father talk to the landlord because I didn't know what to do. It was the worst in winter because it got darker earlier, so we toughed it out for a year. Then the business grew, and we had to find another space anyway. It worked out in the end.

GLEN: It is amazing that you can get everything that you need to do the job, and the place where you work becomes the issue. Usually, it is the other way around. People have decent space or space that is fine to do what they need, and they spend their time trying to build up the business to get the right tools for the job. Do you know how many businesses were started from a garage? Do you know why? Because they

---

88   For Office Use Only

Is Your Work Environment Appropriate For Work?

If the office, store, building, or any other establishment from which you work makes it harder for you to get your job done, you need to assist the company in improving the conditions or move to another company that has it together. Working in an environment that is a negative distraction from accomplishing what you need to do is counter-productive.

We all know the story of the office with the unventilated bathroom or the air-conditioner that never works. Circumstances such as these affect employee concentration and productivity. If you find yourself in this situation, you must alert your superior to discuss improvements.

It is not inappropriate to expect a good work environment. No place will ever be perfect to everyone simultaneously, but there is a standard. Remember that you will be judged on your performance, and if you cannot perform because the environment in which you are forced to work is not suitable, you had better make it known.

Most employers want to create an appropriate work environment because they understand the impact it has on their employees. They will most likely appreciate the information, especially if they are working from another location.

---

are perfect spaces, usually with all of the tools right there.

CHANDRA: That's most businesses. The biggest problem I have had is a good, fast computer that works. How come nobody wants to buy good computers?

VINNY: Nobody needs a computer to do the work. There's nothin' you can't do by hand that you can do on a computer.

CHANDRA: Are you telling me **you don't have computers?**

VINNY: We got'em. But it wasn't like that at first. The only reason I got them is so I could get rid of an extra guy who had to write the tickets by hand. Once I got a computer and the program to print the tickets, I got rid of him.

GRACE: I will tell you it is frustrating to not have what I need to do my job. When I was a temp, it was for a company that was growing, and they couldn't afford full-time help. They were in business about a year doing software development, and I did their accounting and helped them get organized. They were a real mess, and I got them cleaned up in the matter of a month. But they didn't want to even buy a file cabinet.

Erik A. Kaiser

Employer

Do You Supply The Proper Tools To Do The Job?

Companies are like car engines in the sense that they have moving parts requiring attention to keep them running at peak performance. Starve your proverbial engine of lubricants, and it will overheat before it runs out of fuel.

It is vital to understand and supply what your company and your employees actually need to effectively convert their time into your higher value good or service. Improvising is not a long-term or sustainable solution.

Losses are hard to quantify, but you know they exist, with unreliable Internet, inappropriate trade software on slow computers, poor phones, lack of lighting, bad tools, and insufficient workspace.

There is a direct correlation between increased productivity and morale when the proper tools and training are used. Your employees will translate their missing needs as your indifference leading to an infectious low morale. If your employees are on commission, failing to provide necessary tools for their success is your certain death.

Take an occasional survey of your employees to learn about what could make them do their jobs easier and better. You might be surprised that the requests are minor and inexpensive.

This was their problem. They wanted to look professional but wouldn't invest in simple stuff, like basic office supplies. Whenever I needed a pen, I would have to go to the bank and wait to be offered their free pens. I don't think they were cheap. They just didn't understand the value of a file cabinet until I found a free one. Once they saw that it was a value to them and the business was more professional, they would be more willing to get what we needed. No way did they get a copier! Not at least until after I left.

CHANDRA: I would have complained and found another job if they didn't listen.

GRACE: I am not a complainer. I just found another way around the problem. I would tell them every day what we needed, but they just didn't listen.

CHANDRA: I don't keep quiet. If I have a complaint, I tell it to my boss's face.

GLEN: And how does that work?

CHANDRA: He always says the same thing, "Do me a favor sweetheart. Put it in an email and send it to me so we can address it." Nothing ever happens. As soon as I hit the send button, it's like the flush

For Office Use Only

Are You Supplied The Proper Tools To Do Your Job?

Finding yourself frustrated when a task that should take you five minutes to complete takes you an hour? Are you dealing with a company technology that functions sporadically at best? Feeling that your company can't get its act together so you can do your job efficiently? You are not alone.

Not every company can have everything it needs all of the time to be as efficient as possible. Different companies are in various stages of growth, and a lot of times, they have to work the hard way until the money comes in to purchase the better equipment. But working without the proper tools to perform your work should not be the standard expectation.

The employees who suffer most from poorly-functioning or missing tools are those who rely on commissions as a significant source of income. Others are those who work under strict deadlines and find that the amount of work needed to reach the deadline is not commensurate with what is supplied to do the job.

Depending on the cost and the arrangement with the company, many employees who are faced with poorly-managed necessities may take it upon themselves to buy what is needed and then submit the bill to the company. Be careful. Unless you have an agreement in principle or writing from your boss or company, you may never get reimbursed.

"Give us the tools, and we will do the job."
Winston Churchill

lever on a toilet. [laughs]

VINNY: Oh, yeah? My system is perfect. My complaint box *is* a toilet with a cut in the closed lid. **Write it down on a piece of toilet paper** and put it in the slit, press the submit button on the side of the tank, and the whoosh sound is the complaint being delivered to me. Complaint answered! [laughs]

GRACE: Don't you have someone who fields complaints? You have so many people. How do you handle it?

VINNY: We don't have complaints.

GRACE: I am the one who fields complaints to my boss. We have a system in the office that anyone can submit a complaint to me anonymously, and I will look into it. If it is something that needs my boss's attention, then I will discuss with him. It works great.

CHANDRA: If something actually gets

Employer

How Do You Handle Complaints?

Employees want to see the top executives and top managers meaningfully respond to complaints. It promotes morale and gives the employees a sense that someone is listening to them as they slog every day, "working for the man." If an employee complains to you about something regarding company operations or other employees, you have to create a system to appropriately handle the process.

Many times, complaints disappear with a simple explanation of why the contemplated issues exist. Remember that most employees don't know the ins and outs of the company like you do, and they may not understand why something is the way it is.

Consider making a system at your company that responds to complaints in the same effective fashion each time. This way, your employees will know what to expect upon registering a complaint and feel a sense of action.

Be fully aware that a lot of complaints come from subpar employees who use complaints as justification for their underperformance. They are the type who claim that not having business cards makes it impossible to conduct business. Use a complaint system to weed out those losers.

"It is better to light one small candle than to curse the darkness."
Confucius

done, it is great. It takes forever for something to get done, if it gets done at all.
GRACE: It is really satisfying! It is fun to handle them and to fix a problem that is bothering someone. As long as it is a real problem and it gets fixed, people are really thankful!
LENNY: I bet your boss never thanks you, just those people you help.

GRACE: Of course he thanks me! He really appreciates everything I do for him and the company!
CHANDRA: You must get paid a lot or you are sleeping with him or something, because bosses don't thank people.
VINNY: That's right. You're getting paid to do a job. I gotta thank you for doing what you're *supposed* to do? I don't think

---

For Office Use Only

Employee

How Does Your Employer Handle Complaints?

Do you feel like you make a complaint about something valid but your complaint disappears into an abyss of corporate robot babble? Do you feel like your complaints are never addressed or that you don't have a big enough part in the company to issue feedback worthy of consideration?

Most of the time, a very good employer will want to know of your complaints as long as they are productive. Complaining that the water cooler does not produce cold enough water is not a complaint; it is whining. Complaining that you have to stop working in the middle of the day to run to the office supply store to buy copy paper on your credit card because the office is always low on it at critical times IS a valid complaint.

You should not be uncomfortable making valid complaints. If you are, there is a material problem in your organization, or you work in an environment where employees are very dispensable.

If your employer is not responding to your complaints in an orderly and predictable fashion, you need to document your complaints and submit them to your superior, and then farther up the line if no action is taken. Someone senior will eventually care and address the complaints at a good company. If they don't get addressed, one of you will have to go.

---

so. How many times do you think I hear, "Thanks, Vinny" from one of my guys? Right. Zero.

GLEN: I have never been afraid to thank my employees for doing a good job on something. They want to know that they are appreciated.

LAUREN: I tried that complimenting thing with my people before, and every time I said something nice, they asked for a raise. What am I supposed to say? No?

VINNY: I told you before, you gotta train your people what to expect. Here's what my people expect: nuthin'. They don't go looking for anything more than nuthin'. What would you do if I kept thanking you for something? Huh? Your head would swell up, thinking that you were something special.

GRACE: You guys! All those "thank you's" are what keep me going! That's my motivation every day. It is the best thing when I am told I do a great job!

LENNY: Why don't you ask your boss for more money, then?

GRACE: I do ask for more money, and sometimes I get it.

Erik A. Kaiser

Employer

Learn To Give A Compliment

Don't be afraid to tell an employee that he or she has done a great job at completing an assignment or handling a situation well. Most employers fail to ever compliment an employee for fear that the employee will try to hold the employer hostage for more money. They get paid to perform, and they want to know that they are performing as expected. Employees get a huge energy and confidence boost from hearing, "You did a great job. Thank you," or from recognition of the employee's skills and contributions to the organization.

If you give a compliment and the compliment is used to start a negotiation, promptly tell the employee that it is inappropriate to use this time as a platform for a compensation discussion. Remind him or her that compensation discussions are appropriate during performance reviews. If you don't offer performance reviews, you can help insulate against the compensation conversation by telling the employee that you will consider his/her request and that you plan on having a more formal discussion about it in the future. Then you can think about what you need to do without being under pressure.

LAUREN: See, that's the problem. How can they keep giving you raises every time that you do something that they like? That's crazy.

GRACE: Well, I don't ask them on the spot! I always wait until my review.

LAUREN: What do you mean by your "review"?

GLEN: She is talking about a performance evaluation.

GRACE: Yes. Every six months, my boss and management review my job and how I am performing at it. That's how I know where I need to improve and if I am on track to keep progressing. And that's when I ask for raises!

LAUREN: Why don't they do it once a year so they don't have to be asked twice a year for a raise? That doesn't make sense.

GLEN: Performance reviews are super important to us. We give them twice a year, and for new employees, we give them a review after 90 days on the job, then at 180 days, and then every 180 days after that. It is a job, definitely, but it is important for us in management to be able to measure the performance of any employee. You know

Learn To Take A Compliment

If your employer, manager, or boss compliments you on how you handle your job, take that as a great sign that your work is being noticed and that you are valuable to the company. Do not use it as an impromptu platform to demand a pay increase. You are supposed to be doing a great job. In turn, thank your superior for recognizing whatever it was that warranted the compliment, and mention that you appreciate the recognition.

If you feel that you have outperformed your boss's expectations, write down the event and the result. Keep a log of each event that you believe is above and beyond the expectation for your income class, so when you have your next performance review, you can immediately and clearly recall the events that qualify you for increased compensation.

Remember, your position has an income and skill cap. Being the master at your position will only get you to the top of the income bracket for that position, so be careful in asking for more income than the position can support. To get to the next income bracket, you will need to get to the next position and skill bracket.

"Kind words do not cost much. Yet they accomplish much."
Blaise Pascal

the ones who are growing the fastest, the slowest, not growing at all, how they interact with people. It's important.

LAUREN: But how do you keep paying every time they ask?

GLEN: We don't. We have a policy that every year, you are eligible for a pay raise. We can't keep giving raises whenever someone asks. Occasionally, we will override the policy and give a raise to someone who might leave us when we know they are worth it. And we will give bonuses along the way at times as well.

LAUREN: I never thought of that. This is a great idea. Then I can say that I only consider raises based on performance every six months or every year or something like that.

GLEN: If you are going to use reviews, you have to be consistent and be able to back

Employer

Use Performance Evaluations

Performance evaluations of employees are a key tool in understanding your company. Specifically, evaluations help you to determine if an employee is in the proper position, is right for your company, is performing to your expectation, is performing to his or her expectation, is at the proper pay scale, and is doing the job for which he/she was hired.

An evaluation form organizes and helps quantify the value of an employee. By having scheduled performance reviews, employers can control how and when an employee gets a promotion or demotion, gauge improvement from suggestions from the last review, deliver valuable feedback to the employee, and communicate in a prepared manner.

Employees need evaluations to learn if they are meeting your expectations and to understand more about themselves. People want to grow in their jobs, and if you take your business seriously, take your employees seriously by creating an open exchange through a performance evaluation.

It is best to have performance reviews on the 90th and the 180th day after hiring an employee, and then every six months from then on. If you want to arm your new employees with great expectations about your company, include a sample evaluation form in your hire package. They will be clear from the start on what they will be judged.

"True genius resides in the capacity for evaluation of uncertain, hazardous, and conflicting information."
Winston Churchill

up how you rate someone.

LAUREN: OK. What would you suggest?

GLEN: You have to keep notes on your people. You want to remember what they do right and wrong. No one remembers what they did wrong. Everyone has selective memories, and employees think that everything they do right needs to be recognized and remembered.

VINNY: *Whatever* to that.

GLEN: Performance reviews have become pretty sophisticated. **You can really control your employees with it.** We keep notes on every employee. When we see something that impresses us or that they mess up, we write it down. All managers and management is responsible for their people. There is no way that you can keep

Demand Performance Evaluations

Every employee should have a periodic review of how well he or she is performing on the job. There is a lot that an employer has to take into consideration about your performance, like leadership, attitude, ability to get along with others, quality of work, communication skills, and commitment. You may think you are a valuable and indispensable employee, but you may not realize that your attitude brings down the morale of others or that you can improve in areas like organization.

Performance reviews give you the ability to show top management how valuable you are to the organization. They provide a platform in which to discuss your compensation and promotion. Plus, you should want to know areas in which you excel and areas which need improvement.

If your employer does not offer performance evaluations, you should demand that the policy be instituted - even if it is just for you. Without a performance evaluation, you are leaving yourself open to repeating unproductive patterns that may one day cost you your job.

---

track of everything without being able to go back to notes.

GRACE: I agree. I do the same thing. Nobody wants to have to pay me more. I know that. I'm not stupid.

LENNY: [pointing at Stupid at the table] Like this little dude? [laughs]

GRACE: Right. When I go into a review, there are at least three people, and they all have their opinions about me and my work. And **if I ask for a raise, they always fire back** and ask me why I think I am eligible. So I keep notes on everything that I do for the company that is beyond what I think is regular to expect for my position. If I didn't have a record of it, I would have forgotten it. They are always amazed at my ability to recall the times that they should have remembered in the first place.

GLEN: We do the same, but we do it on behalf of the company, especially when we are having financial troubles that we are working through. We try to be as clear as possible about the lengths which we have gone to keep the employees happy with different benefits and features of the job that other companies would not offer.

Employer

Keep Records Of What You Do For Your Employees

In a work environment, people are so quick to forget anything good you did for them because they remember and highlight anything negative that happens. Regardless of whether you are a wonder boss, there will always be employee dissatisfaction at some point in the evolution of your company, and you will be confronted with forgetful employees who consider themselves victims.

A way to level the playing field and defend yourself is to keep a log of what decisions you make on behalf of the employees that you deem to be beneficial. It does not have to be a detailed account unless you want it to be.

Documenting with CRUSH when you do something significant, big or small, that positively impacts the employees is a quick way to keep track. Designate a folder to keep them all in one place. Remember, most employees do not see or hear what goes on in closed-door meetings, and they don't necessarily know how business works. They most likely do not know what your thought process is for trying to keep them happy, and keeping a log of your efforts will give you ammunition against those who do not remember the efforts you make.

LENNY: Yeah, but who cares? It's not their company. They are only there to get paid.

GLEN: Not necessarily. There are a lot of employees who are looking to get into the CEO position one day, and they are working hard to get there. They understand what is expected from a company, and they know very well what is outside that parameter.

LAUREN: But employees always think that the owner makes all this money, and they try to keep the employee's money. That's not the case. Some years, we only make a little bit of money, and other years, we make a lot of money. It all depends on the market and how we get our customers. There is always a lot more competition.

GLEN: Why don't you be open with your employees and show them the books? We have done that a lot of times because they take ownership of driving down costs and getting to a better bottom line, so they know they will be able to get raises. Those are the kind of efforts we like to reward. And you don't have to give raises. You can always give bonuses based on how well the company did in a particular time frame.

GRACE: We never get to see how much money the company is making. I wouldn't

Employee

Keep Records Of What You Do For Your Company

Does your employer forget when you have gone above and beyond the call of duty at your job? Maybe your boss forgets that you perform your job well above the original expectation? Remember, your performance and how you are perceived is what you use to advance at work, to make more money, and to earn more responsibility. Make sure you keep an accurate record of what you do.

There is nothing more powerful than sitting in front of your boss when it comes time for a performance review and listing out months of details describing what you have done to perform above expectations. Your superiors will probably have their own list of what you have done right and wrong.

As you perform your job, keep a log of what you do. Take notes on your phone, and keep them organized. You could be fired one day, and your company resources would be locked by the company with information you might need to appeal your dismissal. You are guaranteed to forget 90% of what you do if you do not write it down. Don't rely on memory.

"My friend has a baby. I'm recording all the noises he makes so later I can ask him what he meant."
Stephen Wright

even begin to guess how much they profit.

GLEN: Companies that make money are going to be less apt to showing you any financial information.

VINNY: Are you crazy? You think I would ever show anybody how much money I am making? The only people who know that are the people in my accounting department and my accountant. That's nobody's business but mine.

GLEN: In some cases, it is the best method to be transparent with your people about the numbers. There are a lot of cases where the employees become vigilant about being part of a successful company, and they control every expense as if it is theirs. It is a very effective way to operate sometimes.

LAUREN: We need to make a certain

Erik A. Kaiser

Employer

Explaining The Company Financials To Your Employees

Very rarely does a company or a business owner share the profit and loss statement or balance sheet with employees. It is none of their business, and it can be very confusing. However, it can be important for your employees to understand some basic information. Many times, they see the money coming through the door but completely underestimate the money going out the door. That is because they do not know all of the costs associated with running a business. When they do understand the costs, they will be more attentive to details and have a better understanding of where all of the money is going.

Many employers are accused of squandering the profits of a company or taking all of the money before paying payroll and expenses. There are many situations in which the lowest-paid employees of a company are making more than the owner or the company because business may have slowed or new costs arose that effectively wiped out the profits.

If you find yourself falsely accused, have a meeting with the top staff to share with them the numbers. You can teach your employees to respect the financial status of the company by becoming more transparent when necessary. When they understand, they will be less accusatory and focus more on the work that promotes profits.

---

amount of money every month just to keep the doors open. I mean, just to have the shop insured, keep the phones, electricity, Internet, and rent costs us a small fortune. Nothing is cheap. And every employee is an additional cost.

VINNY: You are telling me. Do you know what workers' comp insurance costs me every year? For a guy I pay $10 an hour, I have to pay another $5 in taxes and insurances. It's crazy.

LENNY: I thought that if you pay me $10 an hour, that's all you are paying me.

GLEN: No way.

VINNY: Not even close, kid.

LAUREN: No chance. I wish.

GLEN: When you get your paycheck... You do get a paycheck, right?

LENNY: Sometimes I get cash because I

"Beware of little expenses. A small leak will sink a great ship."
Benjamin Franklin

For Office Use Only

Employee

Try To Understand
The Company Financials

Get to know your company's financial condition as well as you can so you can dispel any myths you may have about to where the money is going. Many times, employees will accuse the boss or the company of improperly spending company money without any data to support that argument. There are countless examples of employees seeing what is believed to be a lot of money come through the door but remaining confused about where the money goes. Often, this leads to accusations by employees that financial difficulties of the company are the result of the boss or company spending the money on nonessential expenses. More often than not, this is not the case.

Operating a company - any company - has costs associated with it that would never be known to an employee unless he or she has owned and operated a business. It is amazing how small costs that go primarily unnoticed (like water coolers, postage, and copy paper) add up to enormous sums of money.

To analyze to the company financials is to be responsible. You may not always have access to them, but bosses who are acting responsibly in the management of the business will often share with you the impact of income and expenses.

don't want to pay the taxes. I can't keep up with that stuff. I don't even understand it.

GLEN: Precisely. Whenever you get a paycheck and you are not an independent contractor on a 1099, your income taxes are deducted. Did you know that your employer has to pay taxes on what you get paid?

LENNY: No. That's crazy.

GLEN: Yes. Consider an average of 10% more than what your gross pay is what the company has to pull out of its pocket and pay the government.

LENNY: That's nuts.

GLEN: It is. Then add the benefits you might get from the company, like health care benefits, and you'll find a $10 an hour person will cost the company $20 an hour, maybe more.

LENNY: So does this mean that I can tell my friends I'm makin' $20 an hour?

GLEN: Realistically, you are. There are so many other expenses that go into an employee, like ancillary insurance costs and office space and furniture and electricity costs of you sitting at your desk. Companies have a hard time figuring it out sometimes.

Erik A. Kaiser

Employer

Do Your Employees Know Their Real Cost To The Company?

Don't ever think that employees understand their real cost to the company unless it has been explained to them in exact detail. Even after you explain it, they will conveniently forget at times and need to hear it again.

Employees are not employers. They are not familiar with employer contribution taxes. They don't know about when you opt to pick up increased costs in healthcare, cell phone bills, company car usage, desk space, insurance liability, worker's compensation, unscheduled time off, 401k matching contributions, and other direct costs associated with your business. Employees only really understand the net number they receive in a paycheck and bonus money as true income.

Every company should know the cost of each employee as exactly as can be calculated. With the continued rising costs of health care and other direct costs, companies should provide to each employee a statement with all of the sums calculated so the employee understands that the company pays a lot more than he or she receives in salary.

When employees understand their true cost, you will be able to better manage expectations regarding pay increase requests and other non-cash compensation.

VINNY: You better believe it. You look at the damage these guys cause to equipment and trucks and accidents, and you wonder how the company makes money.

LENNY: Yeah, but that's the cost of doin' business. I am sure you planned for all the problems. That's what everybody does.

VINNY: Oh, yeah, right. How many truck crashes am I supposed to be building into my numbers? Ten? A hundred? And then you guys stand there with your hands out asking for more money. Unbelievable.

LAUREN: I mean, this is one of the reasons that there isn't money for a raise or a bonus sometimes. For me, I want to see that someone is a real value to me and has done an incredible job. Then, I am more open to negotiating a raise.

CHANDRA: It doesn't matter how much I do at work, as long as I get it done. And they made it clear to me how much I could make in the position. I know I can't make a lot of money doing what I do, but the longer I am there, the more money I can make. They will give me a raise every year of something like 4% as long as I am doing what I am supposed to be doing.

For Office Use Only

Employee

Do You Really Know How Much You Cost The Company?

Employers pay a lot of costs associated with your employment that are not evident to you unless you receive a total and complete breakdown of those costs on a quarterly or annual basis. Your salary or hourly wage is only one part of your cost as an employee.

If you employer picks up the tab for all or part of health care costs, that is added to your gross cost. Employers also pay payroll taxes, which are usually around 10% more that the gross amount you get paid. Add to that meals on the company, cell phone reimbursement, insurance related to your line of work, paid vacation days, and any other costs your employer pays on your behalf.

When you add all of that up, you will realize that the amount of money an employer has to spend to pay for an employee is far more than you would ever expect.

It is important to know this information as accurately as possible. You may be able to cut yourself a better deal once you can see all of the costs spelled out. You will be able to understand how your employer analyzes your cost, and you will be able to negotiate pay increases more efficiently in the future. You may discover that your employer would rather pay an expense of yours before giving you any increase. The cost is lower to your employer and the gain to you is usually greater.

GRACE: Don't they give you raises based on your position and what you have done?

CHANDRA: No. These people don't want to spend a lot of money on anything.

GRACE: Why don't you look for a job where you can make more money for what you do?

CHANDRA: Because this job is stable for me. I don't need to make a lot of money. I want more, but even though these people are cheap, they pay and never miss a payroll. I do what I need to do, and that's it.

GRACE: So you don't believe in extra effort?

CHANDRA: If I am getting paid for it, I will do extra if I want. We all get paid the same in my department. I think they pay whatever the position is worth, not by how good of a worker you are. And I think a couple of them are family or something,

"Even though work stops, expenses run on."
Cato the Elder

Erik A. Kaiser

103

Employer

Do You Increase Wages Based On Merit, Tenure, Or A Schedule?

Administering wage increases is either reactionary, proactive, or scheduled. However, maintaining control over policies that determine how and when to increase pay is close to nearly impossible.

Some companies clearly define the range of compensation for each job description and what achievements are necessary to advance. Others keep an open policy to address wage increases when there is a threat of a desired employee leaving or when there is a mutual understanding that it is time for a warranted wage increase.

Productive and vested employees tend to want increases based on either a schedule or on merit. If neither exists, then they prefer using merit as the grounds for an increase. Tenured employees expect CPI to be a customary increase when capped out on total job description value.

Use performance evaluations to identify the best methods to increase compensation to your employees. Evaluations help identify what the employees expect and will help you learn which methods will resonate with your current employee mix.

"Men do not value a good deed unless it brings a reward."
Ovid

because they're awful and they have a job.

GRACE: That seems unfair to you. Why don't you say something?

CHANDRA: Yeah. I think those guys are getting paid way too much. I can do their work, and they can pay me more.

GLEN: Every company has employees who are overpaid and underpaid. The overpaid ones are the worst because that is when the situation for the employer and the employee becomes strained. We see this many times after we hire someone. Even though we have a rigorous interview program, you never know about the person's true abilities until you start working with them. Then you see if they are worth the money you are paying them.

LAUREN: I have had this problem many times over because I was not sure what to even expect with people for the first few years of starting a business. I knew

Employee

Do You Get Pay Raises Based On Merit, Tenure, Or A Schedule?

Your employer should be clear on how pay raises are awarded and instituted. You should know exactly what you need to do to qualify for a pay increase for your job description or responsibilty set.

Some companies only award increases if you are there for certain lengths of time, regardless of the efforts you put forth toward the growth of the company. Other companies don't care how long you have been working there and base increases only on what you do for the company.

If earning up is in your interest, make sure that you know the distinctions between increases based on merit or those based on a schedule. And when your job description is delivering the maximum cap, will you get CPI increases each year automatically? Don't expect that merit is always rewarded unless you can prove it. Maintain an open dialogue with your employer about exactly what qualifies you for pay increases. Then test the policy to make sure that your superiors follow through on what they represented. If they do not honor any increases after you qualify for them, you can be sure that there isn't a policy and the ambiguity is to the benefit of your employer.

---

what I needed people to do, but **I was sold a bag of goods** by a bunch of different people who just overstated what they could actually do. They may not have flat-out lied, but they talked a great game, and I bought into it hook, line, and sinker. One girl I hired was making more than the company at one point. She told me all of these things she could bring to the table for the business, and I figured that she was going to make us a lot of money. Well, it turned out that I didn't know what I was actually doing. She took off for a wedding for a week, and I was forced to do her job. It was so easy, and I realized that I could train anyone to do what she was doing.

VINNY: I woulda sent her a pink slip in the mail.

LAUREN: Well, when she came back, I sat her down and told her that I expected more from her and that until I got it, I would be reducing her pay. I figured I could pay someone half of what she was getting paid. You know what she said? She said, "OK." She said that she knew it was coming and liked the company and liked me and wanted to stay.

Erik A. Kaiser

Employer

Paying An Employee Too Much?

What does one do with employees who are making more money than they are worth? They could be longer-term employees who think they no longer need to put in same time or effort that got them there. Or they could be employees who were getting paid to do a job with more responsibilities, but as the company evolved, they found themselves doing a job that does not match the current pay. Or maybe you just pay them more to keep them retained.

There are risks if you do not align employee overcompensation to the proper pay scale. There may be enormous political and structural consequences for your company when higher-paid employees have to make a transition to a lower pay. The lifestyle and recurring fixed expenses of employees are directly tied to what you are paying them. Rarely does an overpaid employee recognize the sweet deal but personally consume at his or her actual market value. Cutting employee salaries may mean panic for them because it compromises their ability to meet their financial obligations.

If you are unsure of whether you are overpaying, test the market by advertising the position to see the response at a lower posted wage. Also, take into consideration everything your overpaid employee does that you will not expect a replacement to do. You could be getting a bargain already.

GLEN: That says something about you, then.

VINNY: Yeah, it says that you know she hosed you and you caught her and she can't go nowhere else and still make that reduced salary. You could have squeezed her for more, you know.

LAUREN: That is what I thought after she accepted, and I thought about telling her I made a mistake and meant a lower number, but that would have seemed slimy. I don't want to lose credibility with my people.

VINNY: You are probably paying everybody too much. You have to go in low when you offer someone a deal. It's the same thing you do when you buy a car. I want all the bells and whistles, but I ain't paying a lot for that muffler. You know what I mean?

LAUREN: Don't you think that is insulting?

VINNY: Do I look like a guy who cares what anyone thinks? It's business.

LAUREN: I don't think so. Everyone says they are underpaid for what I make them do!

GLEN: Underpaying employees successfully is part art and part luck. You

---

106 **For Office Use Only**

Employee

Feeling Like You Are Overpaid?

Few employees think their value is less that what they are being paid, but there are definitely times when it becomes evident that you can be replaced by someone less-expensive. This is a common experience all the way from the CEO level down to the person who sweeps the floors.

Better technologies or weak economies enable companies to lower the cost of employees through renegotiation of wages or through replacement. You will know this if you are aware of the changes that are happening in your industry. If you feel that you cannot leave your current job and get the same pay or better, you need to be on guard and consider some alternatives.

It is counter-intuitive to ask your boss for a pay cut, but if you see people being replaced by less-expensive workers or positions being eliminated altogether, you should consider an offensive move. There are benefits to approaching your employer and having a candid conversation about what you see happening. Mention that you would consider a pay cut to stay with the company and continue to grow with it if you see future value. Your employer will be impressed and may offer to you other nonmonetary compensation that will help make up for the loss. You should also consider that if company cuts are a result of a bad economy, leave open the right to revisit your old pay once the economy improves.

have to rely on them being too afraid to look elsewhere or too comfortable where they are at the company. You can really keep people underpaid by giving them bigger titles. If they are into titles, they will essentially pay you for the luxury of having it. Give that to them before you have to pay them what they are really worth. Because, what is the downside? They come to you and tell you they are leaving for more money? You can give them more then if you want. You already got a lot out of them. It is like them lending you money and you only have to give a little of it back.

LENNY: That's why I want to get a company credit card. They just won't give it to me

> "Excess generally causes reaction, and produces a change in the opposite direction, whether it be in the seasons, or in individuals, or in governments."
> Plato

Erik A. Kaiser

Employer

Paying An Employee Too Little?

Got yourself a great deal on employees and you know it? Usually, that does not last a long time once the employee understands his or her true value to you. What you don't want is to be held hostage by them for an unrealistic number, especially when your organization will be negatively affected if they decide to leave - especially to the competition.

Don't dig your own grave. Yes, it is great to pay a little and get a lot, but if you make it a long-term proposition, you will usually lose. Instead, begin to recognize the employee with small increases in pay. Try some cash bonuses that equal no more that 0.5%-2% of his/her gross pay. This will make him/her feel recognized and confident that you are serious about fair compensation.

At some point, unless you are a really good dancer, you will end up having to increase that employee's salary to match the going rate. The exchange getting there will likely be uncomfortable. You will earn much more respect and get a lot more from the employee if you end up being the one to institute the increase to a commercially reasonable wage. You will bypass employee disillusionment, and you will have a productive and proud employee. If you are going to end up increasing his or her salary anyway, you might as well get the extra benefits out of it.

---

yet. I figure that I am worth a whole lot more to the company, but they don't want to pay me, so I have to find another way for them to give me what I want. Anything you charge to a company credit card is a write-off for them, so I am really doing them a favor.

CHANDRA: Is it really?

VINNY: What? Who told you that? Now I can't tell which one of you is stupider. [pointing at Lenny and Stupid at the table]

LENNY: That's why people have companies. So they don't have to pay taxes.

VINNY: Oh boy, my blood is boilin'. My Italian half is going to take over in a second.

GLEN: Lenny, that is not the reason people have companies. And you can't write off anything that you put on a company credit

"Folks who never do any more than they are paid for, never get paid more than they do."
Elbert Hubbard

For Office Use Only

Employee

Feeling Like You Are Underpaid?

There are very few employees who feel that they are paid what they are worth. If you want to know your actual value, here are some quick ways to give you an idea:

- Talk to head hunters and recruiters about your position in the market and the value other companies put on it. Understand what other employers would expect of you.
- Look at online job search engines to see what competing companies offer for your job.
- Talk to people in the same position at other companies about their compensation. Understand what more or less they do as it relates to your position.
- Total up all of the company benefits that you receive on a consistent basis (cell phone, car, fuel, health care, vacation days, personal days, etc.) and determine what the cost to you would be if you paid for them independently.
- Determine the hours you work on average per day.
- Quantify the savings and costs to you if you were to switch jobs (longer commute, childcare increases, etc.).

Once you have this all down on paper, you can look at the dollars you are paid on an hourly or annual basis. Then you can assess all of the other intangible considerations, like opportunities to grow and gain experience, to determine if you really are receiving fair compensation.

---

card. That is just false information. The laws constantly change about what is and is not an allowable business expense.

LENNY: All the big guys at my job have them, and I hear they go out to dinner with them all the time. How is that possible?

GLEN: Maybe they are taking out clients or doing other business. Let me tell you about a guy who worked for our company. You want to hear how sensitive business is sometimes and how a credit card helped save us from disaster?

VINNY: I like the way this sounds already.

LENNY: Yeah, me too!

GLEN: We had a guy, Herb, who had been with the company long before I showed up and moved up the ranks. This guy was a legend in the industry. He was an idea machine, and his ideas kept making the company money. And when one idea was getting old, he had another one, and another one. This guy was incredible. If it weren't for this guy, there would have been times that the company would have been in trouble. So, he was in his sixties at the time and **started cheating on his wife.** Things happen. And we all started to panic. It was

---

Erik A. Kaiser

Giving Employees A Company Credit Card

Credit cards are equivalent to cash. By giving employees access to a credit card, you are directly giving the employee a controlled amount of cash. Before you hand out any cards, draw up policies that are signed by the employee detailing the limitations, responsibilities, and guidelines for the card usage, along with the recourse against the employee for any breach of the agreement. This is mandatory, or you are essentially giving away your cash in hopes of getting it back.

Create spending limits for each employee credit card. A suggestion would be to have a spending limit equal to no more than their gross pay just prior to the expected date of receiving the bill. If you pay an employee a gross total of $3,000 every two weeks, make the spending limit on the card the same. This way, if the employee maxes out the card and decides to quit and you get stuck with the bill, you can apply his or her gross pay to the expenses and be even.

When certain employees who have access to credit card numbers leave the company or quit, make sure you call your credit card company and ask them to reissue the cards with new numbers. This needs to be done each time any employee with access to your credit card numbers is no longer with the company. If you don't, expect a random unauthorized transaction with your name on the bill.

---

the *wrong* time for him to be going off and having an affair, and we knew that if his wife found out, there would be too much drama for him to operate properly.

VINNY: So you hired the girlfriend?

GLEN: No, we approached him and talked straight with him. He knew the consequences, but he said after years of no sex and a terrible marriage, he needed a change. We offered for him to use the company credit card to hide all of the activity he was having with his mistress so his wife had to find out the hard way.

GRACE: Oh, that's terrible! You supported what he was doing?

GLEN: We didn't look at it that way. It was a company decision to protect our future. This went on for years. And he started to lose steam in general. He was getting old, he was trying to keep his mistress a secret, and the result was that he stopped coming up with great ideas. The technologies changed, and what he was best at doing was looking more and more outdated.

VINNY: Goodbye. Take 'em out.

GLEN: That was the next problem. He had

Employee

Using The Company Credit Card

The power of a company credit card is often overlooked by most employees. If your company issues one to you, always try to make them responsible for the bill and you the recipient of the benefits, like frequent flier miles and cash back discounts.

Employers who use the benefits for themselves will most likely not give you the benefits, but it is always worth asking. You may also consider using your own credit card to get the benefits as long as you trust your employer for reimbursement.

Some employers will give employees the right to charge up to a limit on the credit card for specific goods and services that the company can write off as an expense; this only benefits you. If you are in the 40% tax bracket, the company may give you $2,000 per month as a personal travel and entertainment allowance. By doing so, the company is spending $24,000 with the ability to write-off a portion. That has a gross pre-tax value to you of $40,000.

If your company allows you to make personal purchases and reimburse the company, you can always rely on the credit card for purchases that you want to keep hidden. For instance, you may want to buy your husband or wife a vacation package or a gift without him or her seeing it on your personal credit card.

---

been with the company so long that we all were faced with a moral issue about what to do. He was once a ball of energy, but he turned into a fossil at the company. The younger generation started accelerating past him, and you could see the effects of age starting to set in. By this time, he was in his seventies, and in a matter of years, he became a clunker.

GRACE: This is so sad. I wouldn't know what to do.

VINNY: I would.

GLEN: With the new generation of people and the change of technologies, he lost his motivation and spent his days reminding us of how important he used to be and what he did for the company.

LAUREN: Wow, I can't imagine that.

VINNY: Fire him.

GLEN: We finally sat him down and told him that the company was extremely

"Remember that credit is money."
Benjamin Franklin

Erik A. Kaiser

Are Legacy Employees Holding You Back?

It takes a long time to build a company, and during that ride, many companies have key, long-term people responsible for contributing to the growth. But those legacy employees can sometimes lose steam. After many years of growth and innovation, legacy employees often find that they have expired their usefulness.

Often, a faster growing organization will rely heavily on certain employees who become legacy employees after about five years. As the business evolves, it may continue without the direct involvement those people.

A good test to determine the present-day value of a legacy employee is to determine if the company can function well by distributing some of his or her responsibilities to other workers. If the company can operate well, it is time to address his or her true effectiveness.

If you find yourself with a ineffective legacy employee, you will face a lot of different emotions. You probably have a loyalty to him or her because of your long history. It is a difficult decision to just terminate the person. You will probably try to find something with less of a sting to make it work. If you decide to keep your legacy employee on staff, he or she must contribute equally to the company. We thank that employee for all the years of dedicated service, but he or she either needs to evolve or move on to the next opportunity.

"There are risks and costs to a program of action. But they are far less than the long-range risks and costs of comfortable inaction."

John F. Kennedy

grateful for his efforts. The board had carefully prepared a very generous compensation package. He felt like he was in the way and was torn about leaving because the company was his home. But, he knew that he was the last of the old guard and that maybe it was time to relax. He accepted, and we got him out of the way.

GRACE: So it was a happy ending, in a way.

GLEN: Yes, because once you lose the motivation to be involved, everything is a downward spiral from there. Sometimes, it takes more energy to motivate someone than you will get out of them. We couldn't

Your Rights As A Legacy Employee

You don't have any real rights for working at a company for a lifetime. There is a legend that if you take care of a corporation for a long time, then the corporation will take care of you for a long time. This is not the case.

You may have been with the company since the inception 20 years ago and have been an important employee for a long time. But if you have not become the decision-maker, you are still as vulnerable to being replaced as you were years ago.

It is sad but true that companies don't always honor their legacy employees. Some do. They will do everything in their power to maintain a great family feeling at the company and recognize the employee's contributions over the years. They will let a legacy person slide during his or her older years and consider his/her lifetime of work enough to relax expectations.

But as companies evolve, get sold to new parties, change the succession of ownership or operation to the next generation, or just go through extremely difficult economic times, no one is safe, regardless of how long he or she has been working at the company.

motivate him, and that affected other people.

GRACE: He sounded like an amazing man.

GLEN: Oh, he was. He inspired everyone around him all of the time. Everyone wanted to work in his division and know what he was doing. **He had this way about him** that made everything exciting, and he could get his staff to find an incredible reason to take out the trash. And they would.

GRACE: Wow!

GLEN: I have not met many people like him again. That is why we were so forgiving with him and his **extramarital** affairs. He was an incredible worker, loved his company, and made an incredible difference. At the time, the company was having a lot of financial difficulty because the management in place was not experienced with a growing company. If it were not for Herb's ideas, the company might not be around today. We learned a lot from him, and he was very open with teaching others. He basically had a fan club at work. You could spend a half hour talking to him, and you would learn more in that time than you would

Employer

Do You Motivate Your Employees?

Employees, like companies, have the tendency to be up and down. When your employees are up and motivated, they are incredible. When they are down and unmotivated, they are miserable, and it seems like the company is falling apart.

One of the attributes of a great leadership is the ability to motivate. Motivation comes from being challenged, enlightened, happy, valued, and competitive. Sometimes you can motivate an employee just by giving him or her some face time over a cup of coffee. Other times, you may need to bring in a motivational speaker to get your employees feeling energized again.

What matters is that you explore and discover what motivates. If you don't have the social skills or the patience to do the job yourself, hire or appoint someone to do it for you. There are a multitude of motivational speakers who will be more than happy to professionally tailor a presentation for your employees. Also, consider a corporate retreat or an impromptu lunch.

If you want to be immediately effective, hold a company meeting and start to talk out the issues that are causing low morale. Be fast on your feet to make suggestions to improve.

"Motivation is the art of getting people to do what you want them to do because they want to do it."
Dwight D. Eisenhower

in a semester of school. I picked up on that vibe, and when I took control of the company, I had him share his knowledge and wisdom with everyone. It was because of him that we completely redesigned our training program.

LENNY: No one teaches us anything at work. We have to learn everything on the job. And anytime I ask about learnin' how to use a piece of machinery or equipment, I'm told that some other guy already knows how to use it so don't bother. It's BS.

CHANDRA: That's sort of like my company. They teach you what they want you to know, and that's really it. But as long as they are paying me, that's all that really matters.

VINNY: Hey, even we have training for

Employee

Are You Motivated By Your Employer?

Your company may be great because it is successful at what it does, but do you find your boss to be a dud? When you are looking for ways to get ahead and stay motivated, are you met with the same glassy-eyed stare, followed by some insignificant cliches that make you wonder why you are actually working there?

A key ingredient to performing your job is to maintain a consistent and ample level of motivation. When you lose the drive to make that deadline or win that sale, it shows.

With hope, you will have a good manager or another higher-up who can help you determine what you need to stay motivated. A review of your position may reveal that you have exhausted the interest in it. New responsibilities and new opportunities would likely be the change that would excite you again.

However, you can't always rely on your employer to be your source of motivation. Your company may have all of the right tools and management, but you are ultimately responsible for yourself. Consider why you are feeling unmotivated to understand if your personal or professional life is the cause.

some of our people.

GRACE: You do, Vinny?! [amazed]

VINNY: Our business is pretty simple, so you can **get monkeys, feed 'em peanuts and they'll do tricks.** You know what I am saying? You don't have to know a lot because in a day, we can teach you how to do it. You got to. You don't want people messing up your equipment and costing you more money.

LAUREN: I have had to teach my staff what I want them to know, but I am not about to teach them how to be my competition or let them go to my competition with my ideas. I had to take a lot of chances to get up and running.

GLEN: But that is business. You have to find a way to make it work for you. Not to hold Herb any higher than I have already, but he always educated everyone around him just by being around him. I am sure it is the same with you. Your people will

"Inspiration does exist, but it must find you working."
Pablo Picasso

Erik A. Kaiser

Employer

Do You Make Learning Part Of The Job?

You will compromise your employee retention, motivation, and interest in your company if you are not providing any opportunities for employees to learn. Great employers know that employees need to be given the opportunity to improve their skills by learning on the job, either through a mentoring process or through company-sponsored education.

Without the opportunity to learn and be able to move ahead at work, employee retention drops significantly, thereby costing the company time, money, and energy. And since there are very few jobs that are forever the same in any industry, you would be remiss not to invest in a learning program.

A learning component will keep your employees engaged for a longer period of time to grow with your company. One of the most powerful and inspiring methods is to have the best people at the company contribute what each knows to a group presentation for everyone else. This also contributes to employee teamwork and building morale.

Other methods would be to reimburse the cost of any classes that the employees want to take related to any aspect of their work. Some companies believe that any education is important and will pay for classes in unrelated fields.

---

learn from you by picking up your habits and watching what you do. It is natural. You are training them each time you are in their presence.

LAUREN: I guess you are right, but I am not about to divulge what I know that they don't know.

GLEN: It depends on what it is. Sure, you don't have to reveal your suppliers, but I bet you they already know. We found that teaching employees the business in and out or not at all doesn't have a real effect on retention. Sure, some of them will try to go out and do it on their own, but that doesn't mean they will be successful. Maybe you just made it look easier than it is.

LAUREN: I have thought of that. What I have seen is that the more that my people have learned, the less I need to tell them to do something.

GLEN: That's right.

LAUREN: My right-hand person is really great because she knows what I need before I even ask. She is invaluable that way. Do you know how much time that saves me?

GRACE: That is one of the work rules I

Employee

Is Learning Made Part Of The Job?

There is always something to learn at work about your job and the company. Always. Businesses change, economic conditions change, legislation changes, and markets change. If you want to move ahead and take advantage of new opportunities at your company or elsewhere, you need to keep learning. If you are not, you are limiting your value.

Good companies want their employees to learn and to be more valuable. They also don't want you learning so much that if they sense you are going to leave the company and go to the competition or start your own company to compete with them.

If you find that there are interests to learn but you are just not given the opportunity, you need to ask to be involved. Good employers will want to help you learn. Most of the time, it is beneficial to them. If you are road-blocked every time that you try to get involved in learning something new, you are working in an environment that will not let you grow. It could also be a sign that the competition at your company is so fierce at every level that you have to work harder at creating value to go to the next level.

"For the things we have to learn before we can do them, we learn by doing them."
Aristotle

live by. I want to know everything about my company and the business so I can anticipate what to do. Do you know how much of a star that makes me look like?

LAUREN: If I had to define one thing about my girl, her ability to forecast what she needs to do is it. She knows my mood, how to avoid problems. She's really great.

CHANDRA: I don't think I can do that at my work. We are fed work to do, and I just have to do it.

GRACE: I think there is always a chance to find how to be one step ahead. You have to **understand the rhythm of the person** you work for. It doesn't take that long, either. You just have to be observant and see what they do and how they react to things. Like, when you know it is going to rain and my

---

Erik A. Kaiser

Employer

Know What Your Employees Want Before They Ask

Being aware of what your employees want and need to keep them productive and happy is part of being a good manager. Understanding how your employees think and operate is something that will help keep your business moving.

Being informed and intuitive will reassure your employees that you are a good leader who can anticipate properly. Also, being able to forecast and act on your ideas before employees need to ask for anything gives you more control.

Take, for example, a slow and rainy summer, during which Fridays are basically dead for business. If you have your employees sitting around with very little to do and the weather forecast for Friday is going to beautiful, you know you are going to have employees ask you for the day off. Instead of waiting, you can approach them and offer the day off. This way, they do not need to make up some lie for fear you will not give them the day, and you end up like a hero with a bargaining chip. You can then leverage your generosity when you need your employees to put in extra effort without having to give them anything for it.

---

boss doesn't come in with an umbrella, I know I have to find him one, so I keep a couple in the closet in the office. Stuff like that. It's simple.

VINNY: You sound like more of a wife in the office.

GRACE: I know, it does! But that is how I got to be the assistant for the CEO. I really worked at it, and that got me noticed. What was cool was that I always got promoted up a level until I reached the big boss. That was awesome because I knew I was being watched and appreciated.

LENNY: I got promoted once, and it was cool. It wasn't nothin' awesome like working for the big man like you, Grace, and it didn't last long.

VINNY: Let's hear it already.

LENNY: I was driving a truck for the tool company going to gas stations in a certain area. My manager quit, and his boss asked me if I could manage the trucks until they could get someone permanent. So I did it, and then a couple weeks later, they brought some new guy in, and **I went back to drivin' a truck.**

For Office Use Only

Employee

Know What Your Boss Wants Before He Or She Asks

Anticipating what your boss wants before he or she asks will make you a trusted hero. Bosses are usually busy and under different types of pressure than you experience. They rely on employee performance because they cannot operate the business alone. Anticipating how you can be helpful is something all employers want from their employees.

The best way to get notice and build value for yourself is to be the person who knows and understands in advance what your boss is going to ask of you. You would rather be the person to hear, "Thank you. You are on top of it, and you just know how to get it done." You don't want to be the person who hears, "Why do I have to tell you to do this every time? Do you know your job?"

Keeping an eye on how your boss operates, anticipating his/her requests, and being proactive rather than reactive will earn you responsibility and build you a great relationship with your boss. Your boss will come to rely on you being proactive, and your value will grow, keeping you ahead of the pack.

"Initiative is doing the right thing without being told."
Victor Hugo

VINNY: That wasn't any promotion. They used you as a band-aid.
LENNY: Yeah, well, it felt good ordering people around for once.
VINNY: Sounds like you were on a power trip.
GRACE: You can't get on power trips when you get promoted. That is the worst.
CHANDRA: Oh yeah, one day you are working next to me, the next you are my boss, and all of a sudden, you seem to know everything overnight.
LENNY: Yeah, well, when you get to be a boss, you get to boss people around. I mean, isn't it pretty obvious when you have the title of "boss"? So if you make me a boss, I am gonna boss. Simple.
GRACE: That's not how I see it. Being a boss doesn't mean bossing people around.
VINNY: Yeah, it does.

Erik A. Kaiser

Employer

Promoting Employees

Promoting existing employees is a great way to grow your company. Regardless of whether your company is growing or shrinking, you will always have the opportunity to promote someone. But it has its own positives and negatives, so be careful.

Promoting comes in many forms. Sometimes, it is a pay raise and title change, and other times, it is as simple as adding on additional responsibility to an employee's workload.

Promoting is a great way to get employees invested in the company. It has the power to give them a refreshed sense of accomplishment. But be careful that you don't set the employee up for failure through a promotion. Make sure the employee is capable of doing the job for which he or she is being promoted. If not, you will become dissatisfied and have to demote the person. Sometimes, that leads to the employee leaving the company, and you lose twice.

"When I give a man an office, I watch him carefully to see whether he is swelling or growing."
Woodrow T. Wilson

LENNY: Yeah, see, I told you.

VINNY: If you are a manager under me, you better be bossing people around and telling them what to do. And you better know how to do it, and you better be right.

GLEN: Therein lies the major issue of promoting someone to a management position when they haven't yet acquired management skills or they have to learn the skills while in the position can be a disaster.

LAUREN: I can tell you that I didn't have any management skills, and by opening up my own company, I had to learn on the job. I am still learning, and it isn't easy all of the time.

GLEN: Indeed. When our company was on a massive growth spike, there was less management than we needed. We started

---

For Office Use Only

Employee

Getting Promoted

It is a great moment in business to be recognized as valuable enough to be elevated at your company. You should be proud, but at the same time, you should be extra cautious.

Your promotion is essentially a new job, one for which you may not be prepared or not used to yet. Take control in your new position, but be sure not to be overly bold or overly confident in territory that is new to you. The result may be that you appear unsuited for the promotion, and you will cause the company more stress. This is usually seen when someone is promoted to manager from a sales position. That person may possess managerial skills that are not yet completely developed.

Do not use a new promotion to gloat or act like a big shot. You can still be demoted. Acting empowered by your promotion usually means that you are immature and most likely not as qualified as expected.

---

taking salespeople who exhibited leadership skills and just promoted them to managers. We needed to do something, and that was the easiest solution which turned out to be the wrong solution.

CHANDRA: Because they didn't know what they were talking about. I've seen this.

GLEN: It was a version of that. They knew what they were talking about some of the time, but then thought like salespeople and not managers. That caused a huge conflict, and we received a lot of information that was not analyzed correctly by them. We started agreeing to decisions, that were driven by a sales mentality instead of a management mentality. And when we tried to implement new management decisions our managers would react like salespeople instead of managers.

CHANDRA: That's because they are salespeople. One of my companies promoted the best salesperson to regional manager only because they thought he could teach all of the other salespeople what he knew. That lasted about a month before they put him back to sales. He was like a fish out of water.

GLEN: That was our experience. We took

Erik A. Kaiser

Employer

Do Your Managers Really Know What They Are Doing?

Are your managers all you hope them to be? Did your managers evolve into their roles, or were they already seasoned and experienced professionals?

Owners and employers depend on the opinion and analysis of their managers to make important decisions. They make recommendations on hiring, firing, disciplining, and rewarding employees. They are in charge of working through day-to-day situations and are required to literally manage the ups and downs of their part of the business.

Many employers rely too much on their managers and give them too much decision-making ability, wanting to believe that they can handle all situations. The fact is, they are, more often than not, in need of a lot more training and experience.

This is especially recognized in the case of a "band-aid" manager who was initially promoted from a lower position to solve a short-term crisis but who has stayed in that position far longer than imagined.

Be careful about the advice from your managers. To confirm accuracy, do your research on their suggestion. Many times, a manager will have a completely different opinion of how a situation should be handled due to his or her lack of experience.

---

a chance, and it worked some of the time, but **overall, it was not a wise maneuver.** It turned out to be a total waste of time for the upper management because we ended up having to spend more time managing the managers.

VINNY: I hope you fired 'em all.

GLEN: We had to shuffle them around and try to come up with "better" positions for them. Essentially, we had to be creative about getting them out of management without shocking the system.

LAUREN: That sounds like more work than it was worth.

GLEN: Not in the beginning. It was a relief. But after awhile, we felt the pains of the decisions. We were bombarded with them on a daily basis, trying to help them along.

> "Experience is the best teacher, but a fool will learn from no other."
> Benjamin Franklin

For Office Use Only

Employee

Do You Really Know What You Are Doing As Manager?

Sometimes, an employee becomes a manager through recognition of hard work or great performance. Companies naturally elevate responsible employees with great track records and the appropriate personality to managerial positions. If you evolve into a managerial position, ask yourself if you have the applicable knowledge to be a manager.

Commonly, great salespeople are elevated to sales management positions. The company believes that others can more easily learn the tactics employed by a great salesperson by giving that person responsibility for other salespeople. This is a mature and reasonable response by the company.

But there are certain downfalls to this. The elevated manager is automatically expected to know and understand how to manage people. If you have become a manager, you will be expected to report back to your superiors with your opinions about what you think and see. Without prior experience in management, you may find yourself delivering information that is materially incorrect or flawed in its analysis. If a more senior and seasoned management person sincerely disagrees with your ideas, you will be smarter to accept the difference of opinion and consider gaining more experience.

It got to the point that they would just walk into our offices unannounced, and we would have to engage in a conversation with them. They didn't understand that we could have been working on something else, and they were always unsure of a decision because they didn't know what to do. They needed help a lot of the times, and it chewed into our time tremendously.

LAUREN: I never mind when one of my people ask me for help or come to me during the day. I think that is a good thing. I have an open-door policy because it gives everyone a sense of comfort. And I don't want to be unapproachable or seem that way, so I always make myself available.

GLEN: Yes, but if your entire day everyday was spent telling managers how to manage, you would find it to be a problem. We should have made it temporary, but once we were into it, trying to unwind them out of their new positions was another whole job.

CHANDRA: Didn't your people complain? That's what I saw happen. We all were forced to listen to one of our own telling us what to do, and everything was turning into a problem. Some people left the company

---

Erik A. Kaiser

Employer

Do Employees Think They Should Have Immediate Access To You?

If you are bombarded with employees who believe they can just walk into your office or workspace impromptu, you have to consider a more formal system. Otherwise, you are being disrupted while doing your work to keep the company going.

Often, employees only need a minute or two or claim that they know you are busy but want to run something by you that instant. Sometimes, it is just being able to get face time with you that is important, and stopping in unannounced is the way.

If you are experiencing this type of interruption, you need to put a system in place that lets employees know that your time is as valuable as theirs and must be respected. The way to not offend your employees with the change is to describe a new contact policy that does not cause an interruption to your schedule. If you have an assistant, make a policy which requires all employees to schedule any meetings with you through your assistant. You can also try making an hour a day an open time during which people can feel free to stop in and talk to you.

You will notice that some of your senior people will believe that the new rules will not apply to them, and they will continue to disturb you if you don't let them know that the rules apply to them as well.

---

because it got to be so bad.

GLEN: Oh yes, people complained. That was another whole management issue. We had to go to the employees to get feedback on the managers we put into place, and they were very open with the information. They also used it as a platform to give us feedback on what we could be doing better according to the other employees, and that was really helpful. We were very happy to hear that they wanted to give us their ideas because it meant that they really cared about the company and about being there.

CHANDRA: That's good that you did something, because nothing ever improved for my company. They left this guy in charge, and he had no idea what to really do. And he would get all bossy. If we said anything to his boss, **we would just get dismissed** like we didn't know what we were talking about. I didn't have a lot of respect for the company after that. You would think they would want to know what is going on, but that wasn't the case. A lot of people needed their jobs, and they were really concerned. I think they made a bad mistake not listening to how it affected everyone.

For Office Use Only

Employee

Do You Expect To Have Immediate Access To Your Boss?

If you expect to waltz into you boss's office anytime you feel like it, you need to take into consideration that you are most likely interrupting him or her from something that might be critical. Your boss's time is generally more important at work than your time because he or she has more responsibility. Be sensitive to the access you have to your boss because too much employee interruption will be considered more of a nuisance if you don't adhere to some simple rules that demonstrate your awareness.

If you want to meet with your boss, send a communication using his/her preferred method of communication (instant messenger, email, phone, et al) detailing the reason for wanting to speak. This way, your boss will have the opportunity to choose a time when he or she will know that appropriate focus can be given to your inquiry. It also gives him or her time to invite other people who may want to be in on the discussion. This will earn you respect because you are recognizing that your boss is not always available on a whim. Following this simple exercise can be a subtle difference between a professional and someone less experienced and less aware.

GLEN: I agree. They could have avoided a lot of problems. Maybe they didn't know how to handle it. Just because you have a company doesn't mean that you know how to run it effectively.

CHANDRA: I think they thought that they knew what to do, but it didn't work all of the time. I mean, they were good at some things and terrible at others. I never really felt connected to them, so if you ask me if I really cared about anything to do with the company after that, I didn't.

GLEN: So is that why you don't care about your new company?

CHANDRA: I think that is part of it. You know, it's weird because I want to like the bosses and everyone at work - and I like my coworkers - but the bosses are usually a mystery. They are just people you hear about and see but never talk to them and never get to know them. They only care

"Lost time is never found again."
Benjamin Franklin

Erik A. Kaiser

Employer

Getting Feedback From Your Employees

Employees are necessary if you can't do everything yourself. Since you have to have these people in your company life, you need to be able to effectively communicate with them about what is happening inside and outside of the company.

Companies should have a platform to be able to capture the feedback from employees about their opinions and ideas. Since bosses are in charge of steering the company, having the eyes and ears of the employees as auxiliary lookouts and problem-solvers should be more of a necessity than a luxury.

Feedback from your employees can come in many forms. The most effective form is through individual and group meetings. Individual meetings allow an open dialogue without the interruption or opinions of others, while group meetings allow people to share ideas and build off of them as the meeting progresses.

When getting feedback, do not be adverse to what you hear. Remember to allow any and all comments to be considered valuable, even if they are not. You do not want to create an environment in which you demand feedback but criticise its quality. You will end up hearing less and less if employees do not feel comfortable speaking up.

---

about themselves, it seems. I hear good things about them, but how am I supposed to believe anything when I can't get a hello sometimes?

VINNY: That's because they don't need to talk to you. You're nothin' to them. You get paid to do a job. This ain't no Christmas get-together.

CHANDRA: [to Vinny] Don't you ever have a company meeting with your employees to tell them what is going on?

VINNY: Yeah, when I am changing something, like how long they gotta work.

It's easier because I make the rules.

CHANDRA: You at least have met all of your employees.

VINNY: I hire and fire 'em all.

GLEN: I try to meet everyone at the company always. I can't do it all of the time because there are thousands of people, but I address them as a group frequently. You have to because **they become invested in the company with you.** You have to give people face time for them to feel part of a company.

LAUREN: I don't have any choice because

For Office Use Only

Do You Give Feedback To Your Employer?

Good work environments make open dialogue with superiors a common exercise. A good boss and company want to know about your experiences performing your job and you experiences in the industry that make a difference to the company. Your company should be looking to be more competitive and require that you be candid about what you see. They should be learning about other potential opportunities for the company to succeed through your eyes.

Many times, the opportunity to express your thoughts about the company operations, procedures, experiences in the market, and experiences at the company is available during office meetings. Sometimes, you may have a one-on-one with your employer, which allows you to talk more freely. You should take full advantage of any open dialogue. It will help you put on record anything that you find to be positive or negative about the company or your job.

Take advantage of offering ideas and solutions to anything that can be improved. When you have the ear of your employer and he or she is genuinely interested in what you have to say, you will be remembered for being interactive and for your ideas. This is a great way to get some recognition and to understand if your ideas and experiences are the same as others.

"The greatest compliment that was ever paid me was when one asked what I thought, and attended to my answer."
Henry David Thoreau

we are only about 30 people, so I see them every day and talk to them in passing and while working. You are right, though. They do want to be able to see you and feel as if they are part of something. My people like what they do, and many of them have been there for years. I have become friends with a lot of them, and they have become committed to what we are doing and growing the company. If I didn't spend time with them and be able to talk about what is going on in general, they would definitely have a different attitude. There is an art to it, actually.

GLEN: Once a month, I have lunch with a group of employees. Managers submit names of people to my office whenever someone deserves some recognition,

Employer

Giving Face Time

Employers and bosses are perceived as important and influential. After all, you are responsible for the employment of everyone under you. It should be no surprise that employees want to spend time in order to be influenced by you in your presence.

It is unrealistic for a CEO to spend individual time with thousands of employees on a regular basis. But it is not unrealistic in smaller organizations to be able to extend a handshake or catch up at the desk of an employee every now and again.

Huge corporations are often addressed by the CEO in super company conferences, where thousands of employees get to see and hear their leader discuss the business that directly affects their daily lives. Smaller companies have the opportunity to have more effective exchanges between the top management and the lowest employee.

Company size does not matter. There is always a way for the boss to be part of the working lives of the employees. Employees appreciate being part of an audience with the boss, and it boosts morale.

"We convince by our presence."
Walt Whitman

and we have a program where I put aside one day a month for lunch with those people. It is really encouraging to them because I am the most senior person at the company, and they feel really special. It is unbelievable for motivation and pushes the other people around them to want to do something extra for the company.

CHANDRA: That would be amazing if my boss did anything like that. What do you talk about?

GLEN: Oh, whatever, really. I usually talk about why they are there at the table and that the company recognizes their efforts. It is perceived as an honor for them and is a big deal with their coworkers. And, I want to meet them. I genuinely have an interest in thanking them.

VINNY: Why is it that it's never the other way around? You have never heard of the

---

For Office Use Only

Employee

Getting Face Time

No matter how big your company is, it is very comforting to know that you are not just another number on an employee roster. With the right attention from the higher ups, a big company can seem like an intimate family. If you feel this way, you are most likely getting enough face time with your employer. But if you feel that your employer is an elusive shadow about whom you really don't know much, you are missing out on some consequential information.

It can be tough working in an environment in which your employer is someone you don't really understand. In this case, it would not be wrong to think that the employer does not have as much of an interest in the company as you think he or she should. If you never hear your boss address your company or you on any level, you have to wonder what is actually going on.

A common downside of not being in touch with your employer is that you will not receive any recognition for a job well done. If your employer has the ability to ignore you, take that as a sign that you are dispensable. That should lead you to seek out a company that does not have a mystery man or woman in charge of your job security.

---

workers coming together and honoring the boss.
LAUREN: That is because employees don't see bosses as deserving of anything. It's true. They think that we are super-human or something. I never got that myself. You know, you bring up a good point. In my case, you go all out for them sometimes, and they just accept it as normal and move on. Sometimes you get a thank you, and people recognize what you have done. But it's really a give/take relationship. We give, they take.
CHANDRA: Why should we care about you? You are the one making more money. Go buy yourself a hug. You don't have the kind of problems we have. If we did, maybe we would all be the boss and you would be working for us.
LENNY: Yeah, you're the lucky ones. And we have to throw you a party? I don't think so.
GLEN: Right. It is never hard work, determination, and discipline. It is always luck. So, it should be the same for employees, then. The ones who get recognized by the company for outstanding contributions are really just lucky people.

Erik A. Kaiser

Employer

Honoring Employees

Do your employees feel like they are important to your company, or do they feel like just a number? It does not matter the size of your company or how you categorize your employees; there is always something you can do to honor employees who deserve some attention. Simple recognition is a very powerful tool to keep spirits high. The return on recognition is very high for the company, and if used properly, will create internal competitions between employees to outperform one another. You will end up winning their respect and loyalty. Your employees will feel recognized and be more engaged at work.

There are some very simple ways to honor employees:

- Recognize an "employee of the month," and put his or her name on a plaque where everyone can see it.
- Create periodic awards that are customized to your company.
- Write a company-wide email about an employee's achievements personally, professionally, or at the company.
- Make a mention of an employee's good work during an office meeting.

"The way to develop the best that is in a man is by appreciation and encouragement."
Charles Schwab

That's like the company giving your paycheck to another employee.

LENNY: That's what companies do. They always give the bonuses and extra days off to one guy.

CHANDRA: That's because you've never done what they are doing. We have salespeople who win the bonuses every month because they consistently bring in the most money. And they work at it.

LENNY: I do as much work as them, and I don't get anything.

CHANDRA: Yeah, right. I depend on sales bringing in the money so I can get paid. I don't care what the company does to keep them happy. I will admit that my company gives them too much in my eyes because even if they don't hit the bonus targets,

For Office Use Only

Employee

Honoring Your Boss

If you like your boss, think that he or she is fair, creates a good environment in which to work, and cares about the welfare of the employees and the company, then it would be a wise idea to recognize him or her. Everyone knows when Employee Appreciation Day arrives, but very few people outside of Hallmark know there is a National Boss Appreciation Day.

There are a lot of different expenses and efforts that go into trying to make employees happy. You should take the time to get together with your coworkers and honor your boss if you are happy. It will go a long way, and you can guarantee that it will be remembered. Bosses want to be seen as doing a great job and appreciated in the same way that you want to impress your boss.

Bosses are people, too. They have the same emotions as everyone else. Just because they have the boss title does not mean they don't desire to be recognized when they do a good job. You don't have to do a lot. You can buy your boss a cake and get together as a group to say thank you. Don't be shy about thanking him or her for a job well done.

---

they still demand them from the boss. I think that is wrong, but they feel like they are entitled to it.

LENNY: See, you are proving my point. If your company pays those dudes, then I should get it, too.

GLEN: He is sort of right, you know. We have gone through this with our top salespeople. They ride high and get recognized every month, to the point they can miss targets but still demand the recognition today based on past performance. That's not how it works. They get spoiled for sure. That is an entire other management issue. You have to keep them engaged and happy to keep producing, so you start cutting deals with them so they keep momentum. It is a sticky issue.

LENNY: Yeah, that's ridiculous. I could save a life at my company, and someone else would get the credit.

GRACE: Oh, Lenny, that's not true. I'm sure if you saved a life, you'd be a hero.

VINNY: Depends on whose life you saved. If it is the life of a guy who owes me money, **I wouldn't be givin' you any high-fives.**

Erik A. Kaiser

Employer

Do You Over-Recognize Employee Achievements?

Giving your employees recognition for a job well done is smart. But since we expect them to grow in their positions or to develop consistency at managing their work, you need to control the type and frequency of recognition.

Recognition in the form of money can be the most powerful, but it can also be the most dangerous. The reason is because employees naturally identify themselves with the recognition that has been given to them. The more that you continue to recognize them, the more they expect it.

When you over-recognize, especially with cash or cash equivalents, employees begin to see the money as part of their earned cash-flow stream. They will believe that their value is greater than it is, and when you decide that you can no longer offer the same cash recognition or you diminish your enthusiasm, they will be left thinking they are being short-changed.

Over-recognition of achievements with rewards that are not cash or cash equivalents runs the risk of becoming counterproductive for employee morale. Eventually, the recognition may become innocuous and not have any real value. You may instead be setting a low expectation for them that will not extract the true value of the employee.

"The only way to escape the personal corruption of praise is to go on working."
Albert Einstein

GLEN: [to Lenny] That's an obvious case, but you have another good point. There are some employees that do extraordinary things for a company, and they have to be recognized. That becomes a personal issue.

GRACE: You better believe it does. There was this woman at my old job who won the Citizen of the Year award for the state. She was amazing. So inspirational. She adopted poor children and raised them as her own. She held charity events at her house for different causes and helped raise money to save local landmarks. She was remarkable, and the state gave her an award for being an incredible citizen. There was a huge event, and everyone from the governor to big business people were at the event. And do you know what she did

---

For Office Use Only

Have You Become Spoiled At Receiving Recognition?

Your company and boss love you. You get awards all of the time for reaching certain milestones, and you get special privileges extended to you, extra cash bonuses, frequent flier miles, trips, and trophies. At first, you thought it was extra-special, but now you expect it and need it to keep you engaged and feeling valued.

There isn't any real reason to think that you didn't earn it, either. If the company is giving it away to you because they think you did a great job or reached certain milestones, then you are worth that much to them at that point in time. But don't get caught in the recognition trap.

Before you know it, there will be a policy change, a change in management, or a financial change at the company. When that happens, the likelihood of you earning the same stream of recognition is bound to slow dramatically or stop altogether.

If you are receiving cash or cash-equivalent recognition, you need to clearly understand the policy under which you are receiving it. Know clearly if it supposed to be an expectation that will continue, or if you should be counting it as a one-time special event.

---

in her speech? She told the crowd that her company was part of the reason for her generosity, and supporting the company would be supporting her. Do you know why she did that? We found out that she knew the company was struggling, and she used her recognition to help the company and the people there keep their jobs. She didn't need to do that. Her event was about her, but she plugged the company.

GLEN: Was that effective at bringing the company business?

GRACE: It was amazing. She was in every social media feed, on the radio, on the television. Anyone who saw the story saw her plugging the company in a compassionate way. The company got tons of new business and so many new customers just because of that. The company really started to make money as a result of that, and the boss felt really indebted to her. The owner ended up putting her son through college and gave her lots of bonuses. It really worked out for both of them.

GLEN: Good for them. That also works the other way around. We paid for the surgery of one of our employees who became sick

---

Erik A. Kaiser

Employer

Recognizing When Employees Go Beyond The Call Of Duty

Let's face it: some employees are enthusiastic about working for the company. We have some clear expectations from them, but once in a while, an employee or a group of employees will go way above the expectation, leaving you wondering what you have done to make them so committed to the cause.

The worst reaction you can have is to do nothing. Employers fear that if they have to recognize anything that employees do that is beyond the call of duty, it will end up costing them in some way. You may think that by recognizing them, it will be used against you. You could be right, but doing nothing is worse than doing something in this case. Not every employee thinks about money as the immediate goal. Sometimes, to be recognized by the boss means a lot at work among coworkers. It gives them credibility and a reason to stand out.

When an employee goes out of his or her way in a meaningful manner on behalf of the company, he or she is doing so to impress you. Don't leave your employee with the impression that it was something that he or she should have done regardless of any situation. That is not the case. Make a point to recognize your employee in the appropriate fashion because he or she really just awarded you.

---

while working at the company.

VINNY: You did *what?*

GLEN: I know this must sound totally crazy to you, but we did. Her name is Sarah, and she was working for us for about a year. She was about 25 years old at the time. She developed a very rare cancer which required her to have some expensive and complicated surgeries that our health care plan did not support. It was brought to our attention through the hierarchy of managers during our regular update meetings.

GRACE: The poor girl! What happened?

GLEN: She became increasingly ill and started to miss days. We followed up and found that her parents were very poor, unable to pay for the surgery, and she was literally dying. The family got together and tried to fund raise, but the surgery was estimated to be about $50,000, and they only were able to scrape up $3,500 so far. So, the second I found out, I spoke to the family, got the doctor's information, and called him. But, their doctor couldn't even do the surgery, and he recommended to us only three doctors who perform the surgery in the country. I personally spoke

---

For Office Use Only

Employee

Do You Get Recognized When You Go Beyond The Call Of Duty?

There are times that you have the option to do something way above the normal expectation for your boss or your company. You should know when and if going out of your way is appropriate or not. There is only one real way to know if going out of your way has value to you, and that is to do it.

When you do decide to do something uncommon, you have to be sure that the recognition you receive for extraordinary acts on behalf of your boss or your company is appropriate. If your efforts are glossed over or, even worse, make you feel as though you should have done it for the company without contemplation, you are wasting your good time.

Great deeds demonstrate your commitment to your coworkers, your boss, and your company. They send the message that you are all for the team and are willing to help out in every way possible. Your boss should be thrilled and want to honor you in some way. If not, you will know that he or she is not worth the effort in the future. Save your dry powder for something that will get you something in return.

"The man who does more than he is paid for will soon be paid for more than he does."

Napoleon Hill

to each one, picked the best one, and put the girl on a first-class ticket the next day to Houston. I negotiated a better price, and our company wired a deposit to the doctor, and she was in surgery the next day.

CHANDRA: That is the most incredible thing I have ever heard a company doing.

LENNY: Yeah, man, that is pretty unbelievable. How long ago was this?

GLEN: Let's see, it was about a little over four years ago, because she had the surgery in May. I remember the month because the entire company was rooting for a "miracle in May."

GRACE: Wow! What happened? Is she OK?

GLEN: The surgery was complicated, and it turned out that she needed another a month after. We picked up all of her

Erik A. Kaiser

Employer

Do Your Employees Know When You Have Gone Beyond The Call Of Duty?

Keeping employees happy and productive is, at times, more important than the bottom line. Most employers pride themselves on a high employee retention rate as a benchmark to demonstrate the underlying success of the company. To keep employees happy, employers many times extend themselves over and above what most other businesses would comfortably do.

What gets lost in translation to the employees are the lengths to which you may go to keep them happy or to protect them. Unfortunately, continued occurrences that are considered above and beyond the call of duty become diluted in meaning and eventually become expected. Do not let this happen. Once employees get used to extra special treatment, they misconstrue it as expectation.

The objective is for all of your employees to understand and to appreciate the extraordinary efforts that you make. You need to explain your efforts in detail and get them to revere you for it. Do not forget to keep a document of what you have done, for you may need to remind everyone of your efforts at some point in the future.

"One never notices what has been done; one can only see what remains to be done."
Marie Curie

medical bills and her rehabilitation. About six months later, she returned to work at our company and has been an unbelievable employee since, from what I hear.

VINNY: She must be Wonder Woman now.

GLEN: That was the report when I used to ask about her frequently. That whole event also scared a lot of people while energizing them about what they were doing. It

created a tremendous amount of motivation at all levels of the company. When the story got out, we had a deluge of unsolicited resumes. And we hired some extremely motivated people who were so excited that a company would extend itself in such a manner to an individual employee.

VINNY: And I bet **they all had a sick aunt** and wanted free surgery.

For Office Use Only

Do You Know When Your Employer Goes Beyond The Call Of Duty?

Most employers care a tremendous amount about the welfare and happiness of their employees. They have to; without you, there really isn't any company. So it should not be a surprise that an employer will go to great lengths to keep an individual or group of employees content.

Often, employers' efforts go unnoticed because the efforts made may be behind the scenes. They could make unnecessary improvements to benefits or retirement plans that cost the company more but benefit the employee more. They could pay for something significant for an employee that far outweighs the employee's value to the company. They could occasionally pay bonuses unexpectedly. There are many examples. But what is important is to understand that you need to recognize the lengths to which your employer has gone to please you.

Without recognizing and admiring the efforts which are obvious to you, your employer will feel as though the effort is unimportant. This is equivalent to shopping for the perfect, most thoughtful birthday gift for another person, and then he or she glosses over it and doesn't recognize the efforts you made. You will certainly not be as enthusiastic about putting forth the same amount of energy next year. The same holds true for employers. When you know they have gone above a standard, recognize it. Your praise will most likely ensure that those efforts are repeated.

GLEN: We considered that, but it wasn't the case. They were really super-motivated people, and we hired and gave them the attention they needed to really grow.
The story was so inspirational to so many employees that we created more work for ourselves. We had groups of employees who were super-eager to talk about their successes at work because of how they felt about the company treating Sarah. We struck motivational gold and created all of these new incentive programs around their enthusiasm. It was one of those benefits that we never planned on.

VINNY: So this girl, Sarah, did you make her sign an agreement that prevents her from leavin' the company? I mean, you just dropped a hundred g's on her, and she was only workin' for the company for a year.

GLEN: No one really cared. The year before she went into surgery, she had excellent reports from her manager, and she never asked for anything. We know she can leave at any time. But we trust her enough to keep giving us her all and to stay and grow with the company.

VINNY: I don't trust nobody. You hear me? *Nobody.* I have been burned so many times

Employer

Handling Super-Motivated Employees

Eager and motivated employees are wonderful to have, but they can be a handful. We want them engaged, but there are some employees who are really motivated and are always working and thinking about work, no matter what time or day it is.

Super-motivated employees are great, but they need a lot of attention and they need to keep getting recharged. In the workplace, they will go to their superior or to the top of the company to continue to share ideas and experiences. Unfortunately, if you are not responsive, you will be sending the message that you are dismissive, and in turn, their motivation will be diminished or lost.

You don't want to appear irritated, but you may not be able to afford the time they demand of you. If you are caught in this bind, you need to find a way to channel their energies away from you. We love a super-motivated employee but not at the expense of your time and energy.

Consider setting up a recurring time to meet with the employee to go over all of his or her ideas. Use this as a platform to consolidate all of the various intermittent conversations that you would regularly have during the day. Make the employee feel that this time is special, and that they should expect your full focus.

"Enthusiasm is the mother of effort, and without it, nothing great was ever achieved."
Ralph Waldo Emerson

that I don't even want to trust any of my people. They will steal from you and lie right to your face.

LENNY: It's no different from any of my bosses lying straight at my face. It's a two-way street. Y'all lie to me, and I lie to you. I don't trust no boss. They're all out for themselves.

CHANDRA: One thing I will say is that whenever I have a problem with my pay or something related to getting paid, my boss never lies to me about what he is going to do. He always does it. But I don't trust him when it comes to other things because he doesn't keep his word. Anything with money, I trust him. Other than that, forget it.

LENNY: You're lucky. I hear more stupid

For Office Use Only

Being A Super-Motivated Employee

If you are always thinking about how you can better your job and your company, or if you are always ready for business no matter when it is, you are a super-motivated employee. You probably have a lot of ideas that you want to share with your superiors at any given time.

Since you have a lot of energy, be aware that not everyone operates in the same manner as you. You may get the boss to pick up the phone on a Sunday morning to tell him or her about your new idea, but that does not mean that he or she wants to be discussing it right then. Chances are, there are better times to make the approach.

If your boss is attentive to you, it is because he or she means to be. But bosses also know that if you are not given the proper attention, you may become less enthusiastic.

A successful super-motivated employee is organized and delivers ideas, messages, and experiences in a concise manner at appropriate times. Your boss may say to call them anytime, but what that really means is that he or she is open to communication freely with you. It doesn't mean that he or she never needs downtime. You don't want to become a nuisance.

---

stories about why my pay is late and why I'm gettin' paid less than I'm supposed to. I've been jerked around more than beef jerky.

LAUREN: I don't lie to my employees. You have to be able to trust one another. I trust my people to do the right job, and they trust me that I will pay them.

LENNY: Well, when my boss takes something from me, I take something from them. If they don't pay me what they said they are goin' to pay me, then I have a right to make up the difference with their stuff. It's simple.

LAUREN: What do you mean?

LENNY: See this t-shirt I'm wearin'? I work at this place right now. They were supposed to pay me overtime a month ago for coming in on Sunday to cover another guy at the counter, and the crooks paid me regular time. So I was supposed to get time and a half, which would have been another $50. I ain't waitin' no more, so I took a box of these t-shirts. I've been selling them to my friends for $5 a piece, and I already sold 20 of them and kept five for myself. Nice and new, see?

LAUREN: So you steal stuff?

Erik A. Kaiser

Employer

Do You Trust Your Employees?

Establishing trust in your employees is essential to a solid operation. Without it, part of your good energy that should be focused on the company or your personal time will be spent on figuring out if you are getting taken advantage of.

Building trust is not quick and easy. And once it is established, it does not mean that it is established for good. Trust must be demonstrated repeatedly, because sometimes a trustworthy pattern can be interrupted by an event in your employee's life.

Employers who do not build trust with employees end up being tied down to the process of monitoring employees. Monitoring comes in many forms. It can literally be video monitoring, or it can mean just being around all the time to keep an eye on everything. This is draining and should not be a big part of your job description.

Sometimes, employers need to hire one trusted individual to watch over the employees for dishonest or opportunistic dealings. Replacing employees who are not trustworthy will help you maintain a level of sanity. But be sure to have a system of checks and balances specific to your business to reassure yourself that the trust you have in others is not abused.

LENNY: Straight out, yeah. They'll never know, and I'm never gettin' paid by them for what they promised. They should expect it. How else am I gonna get paid?

VINNY: If I find out anyone takes anythin' from me, they're fired. We had a guy who was takin' candy when we was filling up the vending machines. He got ratted out by the guy below him, and I fired him.

GRACE: What did the guy say when you caught him?

VINNY: I never caught him, and I never told him. I just fired him.

GRACE: So how do you know the other guy was telling the truth? What if he wasn't stealing anything?

VINNY: I don't care. I don't have time to

"Whoever is careless with the truth in small matters cannot be trusted with the important matters."
Albert Einstein

For Office Use Only

Employee

Do You Trust Your Employer?

There are many potential reasons for distrusting your employer. You may have experienced issues with getting paid. Or you may have been promised a promotion to keep you employed that never materializes. Maybe your employer has not been forthcoming with information that puts your employment at risk. It matters that you identify when, how, where, and with what you can or cannot trust your employer. You then need to analyze if you can operate within those confines and if the effort is worth it for you.

Here are some questions to ask. Does your employer's actions match his or her words? Do you find yourself nervous about presenting new opportunities or contacts to your employer because you fear that they will be taken from you? Does your employer have a track record of not honoring commitments?

There are sometimes rewards to working in an environment where you do not trust you employer. Those rewards could come in the form of a unique learning experience, meeting contacts you might not have had the chance to otherwise meet, or being part of something that is important to your image. Whatever it is, if you don't feel that your employer is trustworthy, you will should explore another opportunity where you can relax and accelerate. Too much energy will be spent protecting yourself.

"Those who trust us educate us."
T.S. Eliot

play Sherlock Holmes and jerk around. It's a 50/50 chance. It don't matter if I am wrong at the end of the day.

GRACE: But, that's not fair! What if the guy who told you was lying, and you fired the wrong guy?

VINNY: If I find out he was lying, I'll fire him, too. Plus, you don't want people like that working together. They were always fightin' about something. Normally, I don't care who gets along with who, but these guys would fight in front of customers. And you just don't do that. We are running a business, not a playground.

GRACE: Why were they always fighting?

VINNY: Who knows? They were both Italian, too. One from the north and the other from the south. They would fight about everything, and it was just annoying after a while. You can't fight in front of a

---

Erik A. Kaiser

Employer

Are Your Employees Stealing From You?

All companies have stuff, from office supplies to inventory to proprietary algorithms. Those assets need monitoring and protection. Employee theft is an enormous problem that can be tough to identify until it is too late.

Employees are known to take home office supplies, toilet paper, and bar soap if it not secured. Worse, they will take cash money or the inventory your are trying to sell. Putting a stop to it is not always easy, so protect yourself with a few common safeguards.

1. Get a fidelity bond or other insurance that covers employee theft, fraud, and other dishonest acts.
2. Install a monitoring system for your inventory.
3. Let it be known that the police will be notified if anyone is ever caught stealing. Enforce this.
4. Buy yourself a loyal rat in the company. For a $1,000, a snitch can help stop a $100,000 crime against you.
5. Have your accountants perform a professional audit of your books and inventory.

Keep an eye out for those whom you know or suspect are on drugs, have marital problems, or have fallen on hard times that might require a quick need for cash. They will be most desperate for anything small of high value like, electronics, computers, and equipment.

---

customer.

CHANDRA: Employees fight all the time. There's nothing new there.

GLEN: Yes, but what Vinny is saying is that it was affecting his business. I would have done a little more investigation, but I understand where he is coming from. More than one problem is solved, as far as he is concerned.

VINNY: Thank you, Glen. [pointing to Glen] Yeah, what he said.

LAUREN: I kind of agree. We are a small company, and when employees don't get along, it is usually the result of one person. I have never had a drastic situation like Vinny's people, but there was a time that I hired a **girl** who started out great but had a **nasty little side to her.** She would do her work and she was good at it, but the way she did it caused arguments with everyone she had to work with. I don't know what it was, but she argued with everyone about how they should be doing their work. Maybe she was trying to be helpful, but it didn't come across that way. She became confrontational, and it affected the atmosphere. So I had to let her go, even

For Office Use Only

Employee

Stealing From Your Company?

The occasional company pen and pad that makes its way into your personal possession is not a crime. But, purposely taking for your own use what your company provides at work is stealing.

You know when you are stealing. If you don't ask to take the laptop which has been sitting unused in the corner of the office, it is stealing. If you intercept a check made out to the company but you can get it cashed at your bank because of a relationship with your teller friend, that is stealing. If your company has information on clients, client lists, lead sources, and other proprietary information that you take without approval, it is stealing. If you use the company credit card to fill up your car with gas but report that it was for a company vehicle, you are stealing. If you take anything owned by the company for your own use without approval, it is stealing.

The consequences to the risks you take range from simple termination to jail time. Some employers will use law enforcement to try to make you pay back the loss.

Most employers do not tolerate theft. But if you get caught, offer your employer something in return to keep your job. Consider working overtime for free if your boss feels compelled to keep you. You can always suggest a payment plan.

"No people is wholly civilized where a distinction is drawn between stealing an office and stealing a purse."
Theodore Roosevelt

though her work was perfect.

GLEN: You made the right choice, I am sure. It brings down morale and eventually, people start to leave.

LAUREN: Fortunately, it didn't get to that point. If it were years earlier in my career, I could guarantee that I would have handled it differently.

GRACE: How so?

LAUREN: Well, for one, I would never had known about the issue until it was too late because I was never as close to my staff as I was at that point. I was only concerned with the business surviving and the numbers coming in, and I never connected with my people well. And my people sort of saw me as a little disconnected from them.

CHANDRA: We call people like you a

Erik A. Kaiser

Employer

Do Your Employees Fight And Argue?

There is nothing more time-intensive and draining than managing the personalities of specific employees so they get along with other employees. You may find that some employees quit because they hate working with one specific coworker. Productivity drops as a result, and your energy is spent on babysitting, not on work.

No matter how great of a worker the employee is, if he or she is the subject of a constant debate and is the cause of drama with employees you revere, you have to get rid of that person. The longer that you keep the person employed, the harder it becomes to retain employees and maintain credibility.

If you agree with the contentious experiences of your other employees, you need to be transparent with them about your plans to replace the disruptive individual. If you cannot be transparent for certain reasons, you will need to move swiftly. Many times, the affected employees will be glad to help with the additional work that will be created when the disruptor is fired. They will be thankful.

Restoration of harmony in your group will eliminate unproductive stress and will allow you to dedicate time to finding the right replacement. Drama is for the stage.

"Weakness on both sides is the motto of all quarrels."
Voltaire

"business biatch."

LAUREN: I know. [laughing] I really wasn't! I just didn't know everything I know now. And I am still working at it. But over time, after building my confidence and dealing with all of the issues of a business, I started to understand my people better. Putting someone between my employees and me made all the difference. So, now I know all the employees, and we have a great relationship. A few of my most trusted people sat me down a few times telling me about the problem we had with the new girl, and I listened. After the regular adjustment period was over, I realized that **I had to get rid of the new girl** to keep my people happy.

CHANDRA: That is good that they feel comfortable coming to you. My boss is all about business. You never get that warm,

---

144   For Office Use Only

Employee

Do You Always Argue With Your Colleagues?

Employers are very sensitive to employee harmony. They do not want warring employees or ones who are disruptive to the operation. If you often find yourself in an altercation or argument with your colleagues, you are probably ripe for a relocation or on your way out the door.

Arguments with colleagues should most often be regarding work. When you have arguments at work, your superiors will certainly be notified, and they will need to get involved to keep the peace. When that pattern continues, and you are always at the source or are always involved, you will most likely be terminated. Companies cannot afford to allow arguments to continue because it will lead other employees to believe that fighting is acceptable behavior. It costs time and productivity, which directly equate to lost money to your employer.

If you are having arguments with colleagues that are not related to work, you can bet that your termination is imminent, especially if you are not professional and debate illogically.

---

fuzzy feeling of anything other than making money. If you want to connect with him, you have to talk about something to do with the business. Everything else is just a waste of his time, and he lets you know it.

GRACE: What does he say?

CHANDRA: You could be in a meeting with him and a bunch of other people, and the topic goes off business for a minute, and he'll say, "Hey! How is this conversation making the company money? We don't get paid for talking about this crap. Focus on why we are here so we can keep things moving forward." Bark, bark, bark.

VINNY: I like this guy. He doesn't waste any time gettin' sucked into stupid conversations.

CHANDRA: Yeah, well, I guess so. It doesn't matter anyway, as long as I get paid.

GLEN: That is his approach, and it may work for the personalities that he has to manage. Did you ever tell him what you think?

CHANDRA: No way. He's not like that. He would probably get mad. It's not worth it.

LAUREN: I took everything personally in the beginning, and if someone told me that

---

Erik A. Kaiser

Employer

Are You Too Business And Not Personal Enough?

There is nothing wrong with maintaining a pretty clear line between your employees and you. But there is a downside to not engaging them on a personal level. Employers build office relationships with their employees but sometimes forget that the simple cocktail with the team after work is an enormous morale booster and can contribute tremendously to their loyalty to you.

Employees want to believe that they have some sort of connection to you. Giving them the opportunity to feel personal works for you in a lot of ways. Once they feel a connection, you become more human to them, and they will take you into consideration more as a person than as an employer. Take advantage of this.

Yes, you may have to force yourself to get involved in the softball game or the occasional beer. But consider your time a direct investment into your company, one for which you can realize an immediate return.

If you know that your employees think that you are a stiff, you should work to improve their opinion of you. Take an hour after work to join them for a drink, get your nails done, hit the gym together, or see a movie. If they are more relaxed around you after hanging out, you have made a positive improvement.

"Perpetual devotion to what a man calls his business is only to be sustained by perpetual neglect of many other things."
Robert Louis Stevenson

I was "too this" or "too that," I would have said something stupid like, "I know what I am doing. It's my company."
CHANDRA: Yuck!
LAUREN: I was inexperienced. It took time for me to trust someone who didn't have an angle with me for me to listen.
GRACE: That's the same with coworkers.

I learned a lot about myself from hearing about what people thought of me at work. I was always thankful that someone would tell me about what they thought about me. **That is the ultimate sign of caring.** If they didn't care about me, they never would have given me any criticism or feedback.
GLEN: We always want to know about what our employees are thinking about the

---

146   **For Office Use Only**

Is Your Boss Always Business And Never Personal?

Some bosses are just plain business all of the time. They have never really make a connection with their employees on a personal level, no matter how many times their employees have asked them to go for a drink after work. You may like your boss at work, but since he or she does not make an effort to see the employees as social humans, consider bringing the party to him or her.

If your boss is a stiff, have a celebration for him or her at the appropriate time. Great times are birthdays, after great business deals, getting engaged, and having a personal victory. Have a party at the office just like you would after work. From that, you will be able to see if you can detect some non-business social behavior. It will put your boss on the spot to interact, and maybe, just maybe, there will be some hope to enjoy the boss's company without business as the focus.

management. It is important. Sometimes there are untrue rumors that circulate that need to be put to rest.

CHANDRA: Like what?

GLEN: Let's see. OK, here is one. There was a rumor between the employees in our headquarters that the former CEO bought a $20 million estate, when the truth was that he built a house that was hardly an estate.

CHANDRA: So what did it matter?

GLEN: It mattered because it was at a time that the company was struggling financially and there were layoffs. Somehow, the word got out about his house, and it escalated to the point that it was a sprawling $20 million Playboy mansion at the expense of the company. Normally, it would not matter, but too many comments were surfacing about it, and it reached the point that it affected morale.

CHANDRA: So how did you stop it?

GLEN: It was pretty ingenious. When the house was built, he held a holiday party for the management and some other select staff. At work the next week, the management talked about it normally to their staff, and the truth was revealed

Do You Wonder What Your Employees Say About You?

The greater the number of employees you have, the more difficult it is to know what their impressions are of you. Knowing how they profile you is important. For the most part, what they think of you is what they think of the company, and vice versa. Having a positive profile with your employees leads to better employee retention, work ethic, and respect.

You can learn what your employees think about you by asking them to complete an anonymous performance evaluation on you. It may seem unorthodox, but the information you learn will be invaluable in understanding how you are perceived.

If you would like a more direct approach, consider appealing to individual employees for a candid appraisal. However, unless you have a very trusting relationship with those employees, you will never get complete information. Employees will not want to jeopardize your image of them or their relationship with you.

Another way to find out is during an exit interview. Their overview will likely be more honest and real because they will not feel that they have to hold back unless there are politics at play. They are already at the last step out of the door.

"If all men knew what each said of the other, there would not be four friends in the world."
Blaise Pascal

that the house was a really nice house in a nice neighborhood. And that was it. Employees wanted to know all of the juicy details about how enormous it was to make true everything they had heard, but the same message was delivered by all of the management.

CHANDRA: So what was the house like?

GLEN: It was a really nice house. It wasn't some opulent mansion or anything like that, but it was beautiful. Relatively simple for what he could afford. It was nice enough without being over the top.

CHANDRA: So people stopped talking about it, then?

GLEN: Yes, and the focus shifted away from him. That's what we really wanted.

VINNY: I would never invite people to my

Employee

Do You Wonder What Your Coworkers Say About You?

You should be concerned about what your colleagues think about you. You can learn a lot about yourself from the people who spend an average of eight hours a day around you. They get to observe you in a variety of situations and can give you free insight into how you work with others, treat others, do your work, and organize yourself, all of which can indicate whether your coworkers respect you.

The relationships that you have with your coworkers can evolve into lifetime relationships. Like minds usually are part of the same team at a job. Empower yourself and learn to be open to criticism because it means that your coworkers care about you and how you perform on the job.

That information is critical to you in your evolution on and off the job. Learn about what your coworkers think about your performance in the areas on which you will be judged for compensation increases and promotions. You are better off correcting your course with their help, before you are asked to do so from your boss.

---

house, no way, no chance. You have to have the right people into your home. I don't trust anyone. Even real estate agents. I had an open house when I moved from my last place, and one of the agents stole my girlfriend's perfume from her bathroom. You know how girls have all those bottles all organized in one spot? Someone just pocketed one. I don't let nobody in my house unless they are friends or family.

LAUREN: I never invite my employees to my apartment. First off, my father bought it 15 years ago, and I have been renting it since. So I can't even say I bought it. And **it is too nice for the kind of money** I make as a caterer. If I had anyone over there, they would think we are making so much money at the company that they would try to go off and start one on their own.

CHANDRA: At least you are honest.

LAUREN: You know, I don't know if I would be inclined to have my staff over my house, anyway even if I lived somewhere else. I am very private, and I don't want to them seeing my whole life and asking me questions. It is none of their business.

CHANDRA: What do you have to hide?

Erik A. Kaiser

Employer

Inviting Employees To Your Home

You may have a lot of reasons why you might want to invite your employees to your home. But be clear on the exact reasons so you understand the implications before exposing the heart of your personal life.

When you allow your subordinates to roam the corridors of your life, you are letting them experience a concentrated version of who you are. We invite them in sometimes to demonstrate they are like family to us, and other times to show them what we have. Don't let it backfire on you.

By letting your employees see most of what you own and the lifestyle you lead, regardless of whether it is better or worse than theirs, you will be stirring up their emotions. Some will have admiration, some jealousy, some disgust, and some a combination of all.

Choose carefully the employees whom you want in your home. You have to expect that after they enter your home and your life, they will form a different opinion of you. Make sure the opinion is better than when they first stepped in. Don't let your willingness to cater to your employees on a personal level work against your efforts at work.

"I think that when you invite people to your home, you invite them to yourself."
Oprah Winfrey

LAUREN: It's not that I have something to hide because I am ashamed of anything. It is just that I don't want my people forming opinions about me because of where I live and how I grew up. I always keep that information to myself.

GRACE: Your personal life is as private as you want it to be. **I keep my personal life pretty private at work,** and I never get into deep conversations about anything. I agree. I, too, don't want people forming opinions about me because of what I like to do or how I do something.

CHANDRA: So you don't tell anyone anything?

GRACE: I do, but I select what I want to tell and who I want to tell it to. Like, I don't want my boss to think less of me because

---

For Office Use Only

Employee

Going To Your Boss's Home

There are times that your employer may invite you over to his or her house. It could be for dinner, a holiday party, a meeting, or because you share the same interests. This is a good sign for you, because it generally means that your employer trusts you and thinks enough of you to enter his or her personal space.

Employers are generally fickle about inviting employees into the nexus of their life. Those employers who have more elaborate and expensive homes and lifestyles run the risk of making you unnecessarily envious of what they have or how they live. You know how hard you work, and you see how hard your employer works, and you may think that you should have the same lifestyle as he or she does. You might feel cheated after seeing what your employer has, since you are making him or her the money, and you may resent it. What seemed like teamwork at work for the company may now just be perceived as exercises to line the pockets of your employer with money. You may start to feel competitive.

If you feel any of these emotions surface when visiting your employer's home, don't let them become obvious. Your employer is welcoming you to his or her home because you are trusted and liked.

---

of something that I like to do that he may look down on.
CHANDRA: Like what?
LENNY: Yeah, like what? I gotta hear this!
GLEN: [clearing his throat, looking at Grace] Yes, like what, exactly?
GRACE: Like different stuff, that's all.
LAUREN: Even I want to hear what it is.
VINNY: Leave the girl alone. She don't need to tell you anything. [shifting his head to Grace and asking softly] Go ahead, tell me, and I'll tell you if I think it's crazy.
GRACE: Oh, my God, you guys! [laughing]
LENNY: You are blushing. I know you got somethin' good to tell. You secretly kill cats or somethin' like that. My old neighbor did that.
LAUREN: You watch Dance Fever reruns to learn the choreography.
CHANDRA: You dress up like a guy, I bet.
GRACE: No! I don't believe this! [smiling]
GLEN: That's enough, spill the beans!
GRACE: OK, OK. I am just going to say it. I have two personal email addresses. One is

---

Erik A. Kaiser

Employer

Divulging Too Much Personal Information To Your Employees

Never forget the continental divide that exists between your work life and your personal life. When you start to become friendly with your employees, you tend to talk about your personal life more. You do this because you want to build a better connection with them or just because you become friendly and don't want to appear as a business stiff.

Be careful about what you divulge. You always need to maintain your image as a boss, and you do not want to taint that image with tales of unsavory experiences and exuberance that will negatively alter the employee's perception of you. What you might believe to be personal information that will inspire an employee may have the opposite result.

Furthermore, your personal life is something that employees can use against you, especially when it comes to money. They may hear about the material fruits of your labor and become jealous. Try not to introduce extravagant lifestyles to your employees unless it is part of the branding of your company.

---

for normal use, and the other is strippergirl.
VINNY: You're a *stripper*?
GRACE: *No!* I like going to girl stripper clubs with my friends. And I go with my guy friends.
LAUREN: You? You go to places like Scores?
GRACE: Yes. Yes, I do. And I like to watch the football games. The place is called Paradise Luverz.
LENNY: You sound like my kinda girl!
GRACE: We have the best time! We go once or twice a year.
VINNY: That's it?
GRACE: Yes. So I don't want my boss to know that, so you all better keep this confidential like we are supposed to. **Could you imagine if he ever saw that email address?**
VINNY: Sounds like he might ask you out.
GRACE: It is so unprofessional, but I use it for fun sometimes.
GLEN: I completely understand your trepidation about revealing your alter ego email address. You might want to keep that

---

152   **For Office Use Only**

Divulging Too Much Personal Information To Your Employer

Don't let your personal life become a topic of conversation unless it is something positive. Employers are concerned about their businesses and any external factor that could affect them. Since employees are the representatives of every company, the personal and professional lives of the employees are important to the boss.

Everyone has a crazy story, and there is likely some shady collateral to accompany it. With social networking websites, your life can be on display in a matter of seconds, and it doesn't have to be you to be the poster. Don't give your boss a reason to monitor you by talking about unsavory details of your private life. Keep your deep, dark secrets in your possession.

Other employees will want to hear your entertaining stories to catalogue for use against you in the future should there be a competitive reason to do so. This should not be a surprise to you, either. If you can be promoted over your competition, you might also use sordid details about your opponent to your advantage. So, if you don't want your boss hearing a story, don't tell it to anyone at work. The person whom you tell in confidence may be the enemy.

"In our leisure, we reveal what kind of people we are."
Ovid

to yourself.

GRACE: I know. It is only for fun. What is yours, Lenny?

LENNY: Mine is scratchnsniff.

CHANDRA: That's gross.

LENNY: That's my dog's name. That's all he did when he was a puppy. He scratched and sniffed everything.

GLEN: That's funny, because you can sometimes tell a lot about someone by their email address or social handles. It is sometimes a shortcut to having to get to know them personally.

LENNY: I thought bosses don't want to get to know workers personally.

GLEN: That's not true at all. Sometimes you have to, and other times, it happens all by itself. Especially when the person is in an important position for the company.

Erik A. Kaiser

Employer

Personal Handles Reveal A Lot About An Employee

Whether you are doing due diligence on a potential hire or you want to find out more about your existing employees, reviewing someone's personal email address and online presence handle is one way to gain some insight.

A personal email address is exactly what it says: personal. Anything personal can be very revealing, the good or bad. It can give you insight into how a person presents oneself outside of work. Social media handles are usually more revealing.

Because there are so fewer unique email addresses and social handles, people have to come up with unusual names or combinations of letters to establish a unique name. Sometimes one's creativity level can be challenged, and the result doesn't match the image someone is trying to promote.

It is a matter that should be important to your company. At times, an employee may use his or her personal email address or communicate through social channels for business purposes. You must prevent a client, customer, or colleague from being offended by your employee's potentially unprofessional choices.

You need to know them personally to see if they are indeed fit for the job they are performing.

LAUREN: You mean, getting to know them is an insurance policy.

GLEN: Exactly. Before I make the decision on someone important for the company, I always want to meet their spouse or significant other. Getting to see what their counterpart is like is more important than a job interview to me. I see how they interact, the choice the person made on a partner, how they respect each other.

CHANDRA: Why do you have to judge them outside of their work?

GLEN: Because people bring their personal lives to work. We try to keep the importation of social issues at a minimum, and I want to see as much as possible about the person to make sure we are making or have made the right decision.

CHANDRA: I still don't get it. When you say "social issues," what do you mean?

GLEN: It means that if they are going through a divorce, having marital problems, are in an abusive relationship, et cetera.

Employee

Don't Let Your Personal Handle Address Make You Look Bad

Regardless of whether you are applying for a new job, don't let your personal email address or social media handles become a topic of unnecessary discussion. It is understandable that many email and social addresses with your name have already been taken, but don't have one that could be a problem for you. There may be times when you need to use your personal accounts for business purposes.

It is not uncommon for corporate email services to be disrupted or not be able to receive a large file because of inbound size restrictions. In such cases, we often just tell the other person to correspond with us through our personal email address because it is the most efficient means to trade information.

If you will be using your personal email or social address for work purposes, make sure you are using an appropriate personal email name that will not be offensive or overly revealing. You do not want to correspond using your inappropriate email or social address on behalf of your company. It will expose you to potential reprimand. Be smart and be professional.

"The way to gain a good reputation is to endeavor to be what you desire to appear."
Socrates

Anything that's distracting from doing a job.

CHANDRA: That seems unfair, but I understand business is business.

GLEN: You have to be careful. We like to understand what we can. You need to take your time finding the right fit. Let me give you an example. My first major hire was after I took a senior management position when I was about 32 years old. I was promoted and became responsible for hiring someone with a lot of experience managing managers in one of the divisions. So I interviewed all of these people, and I made a short list of three candidates, all of whom were women around 40 years old. I had to be smart about this person because it was a representation of my decision-making ability, and I chose one.

Erik A. Kaiser

Employer

What To Consider Before Befriending Employees

Work environments foster new friendships between employers and employees all the time. It is great to build relationships with employees and become friends with them. Time spent will transition out of the office and into each others, personal lives. When building a relationship with an employee, remember that he or she may not consider the relationship in the same way as you do. Remember, your employee still relies on you for income and job security.

There is an inherent conflict when these relationships develop, so take into consideration the worst situations: the employee's performance decreases, and you have to let the person go, or the friendship is used against you at some point.

When you treat an employee like a true friend, you will tend to divulge personal and corporate information that is none of his or her business. You will end up talking to that person in confidence about a lot of different things, like other employees, business dealings, and personal activities.

Even though you may feel that your employee has become a friend, he or she ultimately can cause you tremendous grief by using confidential information use against you to influence compensation increases without merit or to influence other employees against you.

"This wine is too good for toast-drinking, my dear. You don't want to mix emotions up with a wine like that. You lose the taste."
Ernest Hemingway

VINNY: I know where this is going. Name?

GLEN: Tara. Hear me out. So I thought I would get into her personal life and really see what she was like. I invited her out with her boyfriend, and we had a great time. She was excellent and what seemed like a great fit. Her boyfriend was great and in the same industry, having met at work. All seemed good. I hired her.

VINNY: You got your bones jumped.

GLEN: No. So then about six months later, she tells me that her boyfriend is applying for the open position in our operations department. I didn't have control of that department, and it didn't matter to me at the time. The department hired him, and I

---

156   For Office Use Only

Employee

What To Consider Before Befriending Your Boss

A lot of times, you will like your boss a lot, and your friendship will grow out of the office. He or she will spend time with you in personal settings and engage in activities in which you both have an interest. By allowing this, you will both be exposing yourselves to each other beyond a normal employer/employee relationship.

Remember that you are still an employee and that you will still be judged by everything that you do outside of the office. Your boss may intentionally strike up more of a friendship with you to determine whether you are the proper person for the job. You are a representative of the company in which your boss has a different interest, and he or she will be looking for anything you do which has the ability to compromise the interest or objectives of the business.

Being a friend to your boss means that you will talk more freely and openly about yourself and your ideals. If you reveal in confidence that what you really want to do in life is something else and you are just waiting for the right opportunity, don't be surprised if you find yourself replaced. Also consider how you will handle the conversation when you are asked personal questions at point-blank range. Will you tell the truth, or will you lie to protect yourself? Do you want to be caught in a lie? Consider all of the angles.

---

never thought it would be a problem.

VINNY: Until she jumped your bones.

GLEN: No. Tara was more senior than he was by a long shot. She kept growing, and eventually they broke up. Before that, you wouldn't even know they were together. They were discreet and rarely were seen together at work. They would occasionally take lunches together, but work was busy most of the time.

LAUREN: So what was the problem? Did he end up working in her department?

GLEN: No. But this is the part Vinny has been waiting for. She started seeing another employee, and that's when I realized two things.

VINNY: Yeah, you took too long getting to her, and she went for someone else.

GLEN: No. I realized that she met her last boyfriend at work, and it was a pattern. She claimed that the only place to meet anyone good was at work because she was always working. I missed that and learned about that profile because of her.

VINNY: What was the second thing?

GLEN: That you can't have employees

Erik A. Kaiser

Employer

How To Handle Relationships Between Employees

Companies must consider that employees may start dating one another and develop romantic relationships. You will need a plan and preparation. Romantic employees have a greater potential to put your organization at risk by aligning with one another instead of independently with the interests of the company.

When two employees unite, the chance of decreased productivity will rise in the workplace because the couple will spend company time together for personal interests and pretend that time is company-related. Additionally, when the couple encounters normal relationship troubles, the anticipation of the employee couple seeing one another every day is an added stress on the organization. They each may not even want to come to work to avoid the other, and they will feel uncomfortable having one another around if and when the relationship turns sour.

Drama is a certainty, and to combat it, have a clear policy on dating in the workplace. Make a policy that all interoffice relationships must be brought to the attention of a direct supervisor and the most senior decision-maker.

It is common for seasoned companies to have a policy in place that forces termination of one side of the relationship. This is highly effective to control the focus on work and decrease the chance of costly sexual harassment lawsuits.

"While man's desires and aspirations stir, he cannot choose but err."
Johann Wolfgang Von Goethe

dating at work. After I learned my lesson, we made a no-dating policy between employees. I asked other friends of mine in top positions about this problem, and they all had a no-dating policy.
CHANDRA: That seems kind of harsh. What happens if they really like each other?
GLEN: That's great for them. And the company is only willing to keep one of them. There is way too much drama at the workplace as a result. The two will see each other too much at work, get distracted during the day, and then when it doesn't work, the discomfort of trying to avoid each other is unbearable. Then their friends at work take sides and have to hear the chatter of the relationship.
LENNY: I dated this chick at work for like

Employee

Be Discreet About Dating A Coworker

If you are planning on dating or have been dating someone at work, you need to take into consideration the risks involved. The personal and corporate risks that develop from that first after-hours kiss by the photocopier can be powerful enough to make you quit or be terminated.

Many large companies have policies against dating coworkers for a reason: it is highly disruptive to the operation. Consider what happens when your relationship does not work out and you are forced to see your ex every day, during work, when you would rather not see the other ever again. The discomfort is unavoidable, and it detectable by your boss. Your productivity decreases, and there is unnecessary tension.

Coworkers will also be more critical of you because they will feel that you are colluding with your lover regarding work. There is also unnecessary gossip in the office, and coworkers will use your interoffice relationship against.

If you are going to engage in an interoffice relationship, you must absolutely keep it 100% confidential, without alerting anyone at work. Otherwise, when your relationship is discovered, you will have to face potential ultimatums from your boss. Protect yourself from being fired by signing a pact with your new office lover about which one of you will leave the job if one of you is forced to resign.

---

two months, and we had sex all the time at work. She was married, so we could never go back to her place, and I was livin' at my mom's, so we could only hang at work.

VINNY: So what happened to her?

LENNY: I don't know. I got fired, and I never saw her again. After I left, I tried to get with her, but she stopped callin'.

GLEN: You probably got fired because they wanted to keep her and you were the expendable one.

LENNY: She was the boss's daughter, but he never knew about it.

VINNY: Yeah, right, he never knew. He found out what was goin' on, and you got the boot.

LENNY: Whatever. I don't think so. No one ever saw us.

VINNY: Why do you think she never called you back after you were canned? Her daddy told her to stay away from you.

GLEN: He's probably right, Lenny. Don't take it as bad. It was just circumstance. Sometimes sleeping with the boss's son or daughter is as complex as sleeping with the boss. But, the results are always the same.

Erik A. Kaiser

Employer

Are Your Employees Having Sex In The Office?

Companies are breeding grounds for romantic interoffice relationships. It is natural. You can put all of the controls that you want in place, and they will still find their way to each other. Controls like immediate termination upon discovery of the relationship still do not stop them from getting together. They will date secretly and even engage in clandestine workplace sexual activity.

It is a standard practice for a company of any size to have a dating policy, but it is not a regular practice to directly address actual sexual acts in the workplace. Employee manuals rarely have a policy against a make-out session in the elevator. Court cases have been won by employees who have been wrongfully terminated after being caught for sex in the office on the grounds that the manual did not address it.

Have your employee manual distinguish between dating and sexual contact. Too many manuals do not directly address sexual contact, or sex itself, as a prohibited act anywhere on or in company property. The occasional hook-up between employees can be just as destructive to your company as dating.

GRACE: That's not always true. I know of a love story that started with an employer and employee. They are friends of mine. He owns a public relations company and hired a girl he fell in love with and ended up marrying and having two children.

GLEN: That's a small percentage. Most of them turn into a disaster, and it ends by the lower person on the totem pole getting fired. If the owner is sleeping with an employee, when the personal relationship is over, so is the working relationship. It is the same with managers.

GRACE: Is that what happened to that woman, Tara, you hired?

GLEN: Yes, it is. When she started dating a different employee beneath her in her group named Jerry, we ended up instituting the new policies months later. We sat her down and explained the new procedures, and we told her that there was only room for either her or her new boyfriend.

LAUREN: I know who ended up staying.

GLEN: You got it, but it didn't happen right away. She ended up having to suffer through a month of discomfort, and it turned into a problem because he was also

---

160 For Office Use Only

Are You Having Sex In The Office?

You should know the dating and sexual conduct policy of your company before engaging in sexual acts with a coworker. You will be surprised to find that dating may be prohibited but sexual acts are not addressed.

Most companies will have a dating policy that will cause your termination if you are found to have a romantic relationship with a coworker. Since employee manuals are often copies of other companies' manuals or generic documents, the people who made you sign them may not know exactly what they say. Get reacquainted with them to determine if you are in violation. If you are not, feel free to do what you want. If you are, then you need to take into consideration the potential legal problems that can occur as a result of your flings.

The reason why your company has a policy on regulating your romantic interests at work is because it is a nightmare for your company in terms of productivity and legal exposure. Your hot and heavy lust with Jim from the accounting department or with Lana in sales is a distraction for you both. However, there have been court cases that employees have won after being terminated for sexual contact at the workplace. The employee manual discussed dating but not sexual contact directly.

Also, be careful of video recording devices and time-lapse monitoring cameras. Discretion is obviously advised.

"Do not bite at the bait of pleasure, till you know there is no hook beneath it."
Thomas Jefferson

tops at what he was doing. We couldn't really fire Jerry reasonably, and we didn't want to. We talked internally about having him transferred, but it didn't look like that was going to happen. We needed the guy, and his work was excellent. There was nothing wrong with him except that the new policy prevented interoffice relationships.

GRACE: Boy, that must have been super awkward. I wouldn't want to see my ex-boyfriend at work. Once I dated someone and I was done, I was *done*. You know, you want to move on.

GLEN: Well, that's what happened, in a way. Jerry felt like the scorned lover, being younger. She clearly understood that her job was at risk for any relationships at the

Erik A. Kaiser

Employer

Sleeping With An Employee

It is natural to develop a close bond with someone whom you employ. Sometimes, those bonds go beyond the professional level. Here is what to know in advance.

There are only two potential outcomes: marriage or mess. Once you become intimate with an employee, the relationship changes in ways you never thought possible. You change as well. You no longer are objective, but instead react with emotion to the conduct and performance of your lover/employee.

Changing the balance has deeper issues. Your lover may be using you to get ahead but simultaneously also be concerned for his or her job. People do use sex to get ahead at work. Once other employees know of your relationship, they will feel cheated and claim preferential treatment. This lowers morale and creates unnecessary conflict.

Conversely, sometimes bonds are formed at work that last a lifetime. Keep your relationship 100% discreet, until such time that you determine the permanency to make it known to other people at the company.

Know that the risk you take is enormous. You are opening up your company to a sexual harassment claim. Fortunately, you can always terminate the person for work-related reasons, which is a classic fallback position when you are no longer interested. However, retailiation probabilities are increased.

"If passion drives you, let reason hold the reins."
Benjamin Franklin

office, and she was in no way going to jeopardize it again. He, on the other hand, was confused and made advances to her even after the "break up." He would wait for her in the parking lot and they would talk, and then he would argue with her about the policy. Then he made sexual advances to her which, while in a relationship, would be normal. But because they were no longer dating, it was considered sexual harassment.

LAUREN: Oh, what a mess.

GLEN: Total mess. He was really enraged and texted her all sorts of inappropriate commentary about the company and about the newly-instituted policy. He would send her texts, dm's and continue to be non-compliant until it was a true sexual harassment suit. And, of course, he continued to profess his lust for her in a variety of ways to keep her attention.

For Office Use Only

Sleeping With Your Boss

Understand this: your boss employs you, and if you do not care about keeping your job, you will have an easier time with the guaranteed stress that will occur from sleeping with him or her. There are two ways this can go: marriage or unemployment.

To your boss, you could be another disposable link in the chain because you are easy. You, of course, could be sleeping up the corporate ladder because there is something for you to gain. Then again, you could just be attracted to your boss and are having a fling.

Traditionally, these relationships don't work. However, it is not impossible for it to develop into something; it is just rarer. If your boss is married, you are opening up a potential can of worms that can return to haunt you for a very long time.

When you start sleeping with your boss, you need to understand that you are still working for a business and still have responsibility. If your performance drops or the company changes, don't be surprised that you cannot separate business and pleasure. You will take all criticism personally and respond emotionally. Furthermore, if the relationship doesn't work out, you are going to be seeing each other every day, and that will become uncomfortable enough for you to leave or get fired. That's just the way it goes.

VINNY: Fire the clown.
GRACE: Yes, I have to agree with Vinny.
VINNY: There's a first for everything, Grace.
GRACE: Jerry sounds abusive.
GLEN: He was, and it was documented. It was really a shame. We ended up having to let him go, but everything was documented when he began to waste valuable time. We were concerned that if he didn't control himself properly, that there was going to be a lawsuit, and we didn't want anything to do with that. Plus, I hired Tara, and I had to take responsibility for her acts. She remained compliant, and that was what I needed to support keeping her. She was really great, and he was, too. This was another eye-opener for all of us in management. We never had this problem before, and now when we saw the mixture of personal and work lives, we were sure we made the right decision.
GRACE: What happened to the guy?
GLEN: He was somewhat belligerent because he was a top performer in the department. He didn't think that he would be the one to lose a job because he saw his value to the company in dollars as more

Employer

Handling Employee Sexual Harassment Claims

If one employee submits a sexual harassment complaint against another, you have a responsibility to take action. You should be reprimanding the harasser in some manner with a warning or a termination.

If your employee submits a claim through an attorney by way of a letter or a lawsuit, regardless of whom the claim is against at the company, the company bears liability. There isn't an attorney who would absolve the company of having liability. Notify your insurance carrier immediately. There are certain policies that already cover sexual harassment suits and other policies that separately cover them. Be sure that you have a policy coverage.

It is important to maintain a high level of confidentiality to protect the parties involved. You don't want conversation to compromise the employess and have others making judgments about those affected.

Sexual harassment suits, even when not easily proven or valid, can end up sinking managers. Get to know the laws of your region to ensure that you can protect your company properly. Make sure you implement a handbook of employee guidelines that specifically addresses harassment and sexual contact.

"Leave it to a girl to take the fun out of sex discrimination."
Bill Watterson, Calvin in "Calvin and Hobbes"

than hers. It was so difficult having to tell him the general reason for his termination. He was infuriated and embarrassed at the same time, and that was the end of it. He just moved on, and we gave him a good work recommendation so he didn't think we had anything but good intentions for him. We were concerned about a Department of Labor hearing because he could have contested his termination. Fortunately, everything remained quiet.

GRACE: That's too bad for everyone to lose a top employee.

GLEN: That's the twist! We hired a woman replacement, Rebecca, for the position, and she blew the doors off of Jerry's performance. I was amazed at this twist of fate because I had my own fears about getting an equivalent replacement.

LAUREN: That is just pure luck. Maybe it was meant to be that way.

For Office Use Only

Sexual Harassment By A Coworker

Sexual harassment laws are so general that if a female worker does something harassing to a male coworker that does not have a sexual component, a sexual harassment claim can be made simply because of gender differences. Typically, sexual harassment claims refer to sexual touching, jokes, demands, and language used against someone of the opposite sex at work.

Obvious cases of sexual harassment are when a superior demands sex of some sort from a subordinate in order to keep a job or to be promoted. There is always a case any time there is an employment threat used to coerce sex.

Take note that if you begin a romantic relationship with a coworker and he or she ends it, all of those post-relationship grabs, conversations with him or her regarding anything sexual, and any other conversations that include anything sexual, provocative, or uncomfortable is sexual harassment material. You will be in a more sensitive arena for a claim being made against you.

If you encounter uncomfortable sexual harassment behavior, file a claim with your boss. If your boss is the harasser, go to his or her superior or HR. If there isn't anyone higher than your boss, you can consider seeking legal advice from a sexual harassment attorney.

GLEN: I thought the same at the time, but after that incident, I became more comfortable with people leaving the company. You can get comfortable with people, and you can find yourself lowering your expectation of what can be achieved.

LAUREN: But you don't want your top performers leaving your company? I don't.

GLEN: Different people bring different opportunities that you may not have known about before. We didn't think that we could get much better than Jerry, and look at what happened. You would be surprised that it can happen.

LAUREN: So what was the reason why Jerry was never reaching the potential of the position, and why was he exceeding your expectation? Was the bar set too low?

GLEN: It was a combination of things. When we saw Rebecca's performance, we were stunned. And you are right; we did have the bar set too low. The company took advice and direction from Jerry's direct manager in that department. I was relatively new to my position, and once I saw such a huge performance difference, I knew there had to be a better reason why.

VINNY: Let me guess. Jerry was bangin'

You Can Always Hire Better

Don't feel trapped by your employees. No matter how great you think someone is at performing the job or how bad you need the person, there is always someone better. Always remember this when you feel like you are being held hostage by one of your employees or when you know you need to replace one. Yes, there is work involved in finding a replacement and it may take time, but there is almost always someone out there who is more willing and eager to take the position.

Employees come and go, and you are already forced to find replacements. If you have had enough turnover, you should already know that hiring and firing is a job in itself until you find the right person. Usually, you get a better person. Remember, practice in this department makes perfect.

To your surprise, you will find that new people possess new talents that surpass those of the previous person in the position. Don't be afraid to change it up. New people enter the market every day. You should always be interviewing for better talent.

---

his manager before he went for the cougar option of Rebecca.

GLEN: No, but not too far off, if you were to look at the relationships. Jerry's direct manager is named Andrew. It turned out that Andrew was an excellent manager and he was promoted to manage the group. Jerry and Andrew worked side by side for a couple of years and became friends in the process. Then, Andrew is Jerry's boss all of a sudden, and even though Andrew is an excellent manager, he wasn't as tough on Jerry as he should have been. Jerry probably called some of the shots, and Andrew recommended to the management team overseeing him what he thought Jerry's performance should look like.

GRACE: Were they in cahoots?

GLEN: No. I think it was a standard case of having to manage a friend, and the normal breakdowns surfaced after time.

CHANDRA: It was probably a relief for Andrew at some point to have a replacement for Jerry because he didn't have a conscience about setting higher goals.

GLEN: That's right. Anytime one friend has

Employee

You Are Replaceable

When your work performance is excellent and you continue to have good success, sometimes you might become intoxicated with confidence. This may lead you to believe that without you, the company would be seriously impaired or never able to function the same way. There are very unique cases and times when that is true. But, for the most part, it is not. There is always someone out there who can outperform you. If you test this, you will learn your lesson quickly.

Being replaced is especially threatening in lower-paying jobs that do not require a lot of training. Remember that every day, someone new enters the job market and becomes your competition. Do your job and do it well, because even if you are a superstar, your employer is always on the lookout for additional talent. Business changes, and in the future, you may not be the superstar. Someone from a younger generation may have more energy and smarts than you do.

It may not be easy to replace you immediately, but it is certain that you can be replaced. Experienced employers have had a track record in replacing employees either by need or by circumstance. Your value may not be as high as you think.

"Avoid having your ego so close to your position that when your position falls, your ego goes with it."
Colin Powell

to manage another, there is going to be an awkward situation.
LAUREN: I tried hiring one of my closest friends, and we don't even talk anymore because of it.
GRACE: Why? That's terrible.
LAUREN: I figured that if I could hire someone I trust, I could really get the help I needed to manage the company. So I hired one of my college friends, and we were really excited in the beginning. Then I started to have to tell her what to do, and she had her own idea about what should be done. And then it turned into a struggle. She started to become an authority on how the business should be operating, and she had as little experience as me. And she had

Employer

Are You More Of A Friend Than A Boss?

If you are having trouble with managing your employees because you are more of a friend than a boss, you are not a good manager. When you have emotional conflicts about how to treat your friends at work, you don't have controlled employees. What you have are friends who can make decisions about your company without risking the consequences of a bad decision. Your company and you are taking the risk.

If you cannot manage your friends, you need to place someone in between your friends and you to manage. If you don't put someone in the middle as a manager, then you have to come to terms with the fact that your business is not being run efficiently. If your problems stem from the actions of your friends, you are directly responsible for every result, good or bad.

Getting someone in between your friends and you may not be the most comfortable change, but it is a necessary one. The productivity level of your company will increase, and so should your bottom line. You may also find that there are better replacements for your friends that you didn't see.

---

nothing to lose. She wanted to do all of this crazy marketing and make different foods that were exactly the opposite from what I envisioned.

LENNY: Didn't you guys talk about this stuff before you hired her?

LAUREN: Not exactly. I told her I needed help and she offered, and we talked more about having fun doing it. Once it actually started, it got a little weird. And then we would get into fights and she wouldn't come in one day, and I would have to call her and we would make up. It just went around and around until I realized that I couldn't work with friends.

LENNY: I like cat fights. Chicks pullin' hair is the best.

LAUREN: It might as well have been a hair-pulling contest, because that's what it was like. I finally told her that I had to let her go, and she was so offended that she told me off. She called me every name in the book and was holding me responsible for her not taking advantage of other jobs because she was there to help me.

GLEN: Was it true?

LAUREN: I don't know, and I don't think

---

168   **For Office Use Only**

Employee

Do You See Your Boss As More Of A Friend?

Becoming friends with your coworkers is a standard expectation. You may be equal and enjoy the same or similar status at your company. But sometimes through a promotion, your work friend ends up becoming your boss. Or, you may not take your boss too seriously and may instead consider him or her more on your level. If you find that friendship is actually the defining relationship between your boss and you, it is certain that you are not being managed properly.

If you do not take your boss seriously because he or she is too friendly, neither of you is performing well at your job. It means that your boss is soft and most likely afraid of conflict. With a soft boss, your coworkers and you likely call more of the shots because your boss maintains a friendly alignment to you in order to avoid his or her inability to manage.

The downside to you is that you are not being managed to your potential. You may independently realize that you will want more out of the job. If the condition exists, ask to be managed by someone less emotionally connected and more objective.

"Business, you know, may bring you money, but friendship hardly ever does."
Jane Austen

so. I think she thought that I was going to make the business hers and mine after she started working. She assumed a role of being an owner or a partner without us ever having talked about it. The whole thing just got weird, and we haven't spoken since. I look back and realize that we were both young and inexperienced.

LENNY: Why didn't you hire your brother or sister or someone like that?

LAUREN: I am an only child, so the only other person I would go to would be my dad. There's no way I would do that.

GLEN: Why not?

LAUREN: Because that is a cop-out. I had to prove to my family that I could run the business. No one took me seriously in the beginning until I had a bunch of people working for me and because they knew my dad gave me the money to start up. I didn't

---

Erik A. Kaiser

Employer

Hiring A Friend

There are two schools of thought on the topic of hiring a friend. Some say never hire a friend, and others think that hiring a friend is perfectly acceptable. Before you extend an offer, there are a few thoughts to consider.

Friendships outside of work are very personal. Friends have comfortable understandings of one another, and when business interests converge, sometimes it seems like an alliance is a great opportunity. But unless you have hired a friend and gone through the cycle, you could be in for some very unpleasant surprises.

If you are going to hire a friend, be prepared to lose that friend. Once the transition is made to a working relationship, you will each depend on one another in ways that are foreign to a normal friendship. Those dependencies will quickly cause you to become critical of each other, which typically forces you to cast your friend in a new light. Even if you make a pact to remain friends despite your working relationship, you will find that it will still change your opinion of one another, no matter what you say.

---

want their help.

VINNY: Forget family. I've hired all of them, and they are a freakin' disaster. They all think they deserve more or have some sorta special rights because they are related to me.

LAUREN: Did you *"fire 'em all"*?

VINNY: Now you are talking my game. Fired every single last one of 'em. Gone. Out the door.

GRACE: Isn't that uncomfortable when you have to see them? How do you handle the holidays?

VINNY: Hey, I'm not the one who didn't work right. They screwed up, not me. So I don't care what they say or think. I just go on like normal because that's what it was. Normal. I hire, I fire.

GRACE: Why did you have to fire them? What did they do wrong?

VINNY: They just sucked. You can't treat them any different from regular workers just *because* they are family. You know, you gotta treat them harder because they are family, you know what I mean? It shows the rest of the workers that everybody is equal, no matter what.

For Office Use Only

Getting Hired By A Friend

If your friend hires you as an employee, you should be aware that the degree of excitement with which you start a working relationship is the polar opposite of the struggles you'll face at the demise of the relationship. What starts out as an adventure between friends can turn out to be a job loss magnified by a friendship loss.

Before you start working for a friend, you need to understand that your friend is hiring you because he or she wants and expects you to be effective at the job. Because the role of an equal friendship transitions you into being a subordinate, you will have to treat your friend as a superior. If you are not able to conduct yourself in such a manner, you will find your work relationship strained from the start. A strained work relationship guarantees a strained friendship.

Because you are a subordinate, you may not see eye-to-eye on work-related issues. Your way of operating may be different, and you will be subject to the demands of your friend as an employee. Since you are relying on your friend for a paycheck, you will find yourself treating him or her like an employer which will categorically redefine your friendship.

If you can live with the thought of losing your friend, you are better prepared to be in a subordinate position. If not, you will have to weigh the pros and cons as they relate to you socially.

"A friend in power is a friend lost."
Henry Brooks Adams

GRACE: But what did they do wrong? I don't get it.

VINNY: Let's see. My cousin Joey drove a vending van and hit a Escalade. Not too bad, but he got a piece of glass in his eye, and he blamed me for not picking up the hospital tab. He was a nice kid, but he expected too much. He was screaming at me because he didn't have the money for the hospital, and somehow, it was my fault. Hey, I gave you a job. You drove into a car. What do you want from me? So I got rid of him. And I gotta deal with Worker's Comp.

LAUREN: That's borderline cruel. He was your cousin!

VINNY: Like that means something. They all want something from you and use that same crappy "family" line. They are all the same. The truth comes out in situations like that.

GLEN: That part is true about the truth

Erik A. Kaiser

Employer

Hiring A Family Member

Hiring a family member has many pluses and minuses. The real trick is to vigorously manage the downside of having to fire the person and still sit across the table from him or her at family functions.

Usually, if you are comfortable enough to hire a family member, you are already thinking about being able to trust the person more than others. There are many businesses that require trust because the operations may deal with a lot of cash or have other sensitivities. Hiring a family member can mean relief.

Sometimes you may hire a family member to give him or her a chance at a job. Nepotism is normal practice in the workplace, and it happens on every level. Families look out for one another.

Give much thought to the possible demise of the working relationship and the ramifications at the family level. You will see this person at every family function for the rest of your life, and you already have some sort of relationship that brought you together. If the opportunity does not work out, you need to have already managed the downside. When having the initial conversation about hiring, have the conversation about firing and what it will mean. Be 100% transparent and professional with the family member about the downside, and you will determine how best to manage the relationship.

"If a man's character is to be abused, there's nobody like a relative to do the business."
Alexander Pope

coming out. I became very close to one of my employees as a friend. She was great and handled stress really well and knew how to navigate change. The company made a decision to close her division on a Tuesday, and we didn't have a place for her in the company on Wednesday. I took the responsibility of telling her. She went from day to night, and instead of understanding, she lost it. She blamed me, told me she didn't trust me, demanded money she thought was due to her. It was ugly. I tried to help her out after that, and she turned a cold shoulder to the company and me. She ended up doing more harm to herself.

CHANDRA: Why did you close that division, and what makes you think she would do anything different?

For Office Use Only

Employee

Getting Hired By A Family Member

If you are contemplating working for a family member or are already doing so, there are some key elements to the relationship of which you need to be aware.

Working for a family member means potential unnecessary stress both professionally and personally for the family member hiring you. You may be qualified for the position, but so is someone else out there. This means that if your employment does not work out, your family member will terminate you. This will create new familial stress between the two of you, regardless of the realities.

Additionally, a family member hiring you must consider the risks of hiring from family instead of from the outside. There are political consequences of being nepotistic, and often, there is a burden your family member must carry because he or she can be perceived as favoring you.

Getting hired essentially means that you are a representation of that family member, and when you don't look good, your family member looks worse. Most of the time, he or she is taking a bigger risk hiring you than someone else. So understand that more often than not, it is easier for him or her to have hired from the outside. But when a great relationship works out, the power of two can sometimes be the power of three or more.

GLEN: The division was losing money, and she was not performing. She lost interest. It was losing money quickly, without any quick future for a recovery. It was a smart decision and had to be done. It was bleeding money, and the market had changed. And she was a true friend. We spent a lot of time together at work and outside of work. We had a great understanding of each other, or so I thought. You don't know people until times get tough.

LAUREN: It also depends when you fire the person. I would have done it on a Friday. I only terminate on a Friday because I want to start Monday as a fresh start.

CHANDRA: That's the worst. Then you have to sit there all weekend and panic. **You can't go looking for a job on a Saturday.** Why do you people always do that? Don't you ever think about what happens?

"You cannot find peace by avoiding life."
Virginia Woolf

Erik A. Kaiser

Employer

You Don't Know Your Employees Until Disaster Strikes

You will never really know what your employees are capable of doing until they are forced to deal with unexpected events that threaten your company or their employment. You may have a great working relationship with your employees and consider them to be as loyal as the day is long, but when there is a serious blip on the radar and they are affected, prepare for the unexpected.

Like with all people in life, when threatening conditions arise, people have the propensity to act in unexpected ways. Your assumption of how employees handle disastrous situations is only limited to your actual experience with them. Some of the people whom you consider most loyal may be the ones to drop their well-tailored act and expose themselves as disloyal, leaving you questioning your own ability to judge character. In other cases, the people in whom you had the least bit of faith will surprise you by aligning themselves with you to assist in overcoming unfortunate events.

If you feel compelled to test the resolve of your employees, you can easily create an environment to get some insight. Create a shock to their system that will help reveal the real person. If they are aligned already, the tactic will be understood and forgiven.

"Reveal not every secret you have to a friend, for how can you tell but that friend may hereafter become an enemy?"
Saadi

LENNY: Yeah. Well, I been fired on every day of the week, and I will tell you getting fired early is better than later. I can get fired on a Monday and find another job by the end of the week.

LAUREN: Why do you people always quit the day of payroll or on a Friday? It's a two-way street. We have to scramble to find a person over the weekend because you are starting a new job on the next Monday.

CHANDRA: I give my two weeks' notice. If you don't want me around, that's not my problem. Just pay me what you owe me, and I'm gone.

LAUREN: No one gives me two weeks' notice. Plus, if you are leaving, I don't want you around for two more weeks, especially if I am showing new people around to fill

Employee

You Don't Know Your Employer Until Disaster Strikes

Don't be fooled by any of the generous claims of your company. They may color themselves in a light that gives you a false sense of security by claiming to be of a certain character. You might be working at a company that has been fair with you through the up times, but if you have not experienced the down times - the worst-case scenarios - then you cannot be sure about the reaction of your company.

With hope, you will never have to be faced with a disaster that affects your company. But, there is always a chance this will happen, and if it does happen, you may be unpleasantly surprised about how you are handled. What you thought was a great relationship between your company and you may leave you wondering how you got wrapped up with it in the first place.

Since you can't easily test your company to see what will happen if one day the company is forced to fire 90% of the staff or is raided by the FBI, you can always try to safeguard yourself from the aftereffects. Even though you want to make good assumptions about your future and your relationship with your company, you should instead make sure that all promises they make are on paper, along with any other agreements that you have with them. Once the world falls apart, you may be kicked to the side, and any verbal agreements on which you relied will be gone. Get your boss to sign these documents personally. You will be better protected.

your position. The last thing I want is the person who is leaving hanging around talking to the others.

VINNY: There is no such thing as two weeks' notice. You tell me you are leaving, that's the day you're gone. Get out.

LAUREN: I kind of agree. There is a lot to do to find someone new, and you don't need them interfering unless you absolutely must have them around. Or, if you want them around. A key professional will give two weeks' notice, and you will most likely want them around. It all depends, now that I am thinking about it.

GLEN: There is always a lot to do when you lose someone. If you are not always marketing for that position, you have to start up an entire new campaign, and that is a job of its own. We have an HR department, but I know what it is like at a smaller company.

VINNY: We just ask our people if they know

"What doesn't kill us makes us stronger."
Friedrich Nietzsche

Erik A. Kaiser

Employer

The Best Day To Fire An Employee

When you have to fire an employee, it is traditionally done on a Friday afternoon when everyone is heading out the door. You are then off to enjoy the weekend while the employee is left spinning. Choosing a different day may sometimes save the employee stress that may ultimately be relieved on you. Timing is sometimes everything.

There are a lot of opinions about when to terminate an employee. If the event is able to be planned, the best is day is usually on a Monday at the close of work. It is a better situation for the employer and employee for a variety of reasons.

Terminating an employee on a Monday versus a Friday gives the employee a better chance to begin immediately exploring new employment options. On a Friday, the person spends the weekend spinning and worrying about what to do next, whereas on a Monday, he or she can immediately hit the ground that day to start speaking with potential employers. There will be less time for the person to be distracted by unnecessary anger directed at your company or you.

Although you have made the decision to remove the employee, you should wish him or her well on future opportunities and avoid causing unnecessary disruption. Telling him or her the reason for termination on a Monday will demonstrate some respect.

"People are far more sincere and good-humored at speeding their parting guests than on meeting them."
Anton Chekhov

of someone, or I call the parole officers I know and they lead me to someone. Findin' someone is easy.
LAUREN: Maybe for you. We have to advertise. It takes time and money.
CHANDRA: It's the same for us, you know. We have to sit on the computer and look at every stupid job until one looks interesting. And then we have to apply and go through the interview process. It's a real pain. And when it is hard to find a job, you have to find a way to stick out in the crowd. That is an entire other job, coming up with a good way to do that.
LAUREN: When everyone is working and there aren't a lot of people looking for jobs it is the same for us. We have to find a way to become more attractive and it usually

---

For Office Use Only

Employee

The Best Day To Give Your Notice

If you decide that you are leaving your job, give your notice to the company on a Tuesday or Wednesday. You may be in an industry that may have atypical working schedules, but follow this advice for a typical Monday to Friday workweek.

Employers have to make an immediate decision about you remaining at the company after you give notice. There are many companies that must ask you to leave immediately after you give notice, and others that will allow you to work out the two weeks.

Giving notice on a Tuesday or Wednesday gives the employer a chance to organize quickly while the workweek is underway. By telling your boss on a Friday, you will only cause him or her to take time away from work-related responsibilities, and you may even cause him/her to have to work through the weekend to compensate for the new vacancy. You may not care if that is the case, but your departure will be what your boss remembers about you. By giving notice on a Tuesday or a Wednesday, you give your employer the ability to debrief you and share your information with the coworkers who will be responsible for picking up where you are leaving off. Usually within a couple of days, the employer can get the information he/she needs to continue business; by that time, it is Friday, and everyone can go home feeling better.

---

means costing us more either through advertising or paying someone more to attract them.

CHANDRA: You should do a job fair. I found a job there when I was younger.

GRACE: I have never been because I always kept finding work by looking online and talking to friends. But, I hear they are really good.

LAUREN: We don't have time for that. It is a commitment that a bigger company can make. We are a smaller company and when we need extra manpower we call the temp agency. They are fast and cheap.

CHANDRA: Well, it was a great type of first interview because you can meet the people who are there at the company and it is mostly informal. You can ask all sorts of questions and not have to waste time sitting in a waiting room to find out what the people and company are like. There isn't any "being late," and I was more relaxed about seeking out the right job.

GRACE: That seems really productive. I know what you mean about going on interviews. I thought about being a pharmaceutical rep at one time and went

Erik A. Kaiser

Employer

Marketing Your Company For A New Hire

The most popular complaint from employers is being able to find a great staff. The most traditional methods of advertising all have somewhat expected responses. But if you are having a hard time getting noticed through the traditional methods, take some cues from the creative approaches you observe job seekers using to get noticed and come up with your own.

One idea is to incorporate your search efforts as a marketing opportunity to advertise your company. Consider the following:

- Have an outside company create a viral video to reach a mass audience in a more clever way.
- Have a public relations company help distinguish your company in the public eye to get some press.
- Create a contest within your company that rewards your existing employees with cash for the best referral.

If your existing staff knows you are hiring, make sure that they are prepped on how to act when the interviewee visits for an interview or a tour. Clean up your office, and make sure that you have made an effort to create a welcoming environment as much as possible. Remember, your company is not the only company with which they will interview. Creating a good impression will lead to a potential referral from that candidate. Potent marketing is often about first impressions.

---

through the interview period. They had me back time after time, and once I waited three hours for them to finally interview me. Can you imagine that? Three hours! How disrespectful to my time!

GLEN: That is standard operating procedure in that industry. They want to see how you handle waiting in the same way you would in a doctor's office. If you can't be patient for hours, then you are not the right fit.

GRACE: Oh!.... *Uh, oh.*

VINNY: What'ja do? Rip'em a new one?

GRACE: I don't like to wait. I can be patient, but I was actively interviewing and had another interview after that I didn't want to be late for, obviously, and I told the interview team at the pharma company that I only had a half hour left in my schedule for the day. That is probably the reason I didn't get the job. I wasn't rude or anything because that's not my style. They just weren't even sorry for making me wait. Now it all makes sense. Gosh!

GLEN: And that's the reason. They want to know that you have patience.

GRACE: And they asked me all of these crazy questions. I never understood what

Employee

Marketing Yourself For A New Job

If you want to distinguish yourself beyond the basic cover letter and resume, you will have to be creative. If you have any friends in marketing, call on them to help you with some ideas to help you get noticed by potential employers. Here are some example ideas that have received unique attention.

- Send a bottle of decent champagne or a book (like this one) to the head of the company with your resume.
- Record a "video resume;" it is more unique, and you can be seen and heard. If you have great communication skills, your video will be highly effective.
- Have a social media feed for your resume that shows your professional side. Support your resume with content that you believe is important to an employer.

One woman looking for a job as an administrator printed her resume on t-shirts and handed them out. It demonstrated to a employers that she will not stop at the expected methods to get the job done.

But the rule is to be professional in your approach of getting noticed. Your tactic will be remembered, so make sure it is appropriate and is something by which you would like to be remembered.

"Make yourself necessary to somebody."
Ralph Waldo Emerson

they had to do with the job.
CHANDRA: Like what?
GRACE: On one interview, I was asked to write an essay on the ten things that most impacted my life. I was given a piece of paper and told that they would give me a few hours. What's the point of that?
VINNY: They wanted to know what you were really like because you are goin' to be dealing with doctors and drugs. That's why.

GLEN: I think that's right. They wanted to understand your ethics, since they are monitored by the FDA. It is serious stuff.
GRACE: Wow! I totally missed all of that.
CHANDRA: Oh, yeah, employers are slick. The big companies are pros. They know exactly what they are asking.
GRACE: I knew there had to be something, and I was trying to understand it. I had been used to working for much smaller

Employer

Receiving An Interviewee

First impressions can mean everything, especially when it comes to interviewing potential employees. Depending on the type of business you operate, consider what a prospective team member might see that you overlook.

Not all industries conform to general standards of receiving interviewees. Pharmaceutical representatives are sometimes made to wait three hours for the interview to begin in order to test if the interviewee has the tolerance to wait three hours to see a doctor client.

A general standard is to show respect to the interviewee by being on time for the interview and being prepared. With hope, he or she will show the same respect. Don't make the interviewee wait unnecessarily; make sure you treat him or her like you would treat a client. The interviewee, like anyone else, will form an opinion about your company and you based on treatment. The interviewee will be an advertisement for your company even if you do not hire the person, so make a good impression.

Interviewees will be nervous, even though it may not show and even if he or she is regularly confident. You will get more information from them and have a better quality interview if you are able to make him or her more comfortable. Your interviewee will be more likely to display his/her true character, and that is what you really want to judge.

---

companies, and all the process and the questions seemed a waste of time to me.

LAUREN: I probably need to do a better interview job after hearing all of this.

GLEN: I realized that I was not a great interviewer early on in my career. I really worked at it, and I realized that it was a team effort. What one person sees in a candidate, I may not see, and vice versa. There is definitely a skill to it.

VINNY: There's no skill to interviewin'. It couldn't be any easier than takin' a look at the dude, telling them what the job is and what they are gettin' paid. **If they say something stupid** or ask a stupid question, **the guy's stupid.** At that point, you make the call if he's in or out based on how stupid his questions are.

LENNY: What's a stupid question?

VINNY: Like, "Can we take the delivery vans home so I can get to work faster in the mornin'?" That's a stupid question.

LENNY: I don't think that's stupid. If y'all want me to work on-time, then you should be giving me a car to get there. Why not use the company car? I am gonna drive it

---

For Office Use Only

Employee

Going To An Interview

Making a great first impression is important to any potential employer. Besides being prepared with your resume and being dressed appropriately, know exactly where the interview is. Get the exact address and find out where it is the day before. A common mistake made by an interviewee is to underestimate the time it takes to get to the interview.

Arrive at your destination at least an hour before the interview. Hang out in a coffee shop or in the parking lot, but be there an hour before. There are traffic jams and train and subway delays. There are even buildings that have security that will slow you down by twenty minutes. These events do not excuse being late to an interview. Remember, the people you are going to meet are already busy enough to hire someone. They are allocating time in their busy schedules to meet with you. If you are late, you start with an uphill battle.

If you are on time and are made to wait, review all of the information you have gathered on the company and the people with whom you will be meeting. Spend that time looking around and observing what you see and how you are treated.

"Tardiness often robs us of opportunity and the dispatch of our forces."
Niccolò Machiavelli

everyday anyway.
LAUREN: [looking at Vinny] I see what you mean.
LENNY: Is that a dumb question?
GLEN, VINNY, LAUREN: YES!
LENNY: Well, look-it what I learned today!
VINNY: How many jobs have you had?
LENNY: I dunno. Maybe 25.
VINNY: Come by me, and I'll make it 26. In a day, you'll be onto 27. How old are you?
LENNY: I'm almost 30. What does that matter? Is this an interview?
CHANDRA: [to Lenny] Employers can't ask anything they want to in an interview. Like how old you are and if you are married.
LENNY: Everyone always asks how old I

Erik A. Kaiser

Employer

What Not To Ask An Interviewee

There are federal and state laws that prohibit you from asking basic personal questions about: race, color, sex, religion, national origin, birthplace, age, disability, marital/family status. Don't get caught in a trap by having unassuming casual conversation with an interviewee and finding yourself violating the law.

Asking a prohibited question is very easy to do because when we like an interviewee, we tend to become friendly and open with him or her and expect the same in return. You may just be generally curious about the person because you feel a connection. Be careful.

Unfortunately, there are a lot of very savvy interviewees who know the law and look to exploit it if they do not get the job. If you ask a prohibited question unintentionally and the interviewee reminds you that the question is illegal, you need to apologize and move on.

To be sure you are asking legal and relevant questions, have a list of questions prepared ahead of time and have a professional HR individual or even a labor lawyer review them. You can save yourself a lot of potential headaches as well as embarrassment by making sure that you are not held liable for a casual comment as part of a bigger conversation.

"If you want a wise answer, ask a reasonable question."

Johann Wolfgang Von Goethe

am. That's one of the first questions.

GLEN: By law, they can't ask you directly.

LENNY: Really? Can I sue them?

GLEN: It would be for discrimination if you didn't get the job, and it is hard to prove. I don't know what your damages would be.

LAUREN: It is so easy to figure out how old someone is. You just have to ask them lots of questions that get them to reveal times in their life that relate to an age. Like, you know, people generally graduate high school around 18 or 19 years old, so you work backwards if they tell you or write when they graduated.

GLEN: And if you want to know if someone is married, I have an interesting tactic. In the interview, after awhile, you get personal with them and reveal that you are contemplating your own marriage issue.

For Office Use Only

Employee

What Not To Ask An Interviewer

Any interview with a potential employer should be a good exchange of inquisitive questions. Be sure your questions are relevant. Everything you ask can be asked of you, and you will be judged on the quality of your questions. To avoid being judged negatively, refrain from discussing some topics.

- Don't ask useless questions that are not relevant to the job. You will be perceived as a person who is not interested in the company or the job objectives.
- Don't ask if you have to work overtime. It sends the signal that you don't want to put in any more effort than the minimum amount required.
- Don't ask lots of questions about holidays and time off. You will have the opportunity to see all of the policies once you are closer to being considered a candidate.
- Don't ask questions that put the interviewer on guard. For instance, don't ask why people quit the company if it such a great place to work.
- Don't ask prying questions into the personal life of the interviewer by testing their judgement.
- Don't interrupt the interviewer while he or she is talking.

If they start responding about how to handle it, the conversation will reveal if the interviewee is married. They tend to want to reveal it. People love to give advice.

LAUREN: Be clever. Just create a conversation where the other person will want to tell you everything you can't ask.

GRACE: Most smart people interviewing for a job know the basic tricks.

GLEN: I disagree. Some of them know the tricks, and some of them don't. We are pretty good at sniffing out engineered resumes.

CHANDRA: What's an engineered resume?

GLEN: It is a resume that has been glorified and crafted in a way that hides gaps in employment or other notable potential issues. Like overstated responsibilities.

CHANDRA: Why are employment gaps such a big deal? Don't you employers know that sometimes it takes a long time to find a job?

GLEN: Of course. But it doesn't take two years. If there is a two-year gap, there better be an convincing explanation. No one disappears for two years unless you win the

---

Erik A. Kaiser

Employer

Get Answers To Legally Prohibited Questions In An Interview

Legally prohibited questions during an interview often concerns discrimination. Some examples of questions you cannot ask include information about an interviewee's age, marital status, religion, race, and disabilities. However, if this information is important to you, there are ways to figure it out through reverse inquiry.

Most interviewees will provide answers to all of the prohibited questions if you create a conversation where they want to provide the answer. You have to be clever and smart about it. They don't have to answer but may feel compelled to do so.

If you want to know if a person is single or married, engage in a conversation about you being single or married. An interviewee will not sit there silent but feel the need to interact and share stories. He or she will likely reveal information about his or her marital status. If you want to know if the applicant has kids, comment that you have been thinking about putting a day care center for employees with children. They will react if it is applicable information.

There is nothing prohibited about you talking about other people at the company and yourself. Making your interviewee comfortable and unguarded will give you a head start on getting the information you want.

Don't forget to look at any social networking sites to which the applicant may belong. People regularly put their life on display.

"Charm is a way of getting the answer 'yes' without having asked any clear question."
Albert Camus

lottery.

CHANDRA: Two years I can understand. What about six months? I was out of work for six months once.

GLEN: That is not that drastic at all. The ones that scare us are the ones that we find with terrible explanations. We had one applicant for a management position have a three-year hole in his resume. We asked

about it, and he said that he was studying the Bible and had gotten very into religion. He considered a career path in theology.

VINNY: He was in the can.

GLEN: You got it. On the formal application, we have a question that asks, "Have you ever been convicted of a crime?" to which he answered, "No."

---

184   For Office Use Only

Employee

Don't Get Tricked Into Answering Illegal Interview Questions

There are certain questions that are illegal to ask you in job interviews because they deal with issues that are are rooted in discriminatory practice. Your religion and your ethnicity, for example, should be of no concern to your potential employer unless he or she is going to make a judgment for or against you with respect to being hired. This is an illegal and unfair practice. Don't get trapped into answering any illegal questions.

Interviewers will engineer conversations to get you to divulge the information on your own by creating discomfort for you during the interview. Be on the lookout for questions about being able to work on a Saturday or a Sunday. That is a direct question about religion. They may want to know what would prevent you from being able to travel on a whim for the job if it is part of the description. This is a direct question about your marital or familial status.

Get to know illegal questions before your interview. Before you answer suspicious personal questions, think about whether your answer matches an answer to an illegal question. If it does, you are being interviewed by a sharp person who is digging for more than you are willing to offer.

CHANDRA: So he lied on his job application. So what? So will most people if they want a job. How many people *really* look at those applications, anyway? They look all important and make the company look all formal, but seriously, it's all about the interview.

GLEN: Yes, he lied on the application. We are aware that people don't necessarily tell the entire truth. How much time can any company hiring a lot of people look into every detail? Some do for sure, but it depends on the job.

CHANDRA: So did your applicant get caught?

GLEN: Not until the very end of the process. We ran a background check on him and discovered that his "Bible study" was during his stay in jail for a felony. We sent him a letter stating that there were material discrepancies in his employment

"Questions are never indiscreet. Answers sometimes are."
Oscar Wilde

Erik A. Kaiser

Employer

Interviewees With Big Employment Gaps

Successful job postings should yield a lot of inquiries. You will take the resumes and employment applications and begin the distillation process to determine which candidate is best. But as you are get down to making some choices, you my find that you are concerned about big employment gaps on a candidate's resume.

A lack of explanatory information about the gap usually means deceit. You may ask why the candidate was unemployed for three years? Was it jail, rehab, addiction to video games?

Clever applicants know about gaps, and instead claim to have been working at their previous company when they were not. This makes a resume look like stable continuous employment.

Employment gaps also come disguised in another form. When the applicant does not list the month along with the year (August, 2009) as a beginning or completion date of work experience, you have to start to wonder why the months were not listed. A listing of work described as 2009-2010 could actually mean December 15, 2009-January 15, 2010.

Be direct with your questions about the exact dates. Candidates should have valid explanations that can be independently verified if you want proof. If your applicant is not forthcoming, then you can expect the same behavior if you hire him or her.

"When a thing is funny, search it carefully for a hidden truth."
George Bernard Shaw

application, and we retracted the offer.

LENNY: I went to jail when I was a 18 for six months for robbin' a guy's house with my buddies, and no matter what I do, that follows me everywhere. It sucks.

GLEN: You want to hear a good one? Listen to this. There is a major hospital in NJ that hired a doctor to manage one of the medical departments. The woman was administering drugs and making diagnoses.

She had degrees on the wall from a prestigious medical school, and everything seemed legitimate, a great resume.

VINNY: Oh this is a good one. I can smell it already! Who died?

GLEN: No one, fortunately. She was on the job for months, and her friends were questioning how she became a doctor. She claimed she went to night school for years while they were wasting away. It

---

186   For Office Use Only

Handling Employment Gaps On Your Resume

There are times in one's life where (extra)ordinary circumstances prevent you from a consistent pattern of work. You may have become ill, taken time off of work because you were pregnant, returned to school, gone to jail, or traveled. Whatever the reason, if you are putting together an honest resume about your work experience, an interviewer is going to ask you about what you were doing.

Your best defense is an offense. Tell any potential employer the reason for the employment gap before you are asked. You will be perceived as more credible and transparent, without having something to hide.

If your gap is the result of something that you perceive embarrassing to you, and you feel that the truth, under all circumstances, is an employment killer, you are most likely going to make up an alternative experience that will throw the interviewer off track. Common fabricated experiences include attending a school, becoming an entrepreneur (which didn't work, of course) or consulting for a friend who can verify your help. Employers rarely ask for verification of schooling or entrepreneurship. Be aware at many companies that lying can get you terminated at any time for providing false information to induce your employer to hire you.

---

turns out that she wasn't close to being a doctor. She did doctor her resume that the hospital bought and never bothered to independently verify. They hired her for a pretty important position, and it turns out that they never did a proper background check on her. Isn't that crazy?

GRACE: It's scary is what it is! I hope no one was hurt in the process.

GLEN: I don't know, but it was kept a pretty quiet issue. It is a lot easier today with social media, where you can quickly see what a person is all about.

CHANDRA: You go on people's Facebook page as part of the interview process?

GLEN: Well, we don't tell them that. We don't really want them to know because they will prune it and take away all of the photos and information that really tell you about the person.

LAUREN: Oh, definitely! Facebook is probably more powerful than a resume.

VINNY: My girlfriend is on it constantly.

GLEN: We always refer to Facebook and Instagram as the two sources of information about an applicant.

Erik A. Kaiser

Employer

Social Media Tells You All About Your Potential Hire

Fortunately, employers no longer have to rely on overstated resumes and carefully-designed references to limit what can be found out about a potential hire. Search engines and social media platforms do all of the work for you.

Make it common practice for you or your HR department to get online to find every social media platform to which the candidate belongs. There you will witness the activities of your potential hire. Since the legacy founding of MySpace and Facebook, a resume only tells the story you want to hear. Real-live photos and written communications will make more of a difference to you in determining the quality of the information you receive in the interview.

Your best filter of information before you even interview is to find out what you can on social media. Compare the resume to see if it matches up to the real person. The information flow is so positive, that you could make a decision from a phone or video interview if necessary. Plus, you can almost always find out instant answers to federally-prohibited questions without ever needing to ask.

CHANDRA: Don't people know that you are going to be looking?
GLEN: Did *you* know about this?
CHANDRA: Not really.
GLEN: Then there is your answer. Most people think of it *after* they are in the process. We go to it before we even schedule an interview.
GRACE: I don't think most people applying for a job think that a potential employer is going to look them up.
GLEN: That is why it works so well. When we figured out that it is a great site to get the skinny on a person, it was usually after we interviewed them. We would go onto the site, and the person who sat across the table was an entirely different person from the one they promote. It is really surprising.
LAUREN: It is great because you can befriend a potential applicant before you hire them. What are they going to do? Ignore you? And then they give the excuse that they rarely go on it? Yeah, right.
GRACE: I think you have to keep your personal information clean. You never know who is going to be looking at it, and I feel it should contribute to your good side, not

188   **For Office Use Only**

Your Potential Employer Will Find You on Social Media

Don't think your killer resume is going to be the only collateral that your potential employer will see when considering hiring you. Before you are called in for an interview, your potential employer will already know more about you than you think.

After your resume is received and filtered out for consideration, employers will then try to find out everything they can about you on every social media site - just the same way you probably did when you were considering the company.

Smart HR departments and bosses will "friend" you on social networking sites. What happens if you want the job but don't want to befriend them because your profile will reveal compromising information about you? Decisions, decisions.

Instead of running, use your social media as a tool to get a job. Clean up your profiles to be personal but professional. Get rid of those photos that do not contribute to your image in the eyes of your potential employer. And manage your privacy filters.

Consider "friending" them before they "friend" you. It shows that you are not trying to hide the real you. You can tailor an image that supports what the employer wants to see.

"Appearance rules the world."

Johann Friedrich Von Schiller

help people form the wrong opinion.

CHANDRA: I am a little sad to hear this because I wonder how many employers have looked at any picture of mine online and made a decision not to hire me because of my weight.

GRACE: Oh, Chandra, you are not heavy!

CHANDRA: Grace, I am about 30 pounds over what I should be, and I know it. It just makes me sad that my weight might turn off an employer. I understand now why my sister had a very difficult time finding a job.

GRACE: Is *she* heavy?

CHANDRA: Very heavy. To the point she has to wear sandals sometimes because she cannot fit into shoes. My family is concerned that she could be considered disabled soon, but you cannot even mention that to her. She does not think it is a problem. I know any employer that looks

---

Erik A. Kaiser

Employer

Get Background Checks And Credit Reports On Employees

Hiring employees is pretty serious. You make judgments about people from resumes, interviews, and your working experience with them. You entrust them with corporate duties for which they are responsible. We want to believe everyone is honest and has it together, but do they?

Your company should conduct a background and credit check on everyone who is accepted for a job at your company. The reason is simple: sometimes people don't tell you everything if you don't ask. And even if you ask, you don't always get the truth.

Credit reports assist in determining financial reliability. Background checks will give you a history of any issues your candidates or employees have had with crime, possible aliases, addresses, liens, Patriot Act issues, and other data that will help you develop a full profile. Revealing credit or crime issues drive the assignment of types of responsibilities.

If you do not get a background check, there is always a chance that your company will be held liable for a questionable act by an unchecked employee. If you are a bank and you hire a person who has a history of identity theft, without doing a background check and running the person's credit report, you create massive liability. Should that employee be privy to private consumer information they may use it for fraudulent reasons or sell it.

"Fellow citizens, we cannot escape history."
Abraham Lincoln

at her gets nervous.

GLEN: You are right. Health conditions are hot buttons for some employers. But then again, Chandra, it does not matter to others. Did she finally find something? What does she do?

CHANDRA: She is actually a certified public accountant. And she is very good, from what I understand. She does my taxes, but I don't have anything complicated.

GLEN: Why was she out of work?

CHANDRA: Because her company had to downsize. She worked on one big account for a company that merged with a parent company, and all of the accounting work for them went internal. She and about 15 other people lost their jobs. It was legitimate.

GRACE: How long was she at the other company?

CHANDRA: For about five years. She had

---

190   For Office Use Only

Employee

Hiding Issues From Background Checks

Years ago, getting a background check on someone was much more difficult. States and countries did not have a communications platform, and it would have been difficult to find out if you were involved with something like a crime or a bankruptcy. With the consolidation and digitization of public information, your personal matters are available online instantly for a nominal fee.

When applying for a new job, your employer may perform a background check on you. It will tell the employer all about your criminal issues. Your employer may also separately get an authorization from you to run your credit report in order to determine your current financial condition. Banks, for instance, will not have a compelling argument for hiring you to handle cash as a teller if you are 90 days late on your mortgage and you are overextended on your credit cards.

If you do have personal issues that you believe will raise an eyebrow or two, try to find out before the interview if the company runs a background check on the applicants as part of a final approval for a job. If they do, be up front with them, and use the interview as a platform to divulge what they will eventually learn. It will build credibility with your interviewer, and it will shortcut the interview process if there is something that prevents them from hiring you, saving you both resources.

---

to figure out the interview process again.

GLEN: How long was she out of work?

CHANDRA: About nine months. It was terrible. She was so upset. She took a job at a big corporate accounting firm, and she is so thankful they gave her a chance. She really appreciates having a job more than ever now.

GRACE: I can imagine. That is a long time to be out of work.

CHANDRA: She works much harder at her new job because she wants to keep it. She always works late and is really focused. I think she knows she needs to be. She will never answer her cell phone at work. She doesn't even keep it on.

GLEN: Sounds like she isn't taking any chances.

CHANDRA: I would say none. It is actually good for her. I think she was really comfortable at her last job. Now she is in a big corporate firm, and the vibe is different, she says. It sounds competitive, and she is energized by that. She was very upset for a long time after being fired, and now she is back to normal and serious. It is good to see. But she isn't losing any weight.

Erik A. Kaiser

Employer

What To Consider When Hiring Obese Employees

Obese employees cost companies more through higher illness, lost work days, and workers' compensation claims. Companies need to understand the potential financial impact on the company when hiring obese employees if margins are thin and the work has a physical component.

Hiring an obese person needs to take into consideration when the side effects of obesity will cost the company more than it can or is willing to afford. The subject seems discriminatory, but when it comes to the financial health of your organization, every potential expense must be considered including future health costs. You cannot legally discriminate against an obese job applicant, and job applicants who are morbidly obese are protected under the Americans with Disabilities Act.

If you have obese workers, your company should seriously consider learning to become a health-conscious company. You may incorporate exercise during the day and replace the junk food in the vending machines with natural foods that contribute to a healthy lifestyle.

But the reality is that you are a company with a mission; you are not a rehabilitation clinic. Bringing an awareness of being healthy to you employees is a long-term effort that will not have immediate effects on controlling expenses. If you have a company large enough to offer real wellness programs, do it.

"There is no need to worry about mere size. We do not necessarily respect a fat man more than a thin man. Sir Isaac Newton was very much smaller than a hippopotamus, but we do not on that account value him less."
Bertrand Russell

LENNY: I've been fired from almost every job except for the one I got now and a couple of others. You get used to it.

CHANDRA: For her, it was different. She was there for years, and it all happened so fast. She had a little family there and a routine that ended abruptly.

GRACE: I really feel for her. She is back on her feet, so good for her. I don't know her, but tell her I am happy for her.

LENNY: I make friends at work, too, and I don't see them after I work there. That kind

---

192 **For Office Use Only**

Employee

You Are Obese And Cannot Get Hired

You may be as qualified as the next person for a job, but you believe your obesity is the reason why employers offer the job for which you have applied to someone else. You are probably right, and here is why.

Obese employees cost a company more. It has been demonstrated that obese people incur double the claims for workers' compensation, significantly higher medical costs, and greater injuries on the job. Obese employees also miss more work days. Employers consider obesity as a lifestyle issue to which they will end up contributing time and money. Increased insurance costs, especially if the company self-insures, can be a scary truth for employers.

But the obese have rights. Morbid obesity (defined as having a body mass index of 40 or above) is generally a protected disability under the Americans with Disabilities Act. That means companies have to accommodate a morbidly obese person in the workplace. Regularly obese (body mass index of 30-39) and morbidly obese people, who have the ability to perform the advertised job but are not hired because of their weight can claim discrimination and file a claim with the Equal Employment Opportunity Commission (EEOC). Weight-based employment discrimination may be difficult to prove, especially if there are physical requirements for the job.

---

of sucks, but so what? I always get cut off after I am not working at a job no longer.

GLEN: Companies do that a lot. It depends on what you did that got you fired.

VINNY: Yeah, like sleepin' with the boss's married daughter.

GLEN: Right, like sleeping with the boss's married daughter *at the office*.

LAUREN: I always have to do some sort of damage control whenever I let someone go because I have to cut them off completely.

LENNY: I don't get it. Why?

LAUREN: There are a few basic reasons. First is that you can't have access to any of the company information. You can't be sending or returning emails on behalf of the company, even if you have the best intentions. You could create a liability for me, and it is no longer your responsibility.

GLEN: And you need to make sure that any access to anything financial is completely cut off. You can't have former employees walking around with passwords to financial accounts and credit cards.

VINNY: And you gotta get the keys back from any company cars. I fired this jackwad,

---

Erik A. Kaiser

Employer

I Just Hired Someone. Now What?

There are some job applicants who are professional interviewees. They come in, wow you with every answer to your questions, and know how to be that person for whom you have been looking for so long. But don't breathe a sigh of relief until you know that person will perform as expected.

A new employee gets on the job, and you discover that the person in the interview is not the person you hired. They start showing up late, full of excuses that worked on previous employers, and spends time surfing social media and sending personal e-mails and text messages. Their work is sloppy, wrong, or inaccurate, rendering the training sessions little more than glorified babysitting time.

Get to know this person on the job and do it fast, because if he or she is not what you expected, you need to terminate ASAP. Getting rid of a newer employee is easier and less disruptive, and you are still have hiring momentum.

Use monitoring software on your new employee's computer to see if time is spent working or playing. If you provide a company phone, review the records to understand with whom the person is speaking during working hours. If you keep wondering why the interview was so good but the work performance is so bad, consider that your new hire may be most skilled at getting a job, not keeping one.

---

and he stole a van about two months later.

GLEN: And we had a former employee give a rental car agency our company card and rent a car in our name. He didn't return it, and our office was called. Somehow, he still had a credit card. It was an oversight.

CHANDRA: Those are some bad employees. I don't know why people do that stuff.

LAUREN: Because they don't understand the consequences.

GLEN: They don't plan on getting caught. As I gained more experience, I got much better at profiling problem people like this. If you think they are going to be a problem after you fire them, you know they have the propensity to be a problem if you don't have a good termination plan in place.

VINNY: Here's my termination plan. Ready? "You're fired. Get the hell outta here, and I'll break your neck if I see you around here again."

GRACE: That's subtle.

VINNY: Hey, it's pretty effective.

GLEN: I was talking more about knowing how to plan to get rid of someone. Once

---

For Office Use Only

I Just Got Hired. Now What?

The beginning of a new job is a honeymoon stage. You are excited about the new job, and the company that hired you is excited to have the position filled. Life is good, at least until you start making mistakes that draw attention to you.

Until you learn about the corporate culture and about the unwritten rules, you need to do the following:

- Show up early every day and leave after the others leave.
- Stay away from creating alliances with anyone until you have had enough time to get to know everyone.
- Stay away from office gossip.
- Decline dates from coworkers.
- Focus on your work, not the work of others.
- Do not use your office computer for anything but work.
- Do not conduct any personal activities during work time.
- Do not write or respond to personal emails or social media.

Employers are usually sensitive to new hires since to confirm the correct hiring decision was made. All eyes and ears will be on you until everyone is comfortable with one another. Once you get comfortable with the corporate culture, you can modify your behavior to the level you see fit.

"All business depends upon men fulfilling their responsibilities."
Mahatma Gandhi

they catch on that they are going to be let go, you can expect issues. You have to be careful about keeping it completely hidden from everyone but trusted management.

LENNY: This sounds like a covert action.

GLEN: You laugh, but sometimes it has to be. Work needs to continue after you remove an employee. You have to do everything to keep the business running as smoothly as possible with the least disruption. You have to plan and get set up.

LAUREN: So what is your usual plan?

LENNY: Yeah, what's the usual plan so I can figure out when it's gonna happen next?

VINNY: Oh, yeah, [pointing to Lenny] Nostrodamus over here is goin' to figure it out. Are you nuts? It will be invisible to you.

GLEN: That's the point. You need to do all of the work in the background. You need to

Employer

I Just Fired Someone. Now What?

Often after firing an employee, other employees want to know exactly why their colleague was fired if it is not apparent. It is a good protocol to be open to your remaining employees about the circumstances that lead up to the decision. The remaining employees want to understand what occurred because they fear getting fired for the same reason.

You also want to control the rumor mill and false information from being circulated which distracts employees from doing the job. You cannot not be sure what false information the terminated employee shared with the rest about the company or the reason for termination. Terminated employees rarely admit to performing poorly or admit to doing something wrong.

It is expected that terminated employees have a relationship and stay in touch with your current employees. They will talk. Be clear to your staff that the decisions were based on business, not personal matters, and describe the circumstances to them as easily as possible.

You should also have a termination procedure that cuts off credit cards and other accounts, removes software licenses, and forwards communication to others. Don't leave anything critical to the company exposed.

---

do everything like the person being fired is already gone. You have to get everything in order for a new person to come in, and you have to organize the work. And you have to move quickly.

LAUREN: What happens if they catch on?

GLEN: You do what you have to so you avoid any and all dramas. You don't want to disrupt workflow and productivity at work.

LAUREN: But wait. What do you do if they come up to you and ask point blank, "Am I getting fired?"

GLEN: You have a couple of choices.

You could tell them the truth and risk the consequences, or you could be evasive to protect the company.

VINNY: Or, to put it another way, you could lie.

GLEN: You do what you have to do. If an employee asked me, "Am I getting fired?" the answer would be "No." They are not getting fired at that moment. If they asked, "Are you preparing to fire me?", the answer is still "No" because I will not be doing the actual firing.

LENNY: That's what I call real slick.

For Office Use Only

Employee

I Just Got Fired. Now What?

Take a deep breath, because regardless of whether you are happy about it or not, getting fired is an emotional experience that leads to a temporary stressful aftermath. You may have been employed for five days or five years. The firing may have been expected or completely out of the blue. The economy may have been the culprit, or it could have been your performance. Knowing the reasons why you were terminated is important so you can learn from the experience and avoid the same circumstances again in the future. It is time to reevaluate if what you were doing was fit for you.

If your previous job was something that you really liked and you considered yourself good at it, then get out and search for a job in the same industry. If it was a job that did not have much meaning to you, take the firing as an opportunity to do what you really want to do.

Don't spend time being angry with your previous employer or plotting attacks against the company. Focus your energy on getting back on the horse, facing the facts, and moving on. Most of the time, getting fired is a blessing in disguise.

"When one door closes, another opens. But we often look so long and so regretfully upon the closed door that we fail to see the one that has opened for us."
Alexander Graham Bell

CHANDRA: Sounds like lies to me.

GLEN: It's not a lie; it's an adequate answer for the situation. It's business.

LAUREN: I get it. I think that would work for me. I always have to let the person go and then scramble around looking for a replacement. You are doing all of the scrambling and finding the replacement before you fire the person. It's a smart approach, and I am going to use it when I have that issue arise again. Do you still give them a recommendation letter?

GLEN: Of course. We tell them that when we sit them down to let them go. It is a reminder that we are part of their history,

---

Erik A. Kaiser

Employer

Replacing An Employee Without Disrupting Business

You have made the decision that someone has to go, but not without having a good replacement. Keep business disruptions to a minimum by being strategic.

- Do not indicate to anyone that you will be replacing the employee. You do not want the leaked information to undermine your efforts by having the employee resign before you have someone in place to pick up the work.
- Try advertising for the position covertly or employ a hiring agency. Advertising on job platforms with employer confidentiality can be productive.
- Start interviewing. If your company setup is conducive to interviews at your office, then do it there. Otherwise, start meeting the candidates at other suitable locations.
- Learn everything that you can regarding the work of the employee who is going to be replaced. Trim down that person's responsibilities and get full control of what that person is doing.

Once you have made a decision on the new hire, let the employee go on a Monday afternoon and have the new hire start on a Wednesday or following Monday. You can inform your staff on Tuesday and be prepared for the following day.

"Nothing gives a person so much advantage over another as to remain always cool and unruffled under all circumstances."

Thomas Jefferson

and potential employers will call us to get a report on them.

CHANDRA: You always want a good job reference from your last employer.

GLEN: Exactly. Sometimes we show them a draft of a recommendation letter, but we don't give it to them.

CHANDRA: Why not?

GLEN: Because if they do something against the company while they are looking for a job, we won't send the letter out on their behalf. We very rarely give them the letter. If they want a letter of recommendation, we send it directly to their potential employer.

For Office Use Only

Leaving Your Job Without Disrupting The Company

You may not care that leaving your job will disrupt your company, but you should. Your reputation precedes you in almost any situation, and if you are a person known to abort responsibilities, you will not be received as a responsible person. Word gets around, and there is a term called "doing the right thing" which loosely translates into "acting responsibly."

If you are planning to leave your job, don't rely on the two weeks' notice program to give you the time to coordinate your departure with your coworkers and boss. There are potential security issues and policies that may prevent you from staying at work once you have given notice.

Make sure that before you give your notice, you organize all of the work that you are leaving behind. Create a document that details out everything that needs to be known to the company and to your coworkers to continue conducting business without creating an interruption. Organize everything into a format that is recognized for the rest of the team.

Being responsible and organized about your departure from a company will be remembered. It is the proper impression you want to leave behind.

CHANDRA: That seems ridiculous. Why wouldn't you just give the person the letter? Why do you care?

GLEN: Sometimes we do. It depends on the person. In the case we discussed, we had to replace the person because of a problem. We don't want our company to promote them if we are not sure about them ourselves. Remember, we are talking about a person of a certain profile. Like someone who has picked up drug use.

LENNY: There are a lot of people who use drugs at work. I seen it a lot. Guys will smoke pot at lunch.

GLEN: Do they ever get caught?

LENNY: Not really. I mean, no one is looking, I guess. I never got into anything like that, so I don't know what their deal is.

GLEN: Well, you have to understand that at our company, we have a "no drug use" policy. If we know you were clean when we hired you and later you started using drugs, we are going to replace you. That's why we won't give out a blanket recommendation letter. It doesn't make sense for us to put our own company image on the line. Make sense?

Erik A. Kaiser

Employer

Giving Former Employees A Job Recommendation

Once you start hiring, your company is automatically placed forever in the blockchain of work experience that your employees will/may present for the rest of their lives on a resume. Be informed that even if your employees do not ask you for a direct recommendation in the future, other companies that hire them may call you to ask for a review. You will never be liable for giving a former employee a good recommendation, but you can be held liable for negative comments as slander.

Develop a protocol for addressing former employee recommendation requests. If you like the person and he or she did a good job, give a good recommendation. Don't restrict a former employee from finding more new employment. He or she will appreciate it, and it may come back to help you one day.

If you don't like the employee, tell anyone inquiring that your recommendation policy is only to verify date and title of employment of any employee, regardless of position in the company. This is a common practice in the market and anyone calling your company to ask about the employee will recognize this policy and not question you much further. Don't say anything negative or hint at your displeasure through deep sighs, sarcasm, or other indicators. Stay off the liability hook.

CHANDRA: I guess so. I never realized companies think about this stuff so much.

VINNY: If I drug tested my employees, I would have to fire half of them. I don't care what they do, as long as it is not during work. If they want to smoke pot at home at night, go for it. What do I care?

GRACE: What if you find them doing drugs at work?

VINNY: Then I will get rid of them. That's the easy part. Everyone knows that.

LAUREN: I never wanted to do any random drug testing because I don't want to know. If everything has been fine for a long time, why mess with it? I am more worried about people coming in hungover. Then they are a waste for the day.

LENNY: I hate going to work hungover, but it happens. There's no way to get rid of that fast except a good beer and bar-b-que!

VINNY: Anytime I see a guy hungover, I really bust his chops. I will make him work harder than anyone else. It's a reminder that I'm watchin'. You know who the loyal guys are at the end of the day when they don't leave after bein' beat on.

For Office Use Only

Getting Job Recommendations From Your Former Employers

When you begin a new job, remember that if you are not planning to be there a lifetime, you will want to use your employer as a reference for your future jobs. Always keep this in mind because you want positive recommendations from former employers; their opinions make a difference.

Job recommendations can sometimes be the deciding factor on getting hired for a job. Employers talk more candidly with one another because they understand employees and business differently than you do. They can infer from a simple conversation and the application of some industry language the critical information they need to know about your profile.

There is not any true way you can force a former employer to give you a great recommendation, unless it is court-ordered or part of a legally-binding document. But what you can do is ask if your employer will give you a general letter of recommendation (LOR) that you can keep for your records.

Try to get your employer to write a LOR at or very close to the time you are leaving the company. If you are giving your two weeks' notice, ask to have it before you leave. If you can remember, ask for a LOR from the person firing you in a termination. Sometimes, you will get a good recommendation to quell any retaliation.

"When anger rises, think of the consequences."
Confucius

GRACE: I can just imagine what you make them do.

VINNY: It ain't pretty. But you gotta know if they are gonna listen to you or they are gonna roll on you. You can count on those guys when you need 'em. Don't you test your people? How do you know who is really on your side?

LAUREN: I never thought of it that way. I mean, what about working overtime?

VINNY: They are gettin' paid for that.

LAUREN: Not the salaried people.

VINNY: What happens if you tell one of your salaried people they have to work a weekend? Are they gonna do it, or are they gonna kick and scream and say no?

LAUREN: Some will do it, and others I would never ask again. I see what you are saying.

Erik A. Kaiser

Employer

Getting Rid Of Employees Who Use Drugs

Every employer has a rule for employees who use drugs. Some employers don't care what an employee does outside of work, and other employers are random testers who will terminate the employee on the spot if they find that there is hard evidence of drug use. Every industry is different, and different rules apply.

If your employees are operating machinery, tools, or vehicles that are company-owned, mandatory drug testing ensures that your liabilities will not increase as a result of an accident.

The conflict occurs when companies don't want to test for fear of what they will find. For example, top-earning salespeople who are vital to financial survival may be suspected drug users. Employers consciously will not test because if they find out that the employee is a drug user, they may be compelled to terminate cash flow. In addition, once one person is tested, all must be tested because selectively testing is discriminatory.

If you find yourself having to terminate an employee for drug usage, you must clearly document your method of testing and the final result that led to the decision to terminate. Outside testing companies are available for hire to help take the risk out of the equation, and they will provide you with comprehensive information to make sure that you will remain liability-free.

GRACE: I am on a salary, and I will work a weekend. It is a reflection of my job and contributes to my job security.

CHANDRA: I'm not working any weekend unless I am getting something for it. Why would I do that? If they don't want me, I'll find another job.

GRACE: I like my job, and I want to see my company grow. I want to be a part of it. All of that goes into a bonus at some point. And I keep track of it.

GLEN: It depends on your job description. If it calls for late hours and occasional weekends, then that is what it is.

CHANDRA: I don't really care if the company grows or not. It's not my company. I'll do the work during work hours, and I will collect my paycheck. It should be as simple as that. Steady is better.

GRACE: But don't you want to grow in your position?

CHANDRA: I'm good where I am right now. I just want to maintain it. No more, no less. No one told me that I am getting anything for working more.

For Office Use Only

Don't Be Surprised If You Are Fired For Using Drugs

You may work in an environment where drug usage is normal or tolerated, or you may work in a place where illegal drug usage is a "no-discussion" termination event. In either case, you must be careful for many reasons.

Although you may have never been given a drug test, the possibility looms. Your industry standard may change, or your company could be in the sale stage and the buyer has this demand, or the company may decide to make a policy change to lower insurance premiums. The bottom line is that if you are an illegal drug user and you are employed, you are taking some risk of being terminated specifically for that reason.

There are very few tricks that can be played to disguise actual testing through urine, blood, or hair sampling. Your best bet is to remain drug-free if your job is critical to you.

If you are tested, make sure that you receive information that all employees have been tested and that you have not been singled out. If you have been specifically tested because an employer is curious about you, the company has opened itself up to a discrimination claim.

"Drugs are a waste of time. They destroy your memory and your self-respect and everything that goes along with your self-esteem."

Kurt Cobain

GRACE: My boss was very specific to me that he was looking to grow the company, and I knew that meant that if I wanted to grow, that I would put in extra effort when it was needed. I am glad to do it.

CHANDRA: Well, my boss said my job was from 9 a.m. to 5 p.m. I told you this before. I packed up at 5 p.m. and everyone was still working. I wasn't sticking around. Part of the reason I took this job was because I could get home at a decent hour and do what I want to do.

GLEN: Did your boss know that?

CHANDRA: I don't know. He didn't ask me. He told me that there was very little overtime, if any. He told me all sorts of

Employer

Requiring Employees To Perform Loyalty Tasks

Don't make assumptions about the commitment of your employees. Gain absolute knowledge, because you need to know on whom the company can rely when all of the stars fall out of alignment. Loyalty tasks identify resistance in the path forward when the daily work flow is disrupted.

Great employees may show up and leave on time every day. You would expect your most consistent employees to be the ones who might go outside the normal course of business to help in times of deadlines or need, but you will more often than not find the opposite to be true. You might also believe that the employees with the most to gain would be most loyal to the company. Also not necessarily the case.

To start to collect the loyalty data on your employees, you don't have to do anything that is seemingly difficult. Start by getting reactions to the following:

- Ask them to stay later than usual to finish something that is needed but is not urgent.
- Request that an employee move a scheduled vacation for something important to the company objectives.

"Loyalty means nothing unless it has at its heart the absolute principle of self-sacrifice."
<small>Woodrow T. Wilson</small>

other stuff as well that just wasn't the case.

GRACE: Like what?

CHANDRA: Like they were opening up other offices in different cities, and they were close to closing deals with some big companies. I think they said all that because I was looking for steady pay, and they were baiting me to take the job.

GLEN: A lot of companies will overstate their position to attract the right people or different talent. Sometimes you have to.

LAUREN: I did it when I first started out and even when we were growing. I didn't think anything of it, but I wanted to prove to anyone I wanted to hire that we were doing great and were always busy. All I needed to do was get them signed up and through the door. After that, it was what it was. Things

---

For Office Use Only

Employee

Having To Perform Loyalty Tasks

Your company or boss will sometimes ask you to do something on behalf of the company that you don't want to do. It could be to stay late, pick up a client at the airport, attend a function on behalf of the company at your cost, or pick up the tab for your colleagues without expectation of getting reimbursement. There could be many reasons for these requests, including a greedy employer, but more often than not, they are subtle exercises to observe your loyalty.

Often, loyalty tests are used during the process of analyzing an employee for a promotion. The employer wants some additional data to support the decision, and they want to feel comfortable that the company is important to the employee. These tests are also used to help an employer collect loyalty data to determine on whom they can rely and who is more worth their time.

Be sure to determine that the company is not just trying to take advantage of you. When you feel that you are the subject of a loyalty test, keep a written log of your experiences and actions so you can reference it later.

---

change. But my intentions were right.

GLEN: It doesn't matter if you are hiring someone or you already have a bunch of employees. You are always going to be selling to them. It's called motivation, and you need to motivate people. They want to be part of something bigger. It's the same thing as selling a client on why they should use you and not the competition.

GRACE: But doesn't that interfere with the idea of real job security?

VINNY: There ain't no such thing as job security. Where do you people get these ideas? You think you are gonna live and die at some company because that's *your* plan? If you ain't drivin' the bus at the company, it means you are goin' where the driver is takin' you.

GLEN: There is some truth to that.

VINNY: More than some. Come on, you're tellin' me you can look your people in the eye and tell them that their job is gonna be there as long as they keep doin' what they're doin'? No way. It's impossible.

GLEN: There are variations of it. Of course, companies sometimes close or get bought

---

Erik A. Kaiser

Employer

Did You Lie To Your Employees About The Prospects Of Their Job?

It is not uncommon to oversell potential employees on the great benefits and opportunities your company has to offer, even if it is not true. When you need to get employees through the door to keep the company moving, you might say anything to get it done. Usually, once they are working, they will get used to what is going on, and you can later make up some excuse as to why the opportunity changed.

Promises of promotions are the easiest to offer because you can always come up with a reason why you cannot follow through. The same is true for pay increases. There are always cash concerns, no matter how much the company is making.

Once an employee makes a transition to your company, he or she is less likely to pick up and leave two weeks into the job after finding out that some of what was promised was a stretch. They made a commitment and will try to make it work.

When you are selling potential candidates, be general and vague, and talk in big ideas. If you claim something specific, like working from home four days a week when it's actually zero, you will be called out. Paint with big strokes, and you will have an easier time with any direct questions about why the picture you painted isn't what was delivered.

"Everyone lives by selling something."
Robert Louis Stevenson

by other companies. But you are right. There is no such thing as security in a job. That is largely a myth.

CHANDRA: I don't count on any company for more than a couple of years. Who knows if they are going to be in business?

GRACE: I think it depends on the business.

VINNY: No, it don't. You would think that after a 100 years in business, a company like Lehman Brothers would still be around. I bet everyone there was totally convinced that they had lifetime job security. And then, kaboom! They disappeared in a week. If that don't tell you there ain't no job security, then you got a lotta learnin' to do.

LENNY: I been fired so many times that I wouldn't even think of working someplace more than a year. Are y'all tellin' me that people think they are gonna work for a place forever? That's crazy!

For Office Use Only

Did Your New Employer Lie About The Prospects Of Your Job?

You may find out that the promises, promotions, learning opportunities, and other benefits a new employer discussed in your job interview do not match the reality of your experience. In the corporate world, you just got punked. You left another job for this one based on the cornucopia of benefits that do not exist as described. If you find that you are not getting what was promised to you to induce you to take the job, you have a few choices.

- Get back out there and find a new job.
- Approach your employer, describe what it was that was promised, and have him or her devise a plan to compensate for the discrepancy.
- Find others in the company who are also experiencing the same misrepresentation and form an alliance to exert some influence.

Unless you have documented specifics regarding the benefits you were to receive by the company as part of your hire package, you really do not have too much recourse against the company. Fighting a claim against them would most likely not be worthwhile unless there is a contract on which to rely.

GLEN: Oh yes, they do. And in many cases, it happens. Not every company closes or changes up people. That's why employees become partners. Like in law firms. There are many examples of firms that have retained people for decades, and they retire from there. Big institutions like museums last for centuries. It is possible, of course, and not as rare as you make it. But it is a gamble, one that you need know about.

GRACE: [looking at Lenny] Lenny, why do you get fired from every job?

LENNY: [head down] I'm not sure.

VINNY: Yes, you are. What is it?

LENNY: It's not that I don't know. It's just that no one gets me. It's like, once you get into the routine of gettin' a job and then gettin' fired, it becomes just what I do. I don't expect anything more. And the weird thing is that I sort of like being fired. I am a pro at gettin' jobs and a pro at leavin' jobs. I don't care about gettin' fired because every time I leave a place, I feel like I'm doin' something new. Is that weird?

VINNY: [speaking to Lenny] Hey, kid. Let me tell you something. Gettin' fired just ain't no fun, even if you are better than

---

Erik A. Kaiser

Employer

Do You Have Employees Who Think Their Jobs Are Secured Forever?

Employees create their own sense of job security, and they sometimes believe it is less or more secure than it is. Trying to keep them balanced between zero and full job security is an auxiliary job. You don't want them so fearful that it causes them to feel undervalued, unmotivated, and ready to look elsewhere. On the other hand, you do not want them so comfortable that inspire complacency.

If you end up with employees who feel entitled to remain employed under all circumstances, you have probably done a great job at bonding with them and building morale. You have also instilled a confidence in them and have recognized them repeatedly to make them feel ultra-valuable. In doing so, however, you may have given them a false sense of security.

When this occurs, you may detect a loss of work ethic and production. They will feel as though they can take advantage of their positions and not have to work as hard. They don't feel the need to take orders from others and may start acting with entitlement.

Getting them back to a place of reality can be very abrupt. One of the best solutions is to have a very candid and frank conversation about how much you revere them, but that their job is at risk if their attitude does not change. Usually, this gives them a much-needed dose of reality.

---

them. Nobody likes rejection, because that's what it is, and it don't feel good. It's like dating a girl, and you get in a fight, and she throws your stuff out the second story window of a two-family house right onto the sidewalk when it's rainin' out. And she changes the locks, so when you come home tired from a freakin' long day, you gotta stand out there feelin' like a jerk, screamin' until the neighbors call the cops. So you gotta turn around and grab your stuff, and your cell phone is dying because you been on it all day trying to calm the bitch down. You know what I'm sayin'?

LENNY: Yeah, it sorta sucks.

VINNY: A *lot*. You seem like a good kid; you just got rejection issues. And you probably do stupid crap because you aren't thinkin' about your future.

GLEN: [to Lenny] Lenny, did you know that companies face the same feelings that you do when you get fired? When a company loses someone, it means that the employee is firing the company for something better. For people like me who have to manage a large company, losing someone really good to the competition means a whole lot more to employers than you can imagine.

For Office Use Only

Employee

Do You Think Your Job Is Secure Forever?

There will be times that you will be able to jockey into position to be a valuable star at your company. You will earn recognition, possibly some extra money, and you will feel more rooted in the company. Your relationship with your employer will grow stronger, and you will begin to realize your own value to the operation. This is a great achievement. But be careful not to think that your status will last forever and you no longer have to work at it.

Companies change for the better and worse. You may be the reason for the recent change to the better, but the effects don't earn you a place on the list of people who can never be fired.

If you find yourself gloating and proud about a recent achievement at work that has earned you significant recognition, don't let it trick you. You may not be able to reproduce the event, or someone else may one-up you, making your achievement less memorable.

Job performance is not the only prerequisite for job security. Your personality, skills, attitude, ability to grow, and ability to work with others are also factors that are taken into consideration.

"The only real security that a man can have in this world is a reserve of knowledge, experience, and ability."
Henry Ford

GRACE: [to Lenny] Have you ever asked for real feedback from any of your employers? You know, to know really what they think about you in an effort to help you?
LENNY: I don't wanna know.
GRACE: You should know, even if it hurts. Find someone that cares. They will tell you.
VINNY: That's a *really* good idea.

GRACE: Thank you, Vinny!
VINNY: [to Grace] Don't think nothin' of it, babe. We got a connection, me and you.
GLEN: I like Vinny's idea, too. When we have someone leave the company, we always sit the person down for an exit interview. We want to know what decisions led to leaving the company and what improvements can be made, because if one

Erik A. Kaiser

Employer

How To Fire Someone

If you don't have an HR department at your company to handle hiring and firing, and you have don't have a structure in place for someone else in your company to handle these situations, here are some tips. To be most effective and limit the downsides to firing someone, consider the following:

- Find a place where you can fire the person without causing disruption.
- Consolidate all of the employee's personal belongings.
- Lock the employee out of the company computer system.
- Retrieve any sensitive company information beforehand.
- Have the final paycheck or commission check ready.
- Call on law enforcement to monitor the process.
- Have any documents relevant to the employee's dismissal at hand.
- Keep it friendly, sympathetic, and short.

Immediately after you part, take notes of what occurred, good and bad. Include the time you met and the time you finished, the date, the weather, what the person was wearing, anything threatening or off-color that was said to you, and your conclusion.

Remember, you are freeing this employee to find a better opportunity. Don't hang on to an employee you when there is something out there that would be better for both of you. But, if there is retaliation, your document of the termination will be important to any legal proceeding.

---

person is unhappy enough to leave over something, then there a lot of people who are unhappy. It is up to us to monitor and address the situations we hear about.

LAUREN: I bet people just spill their guts about their experience.

GLEN: Some do. Some tell us everything they think in an emotional manner, and others have targeted issues. Sometimes it is money; other times is it is more perceived opportunity. And you know what? Other times, the competition did a better job at recruiting an employee of ours than we did at retaining them. We find exit interviews extremely valuable.

CHANDRA: So you guys are finally in the hot seat for once.

GLEN: That is the case, and we want to be there. The truth hurts sometimes. Without it, we are flying blind sometimes.

VINNY: Well, the truth is that having employees sucks. I am sick of them, and I couldn't do what you do, Glen. I am good at managin' the truck drivin' type. It's just my personality.

GLEN: So why do you do it if you hate it?

VINNY: I gotta do something. What am I

What To Do When You Get Fired

Getting terminated from any company, even if you wanted to be fired, has an unpleasant feeling associated with it. The action of being fired elicits feelings of rejection. You may feel unworthy, your confidence may drop, and you may start to panic. Remember that when you are getting fired, you are being judged again. Keep your emotions in check.

When you are told the news and it is shocking, immediately remember that there is a high degree of likelihood that there is a law enforcement agent waiting to escort you from the building. The reason is because employers have had enough bad experiences with property damage and unpredictable behavior from previous firings that the law is asked to help maintain control if the anticipated calmness goes awry.

Don't get yourself into a legal issue by trashing the place or attacking the person who is delivering the message to you. Remain clam, follow your employer's instructions, collect your belongings, and get out of there. When you are in the clear, immediately write down notes on the event to keep a log of what occurred.

After a few days, if you believe you have been terminated wrongly, you will have your notes to which you can refer with the reasons as you remembered them immediately after the firing, and you can consult a labor attorney about your case.

"March on. Do not tarry. To go forward is to move toward perfection. March on, and fear not the thorns, or the sharp stones on life's path."

Kahlil Gibran

gonna do everyday if I'm not working?
LAUREN: If you don't like it, then find a business you like.
VINNY: It's just too much sometimes. I like making the money, but I'm sick of dealin' with the babysitting and the BS. I don't even need the money no more. I've made more than I ever dreamed I'd make. After listening to Glen and you, I feel like I'm just good at workin' hard and yellin' a lot. But I know how to do a lot. I'm good at it, and I got a lot of people.
LENNY: And my boss sucks. No, I mean it, for real. I'm not just saying that because I suck as a worker, but I know this job ain't takin' me anywhere. Y'all are right, and I feel

---

Erik A. Kaiser

Employer

Get An Exit Interview

If someone is leaving your company, you'd better find out the reason, especially if the person is leaving for the competition. It is hard enough to find employees you want to keep. Losing one of that profile can be a shock to the identity of the company and to the management responsible for retention.

Exit interviews are conversations that HR or management have with a departing employee. The purpose of them is to get free information from the employee about his or her experience at the company. You need to know what events contributed to the decision to leave.

In an exit interview, you want to ask the employee to where he or she is going and why. If possible, you should ask about the compensation at the new job and what compelling arguments were made by the new employer.

Don't be surprised if the departing employee lays his or her disappointment out on the table for you to digest. Do not take offense to it. Listen to the reasons and act unemotionally. You may be hiring that person back one day.

If the departing employee is leaving for wildcard reasons, an exit interview has the potential be extremely revealing. An employee changing industries altogether or moving to another state may be more open and candid for they do not have fear of needing you for anything further in life.

---

like I'm wastin' time. I gotta make a change, too. I gotta get it together.

GLEN: I know you can do it, Lenny. You just need to know that you can break that pattern of working for bad people and bad companies. Take yourself more seriously.

VINNY: Yeah, and you gotta clean up your act, too. You gotta learn to be a good worker, like that Grace over there.

CHANDRA: [to Lenny] You have to make some steady money. That's all I care about. Find yourself a decent company where you can stay, and get steady income. You decide if you want anything more from there. Take it one step at a time.

LAUREN: I like that. Take it one step at a time. But find something you really like doing. It won't be work for you, and you might really do well at it.

GRACE: Well, I feel really lucky to absolutely love my job and love the company I work for. They are fantastic, and after working at other places, I know what is good and what isn't. Meeting all of you made me appreciate more what I have and the people I work with.

For Office Use Only

Employee

Give Your Company An Exit Interview

So you have decided to move on from your current job, and you are giving notice. Don't be surprised if your company interviews you about why you are leaving. They may do so in an effort to salvage a good employee, but they really want to know the exact reasons that you are moving on.

Companies identify with their employees, and employees are the image of the company. When you decide to leave, you are firing the company. They will want to know what circumstances exist that influenced your decision. They may ask you about the offer you received from the competition. If you like your company, you should tell them, but you are under no obligation to do so.

Your company will want to know any and all details of your decisions and new position because they will want to determine if there are improvements they can make to their company. They will want to know the compensation you will receive at your new job to understand what the competition is doing.

If you are leaving for a completely different career, your information will be noted, and it may be more effective for them to know your total thoughts. If you feel you no longer ever need them in life, you can be more candid and open. They will detect if you are leaving the industry because they burned you out. This information will help them learn about how to better treat employees for better retention.

"He was always smoothing and polishing himself, and in the end, he became blunt before he was sharp."
Georg C. Lichtenberg

LAUREN: I feel caught in the middle because I love my company and I love what I do. But I know that some days, I want to pack it in, but I keep going. But I don't want to do anything else! And I am good at it. I think I can change it because I know what is bothering me about it.
GLEN: What is it?
LAUREN: I need a new senior person who can do a lot of what I do every day. My company can afford it, and after listening to everyone tonight, I need to focus on all of my strengths and not get caught up in small details all the time. That's how I am going to "grow" to the next level.
GLEN: That is the sign of a business reaching maturity. And I have to agree with Grace. I feel really lucky to be doing what I

Erik A. Kaiser

Employer

My Employees Suck

Hey, you hired them. If you don't like them, hire new ones.

Sure, it can be a lot more complicated than that, but if they suck, and you think they will always suck, then stop bitching and start replacing. Figure out what you are doing wrong to attract such losers and invest the time to make the necessary change.

It may come as a surprise to you that you attract look-alikes. Or the one person who sparks a hiring spree attracts people who look like them and not like you. Maybe you do not know what good employees look like. Or, maybe you just cannot get the type of talent you need because of your geography or type of business.

Always be interviewing, and always be looking for new talent.

"Waste neither time nor money, but make the best use of both. Without industry and frugality, nothing will do, and with them, everything."
Benjamin Franklin

like doing. It hasn't always been the same, but I learned to surround myself with good people who make my job exciting and new every day. I hear of Lenny's experiences, and I want to work harder on making our company an even better company.

LENNY: And I gotta start doin' stuff right.

GRACE: [to Lenny] Oh, yes! You just have to find a great company. Be honest with them, and be honest with yourself! You can do great things! Look at your girlfriend!

GLEN: I really look forward to work. It can be a lot of fun and very satisfying setting targets and hitting goals.

LAUREN: That is so true! I can't wait to get back to make some changes. Some

---

For Office Use Only

Employee

My Company Sucks

If your valid complaints have gone unsolved and your company sucks, don't waste the time and energy complaining about them when you can dedicate your efforts to finding a real company. Don't get caught in the death spiral of a bad company.

There is no telling exactly what landscape for any business will be, and ups and downs are a natural part of engaging with anything. But there is a point on the curve where you will cross into territory that continually bothers you about either the team on which you work, the company structure, or even customer base. You might also be mismatched with your company, responsiblities, or industry.

Turn your unpleasant emotions into action, and get out there to see what else the world has to offer you.

---

positive changes! Like those performance reviews!

GRACE: Wow! I learned a lot. This calls for a toast! [holding her glass high] To being happy, and good at work, and... and to all of us! [cheers from everyone]

VINNY: Hey, Glen. My glass is gettin' kinda empty.

GLEN: Well, I have been waiting for dessert, and I think I brought the best drink for everyone. It is in my bag, so let me run upstairs and get it.

CHANDRA: If you brought it, I know it is going to be good!

By this time, the group was on dessert, and I remained in the background clearing plates and cleaning up. The conversation continued to personal topics, and it looked like some interesting new bonds were forming. I could see that Vinny and Grace really seemed to like each other in a non-romantic way. It was funny because it reminded me of when I first met him and how unlikely it was that we became friends. Their newfound friendship had to have started when they took the drive up to the lodge, because Vinny never pulled me aside and complained about "the chick."

Erik A. Kaiser

Employer

My Employees Rule

There is a complete satisfaction to having a really great employee base. It does not matter if you have one employee or thousands of them. Great employees beget great employees. All of them are a reflection of you.

It is a lot of work to get stellar employees, and you should be proud. You have done a solid job at attracting and retaining great people. Go ahead and gloat. You deserve it. It is a testimony to your skills as a manager and employer. Keep it going.

"There are a lot of things that go into creating success. I don't like to do just the things I like to do. I like to do things that cause the company to succeed. I don't spend a lot of time doing my favorite activities."

Michael Dell

I wondered if she happened to press one of his buttons, like I did the night we first had dinner.

Moments later, Glen returned to the kitchen, armed with a plain wooden box with "Gran Patron" stamped on the front. He marched in with a smile and walked over to his bar area.

LENNY: Hey! That's a bottle of tequila! I love Patron!

CHANDRA: OMG, so do I!

GLEN: Oh, but wait until I get the bottle out of the box. This is a very special tequila. This

---

For Office Use Only

My Company Rules

Employee

With zillions of companies out there, you have found one that you love. Congratulations. Take a survey of your friends, and you will find that at least 70% of them don't feel the same way.

Working for a great company is exciting and tells a lot about you. After all, a strong company is made up of good people, of which you are one. Keep doing the great job that you have been doing so the company stays great.

---

is the best tequila you can get.

VINNY: [seeing the black velvet bag emerge from the box] Hey, that's Patron Platinum! That's the best stuff money can buy! That's like a $200 bottle.

GLEN: You got it. It is the best, and we're going to share it right now.

GRACE: I have never had it. I hope it is good.

LAUREN: Oh, it is so good, Grace. You will love it.

VINNY: It's unbelievable.

Glen poured six small glasses and proudly handed each one out. He explained that it is to be sipped and enjoyed.

GLEN: I also would like to propose a toast.

VINNY: Let's hear it, because I want to drink this stuff already.

GLEN: Let this tequila remind us of our conversation tonight. To distilling *our* thoughts and learning from one another. To conquering new frontiers. And, to new friends. Cheers!

LAUREN, VINNY, GRACE, CHANDRA, LENNY: [very loud] *Cheers!*

Erik A. Kaiser

With everyone's glasses hoisted high and touching, I took the second most memorable photograph of the evening. It stands in sharp contrast to the photo I took after Lenny showered everyone with flour earlier that night. The six of them started off in different poses as a mess and ended the evening in unison. I couldn't help but think that even though there were underlying differences in all of them, they were able to unite through meaningful conversation. All they needed was to be able to share information openly with each other in a way that didn't make anyone feel threatened.•